# Black Religion in the Madhouse

*Race and Psychiatry in Slavery's Wake*

Judith Weisenfeld

NEW YORK UNIVERSITY PRESS

New York

NEW YORK UNIVERSITY PRESS
New York
www.nyupress.org

© 2025 by New York University
All rights reserved

Please contact the Library of Congress for Cataloging-in-Publication data.

ISBN: 9781479829781 (hardback)
ISBN: 9781479829804 (library ebook)
ISBN: 9781479829798 (consumer ebook)

This book is printed on acid-free paper, and its binding materials are chosen for strength and durability. We strive to use environmentally responsible suppliers and materials to the greatest extent possible in publishing our books.

The manufacturer's authorized representative in the EU for product safety is Mare Nostrum Group B.V., Mauritskade 21D, 1091 GC Amsterdam, The Netherlands. Email: gpsr@mare-nostrum.co.uk.

Manufactured in the United States of America

10 9 8 7 6 5 4 3 2 1

Also available as an ebook

*For my parents, Barbara (1930–2022) and Bernard*

CONTENTS

# LIST OF FIGURES

# Introduction

It was one of the last files I opened in my research for this book. I had spent time in the archives of state hospitals reading materials related to Black patients in the late nineteenth and early twentieth centuries, and thus the records it contained were familiar to me in form. As familiar as its elements were, however, I was still startled by one item. Case 3985 at St. Elizabeths Hospital, the Government Hospital for the Insane in Washington, DC, is that of Judy B., who had been admitted in 1875 at the approximate age of fifty-five with an initial diagnosis of chronic dementia.[1] Upon opening the file in the National Archives, I encountered two oval photographs of Judy, one in which she is facing the camera and the other in profile. They are set next to each other on one card, as in a mug shot. The back of the card contains blanks for the patient's name, case number, negative number, and information about when the photograph was taken, in this case, August 1912. There are photographs preserved in many of St. Elizabeths' patient files from the early twentieth century, some, like Judy's, capturing front and profile views. Photographs in the files of other patients are single frontal views, either close-up or medium-distance shots, reflecting the varied conventions of medical photography.[2]

St. Elizabeths' staff had seated Judy B. against a black background with bright lighting directed at her dark brown skin, making her short gray hair stand out and highlighting her gingham dress. Her lips are pursed, and her eyebrows furrowed, registering what seems to be discomfort, fear, anger, or perhaps all three. In profile she appears proud and defiant. I wondered what Judy's doctors thought they might be able to capture, discover, or demonstrate through these images and to what uses hospital staff might have put them. But Judy is not the only person in the photograph. What struck me in the archive that day was the presence of a white man's hand on Judy B.'s head. In the front-facing photograph the man's hand grips the top of her head, and the flex of his thumb seems to indicate that he is exerting pressure on her as she stares into the camera. In the side view, both of his hands hold the back of her head, and we can see the fingers of his right hand pressing into her hair. Judy was approximately ninety-two years old when these images were taken and had been in the Government Hospital for the Insane for thirty-seven years. The controlling hand that fixed her in the frame seemed to also tether her to the institution.[3]

While I did not learn more about how Judy B.'s image was used within the hospital or whether it circulated beyond her patient case file, I do know how her story circulated or, rather, a story about her and a claim about religion, race, and her institutionalization. Judy's file contains no clinical notes prior to 1906, when hospital physicians began recording observations as part of staff conferences at which they discussed patients. The absence of records of her condition and treatment for the first thirty-one years of her confinement might be attributed to the institution's failure to retain case materials; it might also be that there was simply not much to keep, something I had found to characterize record-keeping in other hospitals in the same period. In this case, however, the first entry in the conference reports in Judy's file calls attention to the absence of prior notes. The description of Judy's physical and mental state in this first entry encapsulates the tenor and content of the assessments St. Elizabeths' psychiatrists would record periodically until her death in the hospital, ten years later. The doctor who wrote the brief report presented her as in good physical health, tidy, and with good appetite and able to work in the hospital laundry, but showing marked deterioration in memory and an emotional state they described as one of "absolute indifference." The report continued, "She entertains numerous ill-defined flighty delusions; she walks around and imagines she is catching witches; will hold out her hand to get them—apparently has delusions of sight."[4]

Subsequent entries highlight Judy's attempts to catch witches, her auditory and visual hallucinations, her conversations with absent relatives and, at one point, with the man who had enslaved her in Virginia.[5] It is difficult from the clinical notes to determine the degree of Judy's memory loss. The doctors reported that she was unaware of her age or how long she had been in the hospital, and sometimes she could not identify the day of the week or the month. At the same time, it is easy to imagine disorientation to time after so many years of confinement. In addition, the standard memory tests psychiatrists began using in the early twentieth century called on patients to recall information that someone who had been enslaved might never have known, including their exact age. But St. Elizabeths staff did not see Judy's memory as the main problem. One year before her death, when she may have been as old as ninety-five, one of the doctors wrote that "her memory is very poor as the senile changes are engrafted upon the original psychosis."[6] Judy's daily activity of "catching witches"—who, in her descriptions looked "right nice," "some like persons, chicken gizzards and dresses, parrots and trees"—was, for the doctors, the primary manifestation of her psychosis.[7]

Arrah Evarts, a white physician at St. Elizabeths and a Methodist from Minnesota who was active in the Woman's Foreign Missionary Society, was particularly interested in the larger significance of Judy's relationship with witches.[8] In her clinical notes, Evarts cataloged what she described as the "stereotyped set of movements" Judy used to catch witches, consisting of "clutching some object and pull[ing] it from the invisible air." She recorded what she characterized as the "soulless incantation" and "senseless" verbal formula of "Chrysanna—chrysanna—chrysanna" that accompanied this activity.[9] Evarts was not alone among St. Elizabeths' psychiatrists in highlighting this patient's occupation with witches, both in terms of her belief in their existence and engagement with people and her practice of catching them, but she used Judy's story in a 1916 article in which she made broad claims about race, religion, and mental normalcy.[10] As Evarts explored the relationship between evolutionary and inherited factors, on the one hand, and individual developmental factors, on the other, she foregrounded literature on ancient forms of myth, religious ritual, and taboo as offering critical insight into the manifestation of "psychoses in the colored race."

Judy B.'s was among several cases Evarts included in the section of the article in which she considered evolutionary factors and mobilized ideas about ancient myth and ritual as providing useful clues to these inheritances. Evarts addressed her presumed white readers, encouraging them to "recall our own childhood with its belief in witches, their tricks and their slavery to whoever knew the proper motions and spells." She invoked her own and her white readers' childhood belief in witches not to identify connections or parallels to Judy's preoccupation with witches but to draw a racial distinction. *We* need only remember *our* childhood belief in witches, she wrote, "to understand that this little brown woman has reverted not to a childhood like *ours*, to be sure, where there would be a questioning unbelief of these things, but to *the early life of her race*, where belief in witches was positive and means taken to control them invariably effective."[11] For the Methodist Evarts, not only did Judy's belief in and catching of witches represent primitive, childlike religion, but she took it to reveal something significant about the nature of Black religion and its role in "psychoses of the colored race."[12] In this, Evarts contributed to a body of medical theory and standards of practice that had long histories in the United States but that had become of greater significance in the years following the end of slavery. As the historian Martin Summers has argued, "Ideas of racial difference were foundational to the production and deployment of psychiatric knowledge from the mid-nineteenth to the mid-twentieth century."[13] Evarts's assessments reflect those foundations, with African American religion and spirituality offering key evidence of racial difference.

## Pathologizing Black Religion

This book charts how ideas about religion came to occupy a central place in late nineteenth-century and early twentieth-century white psychiatrists' theories of the nature of the Black mind. It shows how racialized medical understandings of mental normalcy pathologized a range of Black religious beliefs, spiritual sensibilities, practices, and social organizations and framed them as manifestations of innate racial traits. The theoretical frameworks white physicians developed intersected with contemporaneous representations in American literature, journalism, politics, popular culture, and social sciences that also characterized Black religions as backward or deviant.[14] This book explores the purchase and power of such characterizations within the American medical context, attending to how white psychiatrists' theories about Black religion and mental illness promoted claims of African Americans' unfitness for freedom and bolstered broader arguments for political disenfranchisement and social marginalization.

This was a period of change and transition in African American religious life as many formerly enslaved Black Christians gathered into churches, formalizing religious communities that had taken shape in secret worship in "hush harbors," away from the surveillance of their white enslavers whose Christianity aimed to convey that their captive status was part of God's will and order. As the historian Nicole Myers Turner describes, "The hush harbor independent and clandestine worship spaces were characterized by enslaved people's resistance to white domination through the act of 'stealing away'—secretly removing oneself from the plantation."[15] In the post–Civil War period, some African American Christians transformed these hush harbor communities into independent or Baptist churches, joining the ranks of several independent Black Baptist congregations that had existed in the South before the war. Others affiliated with the African Methodist Episcopal and African Methodist Episcopal Zion churches, both older Black denominations founded in the early nineteenth century North. In yet other cases, African American Christians worshipped within majority white denominations, including Congregationalist, Methodist Episcopal, Episcopal, Presbyterian, and Catholic churches, often in relationships of what Turner describes as "interdependent independence."[16] In addition to proclaiming a Christianity that challenged white supremacy, Black churches fostered collective political, economic, educational, and cultural development in slavery's wake. The growing social power of Black churches in this period sometimes stood as both a political and a theological threat to continued white domination in American society.

Christianity among the enslaved had never simply mirrored the theologies or forms of worship presented by enslavers, and the religious approaches crafted in slavery shaped post-emancipation life. As Alexis S. Wells-Oghoghomeh, a scholar of Africana religions, argues, enslaved Black people "redeployed Christian vocabularies and participated in Christian rites to access various forms of spiritual and material power," understandings of which were shaped in significant ways by West and Central African cosmologies.[17] In the practice of conjure, enslaved Africans in America and their descendants combined material objects—hair, bones, nails, dirt, roots, herbs—in bundles to activate spiritual power, understood to be neutral, on their behalf. Sometimes also called rootwork or hoodoo and performed through the expertise of the conjurer or root doctor, conjure empowered people to protect, heal, or harm. Protection might be mobilized against other people's malicious conjure aimed at harm or revenge or against the power of malign spiritual forces like hags, witches, or the devil. The spiritual sensibilities of enslaved Africans and their descendants also valued the skills of members of their community who were gifted with "second sight," or the ability to see into the spiritual world, those who received spiritual wisdom through dreams or visions, or those who were able to interpret signs and portents the natural world. These and other modes of what the religious studies scholar Yvonne P. Chireau calls supernaturalism in African American life, or ways of engaging "unseen powers or spiritual forces," existed "within and outside black spiritual traditions" and are "creations that black people have woven into their quest for spiritual empowerment and meaning."[18]

Enslaved Africans and their descendants employed their bodies as conduits to engage the spiritual world in ways that also shaped the character of the post-emancipation religious landscape of Black Christianity. In the ring shout, in which ecstatic worshippers sang and moved in a counterclockwise circle, and in revivals and camp meetings during slavery and after emancipation, as well as Holiness and Pentecostal worship in the late nineteenth and early twentieth centuries, African American Christians sought to make the Spirit present among them and in their very bodies.[19] As the historian of religion Clarence E. Hardy III shows, the religious value placed on embodiment in varied Christian contexts was also present in the religious innovation of Black new religions of the early twentieth century, like the Nation of Islam and Father Divine's Peace Mission. In their theologies focused on God in the flesh among them in the person of their founders and in their embodied practices of dress, diet, and worship, members of these groups rejected bourgeois respectability and reimagined race through religion.[20] The late nineteenth-century and early twentieth-century African American religious landscape was varied and dynamic, marked by the continued presence of Black supernaturalism, African American Christian institutions, and new religious movements and other forms of religious creativity, sometimes distinct from one another and sometimes overlapping.

In American popular and political discourse in slavery's wake, African American modes of connecting to and deploying spiritual power were framed as fetishism and superstition, embodied worship characterized as excessive or fanatical, and new religious movements labeled "cults." Some Black religious and political leaders contributed to these framings, seeking to make African American religion into an arena for unified demonstration of fitness for citizenship, but their approach differed from assessments in white public culture. As the historian of religion Curtis J. Evans argues, "White interpretations of black religion or spirituality . . . rarely involved the specificity that attention to actual black churches entailed for black leaders concerned with the concrete problems of their communities."[21] As white psychiatrists turned their attention to analyzing African American religion and theorizing about its impact on the psyches of their Black patients, they reduced the variety and complexity of African American religious life into claims about racial traits. These theories underlay the widespread institutionalization of African Americans on the basis of religious orientations and practices unfamiliar or objectionable to many white Americans. African Americans who mobilized spiritual resources of African origin, participated in forms of Christian enthusiasm, and promoted novel theologies and alternatives to dominant religious forms were all subject to scrutiny and discipline within these psychiatric frameworks. As this book shows, there was no other group in American mental hospitals in the late nineteenth and early twentieth centuries for which the attribution of mental illness to religious causes was as prominent as for African Americans.

While not all legal and medical determinations of insanity or commitments to hospitals in the late nineteenth-century and early twentieth-century United States can be attributed solely to white political and social efforts to marginalize and oppress Black people, racialized psychiatric theory about disordered religious minds certainly affected individuals within the legal systems that evaluated Black sanity and medical institutions that provided care and treatment. In short, this book is animated by the question of what it meant for a Black patient like Judy B. to encounter a world of medical theory and practice in which racialized ideas about what constitutes authentic and beneficial religion, both for individuals and for the social order, shaped the course of their diagnosis, care, and treatment.

The pathologizing of Black religious expression in late nineteenth-century and early twentieth-century American psychiatry, whether communal ecstatic worship, individual visionary or prophetic experience, or appeal to the supernatural power of conjure, sits in a longer and broader history of medical authorities framing a variety of individual and group religious expressions as forms of insanity. In the United States, some medical, religious, and cultural authorities deemed new forms of religious expression manifestations of disordered minds or liable to promote insanity. These included Shakers in the eighteenth century; Christian Scientists, Millerites, Mormons, and Spiritualists in the nineteenth century; and Pentecostals in the twentieth century.[22] Yet even as white physicians evaluated varied religious groups in American society as disordered, their ideas about how religion interacted with what they argued was a distinctive Black mind positioned African Americans uniquely within prevailing diagnostic and treatment frames. The very notion that "psychoses in the colored race" represented a discrete field for research, as Evarts and many other white physicians pursued it, and that something unique about Black religion contributed to these psychoses distinguishes the pathologizing of African American religions from judgments of most other religious groups in this longer history and broader US context.[23]

The case of Arthur K., a white patient admitted to St. Elizabeths Hospital less than two months after Judy B. and diagnosed with chronic mania, is instructive here, despite the different diagnoses. Like Judy, Arthur remained in the hospital until his death in 1910. Clinical notes in Arthur's case begin around 1906 and indicate "delusions of grandeur." Doctors recorded that the "patient believes he is the ruler of a vision world which extends through the whole universe. He is dealing with spirits who live in the ground. They are his friends but are too strong for him. He has the power to make planets, comets and stars."[24] Because, as Summers shows, "the American psychiatric profession engaged in an (often) unarticulated project that conceptualized the white psyche as the norm," Arthur's doctors did not see his case of visionary religion as reflecting something essential about "the white race."[25] In contrast, while staff attended to Judy B. as an individual in the hospital's racially segregated wards, her doctors diagnosed and treated her through the lens of theory about the mind and religious predilections of "the colored race."

## Becoming Race Experts

Judy B. was born into slavery in early nineteenth-century Virginia and grew to adulthood and formed a family within slavery's hold.[26] She entered St. Elizabeths Hospital in the decade after the Civil War when southern African Americans deemed mentally ill were being treated more commonly in public hospitals and encountered racialized medical frames that shaped their experiences. In slavery's wake, white asylum physicians and neurologists studied their Black patients and produced a theoretical literature on race and mental illness that had implications beyond the experiences of individual patients.[27] The attention white doctors devoted to the question of mental illness among African Americans in the late nineteenth century coincided with the development of psychiatry as a distinct field of medicine that claimed disciplinary authority to determine the bounds of both the insane and the normal mind and behavior.[28] Most of the white physicians who developed, propagated, and deployed theories about race, Black religions, and mental disorder in the late nineteenth century were connected to state mental hospitals in the South, where the majority of African Americans lived. In the case of the Government Hospital for the Insane, which served residents of the District of Columbia, federal territories, and military personnel, many of its Black patients had been born in the South. These doctors fashioned themselves as experts on the Black mind and promoted their views through articles and studies published in leading medical journals and through lectures in contexts like meetings of the National Conference of Charities and Correction, where they influenced physicians, hospital and prison administrators, and charity workers representing institutions across the country. As the field of psychiatry developed, the early theories put forward by white southern asylum physicians reached psychiatrists and other physicians from a range of backgrounds nationally, and their works were cited widely and repeatedly in later studies. Thus, these early psychiatric views on race, Black religions, and mental disorder formed the ground for future studies, such as Evarts's, persisting in significant ways and shaping changing approaches to diagnosis and treatment into the twentieth century.

Many of the white southern asylum doctors who developed and circulated these theories had clear investments in or were shaped by their privileged location in the American racial hierarchy. Some had been enslavers themselves or had grown up in families that enslaved Black people. Some had fought for the Confederacy to maintain slavery. Most were Protestant, with active connections to Baptist, Episcopal, Methodist, and Presbyterian churches, missionary societies, and social reform committees and highlighted their denominational connections in many aspects of public life. As such, they were oriented toward what the historian Timothy Gloege characterizes as "churchly" Protestantism and "assumed that an authentic faith required sincere and active membership in a particular church," the health of which supported community and government.[29] The authority these physicians lent to interpretations of certain Black religious beliefs and behaviors as promoting psychic disorder, in turn, helped to shape the bounds of acceptable religion in American life. Their characterizations linked ideas of good and healthy religion to mainstream white Christianity, which they viewed as rational and moral in contrast to what they framed as Black religious excess and absence of ethical content. In addition to adhering to the specific theological precepts of their denominations regarding membership, clerical orders, worship, and institutional organization, in the post–Civil War period many white southern Protestant leaders sought to maintain the social and spiritual hierarchy that had characterized antebellum southern Christianity and to continue to exercise paternalistic control over African Americans, if not in shared churches, then in the broader social order. Even those who repudiated the violence of the Protestant terrorism of the Ku Klux Klan "seized on segregation and disfranchisement as God's plan to preserve racial peace through white rule," as the historian Paul Harvey argues.[30] Moreover, as the historian Elizabeth Jemison describes, in the 1880s southern white Protestants "invented historical narratives of continuity with the antebellum period" that "constructed fictions in which enslaved people had been happy recipients of their white owners' generous benevolence."[31] Such invented narratives are prominent in late nineteenth-century and early twentieth-century white psychiatric theory about the Black mind.

Along with endorsing the predominant racial conservatism of most southern white Protestant churches of the time, these early psychiatric theorists embraced science, and many were advocates of Christian social reform, placing them among those who sought social solutions to problems, including "the Negro problem," rather than emphasize change primarily through evangelism and conversion of individuals.[32] The social, racial, and religious locations of the white physicians who established themselves as experts on the Black mind and foregrounded religion in their theories did not determine the kinds of psychiatric theories and practices they would develop. Nevertheless, the contexts of the enslaving and Jim Crow South and Protestant denominations that supported slavery and segregation most certainly influenced their medical views of the capacities of Black people in the years after the Civil War and emancipation. Recognizing their religious affiliations and connections suggests the influence of their understanding of religious norms and goods, as much as their ideas about race, on the medical theories they developed and embraced.

Attending to these multiple investments highlights how early racialized psychiatric theories that centered Black religions were not a contest between white secular medical authority and Black religious ways of knowing, but the engagement of two broad religious worldviews with unequal power and access to authorizing structures. As Terence Keel, a scholar of religion and science, writes, "the secular acts as a mask for the religious"; he argues that "our beliefs about science as secular have been configured specifically to prevent our awareness of those Christian forms that continue to animate scientific thought."[33] White psychiatrists diagnosing, treating, and writing about Black religion and mental illness brought their understandings of what constitutes true religion, authentic theology, and appropriate expression to their encounters with Black patients like Judy B., and they had the power to embed these purported norms in medical theory and practice. Late nineteenth-century American psychiatric theory about Black religion and mental illness contributed to the social and political contexts in which African Americans worked to make freedom in slavery's wake and to the new mechanisms for maintaining racial hierarchy that took shape in this period. The figuring of Black spiritualities as mind and matter out of place worked in tandem with direct means of coercion and violence that, as the Black studies scholar Rinaldo Walcott argues, functioned to refuse Black people's entrance into civic and social participation and "tutored" them, "in often degrading fashion, into a new reorienting political and social polity."[34]

Pathologizing Black spiritual sensibilities and religious expressions contributed to broader claims of African Americans' inability to manage freedom and bolstered arguments about their unfitness for participation in American political and social life in the decades following the end of slavery. White psychiatrists' theories strengthened efforts to limit African Americans' access to civil rights through assertions that their religious predilections could produce mental instability that endangered the safety and security of the white body politic. In this way, psychiatry functioned to discipline aspects of African American religious life, and this disciplining work coincided with the rising authority of psychiatry as a scientific field. This book exposes how the racism embedded in these theories of religion's place in African Americans' purported mental instability in freedom was an important factor in the rise of psychiatry as an authoritative and powerful profession in the postslavery era.

African American religious and political leaders, social scientists, and by the 1930s Black psychiatrists, engaged prevailing white psychiatric theories about the role of religion as a precipitating cause or manifestation of mental illness. They challenged long-standing psychiatric claims about the disordered nature of Black religions, a racial propensity for religious excess, and the absence of ethics and morals in Black Christianity. Many did so even as they were invested in promoting what they understood to be respectable, restrained, and rational religion for the good of racial progress. The dominant public perspective among Black physicians, social scientist, reformers, and religious leaders identified racism as the cause of poor mental and physical health among African Americans, affirmed a need for moral and educational development, and rejected claims of innate racial traits that fostered the development of mental illness. In the post–World War II era, Black clergy, physicians, and cultural leaders increasingly called for access to mental health care outside of large institutions and offered critiques of the prevailing psychiatric theories about the relationship of Black religion to mental health.

The development and deployment of racialized psychiatric frames foregrounding ideas about Black religion has not been limited to the United States. As Rana Hogarth shows, medical ideas about Blackness and racial difference circulated across the late eighteenth-century and early nineteenth-century Atlantic world, shaping the experiences of enslaved people in the Caribbean and the Americas.[35] Racialized conceptions of Black people's mental capacities were part of these discourses, and concern about the destabilizing influence of Black "witchcraft," "obeah," and spirit possession occupied white physicians in Jamaica,

Trinidad, and Brazil, for example, in ways that had much in common with discourses about "Negro superstition" and "emotionalism" in the United States.[36] Historians have explored similar questions in scholarship on race and psychiatry in several European colonial contexts, including colonial Zimbabwe, East Africa, Southwest Nigeria, and North Africa, for example, in which racialized constructions of insanity supported colonial administration. As these scholars show, psychiatry and psychiatric institutions served as sites through which we can see contests over authority, knowledge, and power, with religion—varieties of Christianity, Indigenous religions, and Islam—often a significant factor in these contests.[37]

## Racialized Religious Excitement and Its Afterlives

Even while recognizing overlapping histories and thematic connections with similar histories in other colonial and national contexts, this book focuses on the United States and the social worlds of formerly enslaved Black people and their descendants. It offers a broad analysis of the significance of religion and race to early American psychiatry; of white psychiatrists' roles in defining religion and shaping the possibilities of Black freedom in slavery's long wake; and of how Black patients, their families, and communities navigated institutions of care and confinement. In concentrating on the United States, the volume charts how late nineteenth-century and early twentieth-century white doctors' ideas about religion shaped their conceptions of the Black psyche. It shows how emerging racialized medical understandings of what constituted the normal mind relegated a range of African Americans' religious affects, beliefs, practices, and social organizations to the realm of the disordered and pathological. Moreover, it highlights how racialized notions of good and beneficial religion helped to constitute psychiatric understandings of the normal mind. These racialized psychiatric conceptions of mental normalcy and deviance, grounded in significant ways in assessments of Black religion, helped to limit the possibilities for African American participation in American political and social life and constrained paths to self-determination.

This volume benefits from recent works on African Americans, race, and psychiatry as well as scholarship charting the broader history of race and medicine and medical racism in the United States.[38] The study of religion and mental health also provides an important backdrop to this book, including historical studies, ethnographic studies, and works that emerge from clinical contexts and consider questions of religious diversity and patient care.[39] Attending to the history of psychiatry and African American religions reveals much not only about how ideas about race, religion, and mental normalcy shaped African American experience in courts and mental hospitals but also about the role the racialization of religion played more broadly in American medical history.

The book begins by exploring how conceptions of inherent Black religious fanaticism, marked by what white commentators described as savagery, barbarism, and excess, helped to configure the broad American cultural discourse about the state of Black mental stability in this period and helped white medical, legal, and political authorities racialize the notion of "religious excitement" as a cause of insanity. Focusing on events in Liberty County, Georgia, in 1889, the first chapter shows how popular claims of inherent racialized religious fanaticism contributed to broader discussions about Black freedom and citizenship. The second chapter moves from political, religious, and popular discourse to the medical context to chart how, over the course of the late nineteenth century, white physicians racialized as Black the idea of "religious excitement" as a precipitating cause in what they argued was a dramatic increase in cases of insanity among southern African Americans in the aftermath of slavery.

The next three chapters examine key components of white psychiatric theory about racialized religious excitement. Chapter 3 explores how the pathologizing of Black supernaturalism through ideas about a racial propensity for superstition among Black people served as a building block in theory about African American insanity from the 1890s through the first decades of the twentieth century, persisting even through a significant shift in diagnostic categories in American psychiatry. Along with the idea that superstition was an inherent characteristic of the Black mind, an innate emotional nature was the most prominently featured argument in psychiatric discourse about race, religion, and mental illness. Chapter 4 examines psychiatric approaches to Black religious emotion in collective worship and in individual prophetic or visionary experiences across this period, highlighting the mental hospital as a site of disciplining what psychiatrists framed as unruly Black religious emotion. The fifth chapter focuses on the gradual shift in the 1930s from theories about innate racial characteristics and religious propensities that had the potential to precipitate mental illness in African Americans to arguments about how the social environment contributed to the development of mental disorders. Black and white psychiatrists and social scientists advanced this work, looking to African American migration to northern cities and the proliferation of Black new religious movements as laboratories for testing their ideas. The final chapter highlights African American participation in the mental hygiene movement and the establishment of a community mental health clinic in Harlem, both in collaboration with Black religious leaders, as cases that highlight work to shift mental health treatment from hospital commitment to preventative therapeutic care.

Locating racial commitments at the center of a story about the place of religion in American psychiatry's theory and practice brings into sharp relief the profound entanglements of race and religion in American history.[40] In making claims about race and African American religion, white psychiatrists simultaneously constructed Protestant whiteness as normal, reasonable, morally good, and capable and deserving of freedom. The scientific frame of psychiatry cloaked the religious labor of constructing race in the aura of the natural in ways that highlight what Terence Keel argues is the "Christian intellectual inheritance that has shaped Euro-American science."[41] Keel shows that Euro-American scientific ideas about human origins and race did not represent a break with Christian ways of knowing. Similarly, American psychiatric theory about what constitutes insanity depended on religious notions of the normal that, in the American context, were racialized as white but projected as universal. Examining American psychiatry's racial commitments offers a window on the enduring power of religion in what we might take to be secular science, free of religious and moral claims. It points us to consider other sites for uncovering how religion and race entangled have produced a scientific authority announced as secular, understanding this process instead as what the religious studies scholar John Modern frames as "the production of religious-secular difference."[42]

## Notes on Sources, Approaches, and Language

I have drawn on a variety of available sources, including court and hospital records, annual reports, newspaper and journal articles, published psychiatric studies, memoirs, and autobiographies to offer insight into the stakes and consequences of Black people being characterized as suffering from or manifesting a religious insanity in this period. It is difficult to learn much about the interiority of most Black patients who were diagnosed with religiously grounded mental illness and consigned to state hospitals. Judy B. remains an elusive figure, as do so many other patients whose files I have handled and read. The records of the legal process through which people were committed to state mental hospitals, whether initiated at the request of family members or a directive from white authorities to evaluate an individual held in jail or resident in an almshouse or other institution, privilege the voices of witnesses, particularly of local white doctors, as well as family, neighbors, and sometimes employers. When patients' perspectives are represented, they are generally secondhand accounts offered by police, examining physicians, family and community witnesses, and journalists, if the case became public. Patient records from state hospitals in the late nineteenth century often contain little more than information transferred from the commitment paperwork and sometimes daily ward logs in which attendants describe the individual's physical health; medications administered; and their participation in work or recreation, attendance at religious services, and compliance with hospital rules. On occasion, patient files contain correspondence from family members and sometimes from the patient to relatives; by the early twentieth century, they might include photographs and more extensive case histories. Many records from state hospitals, particularly those for institutions that housed Black patients only, have been discarded; in other cases, health privacy laws restrict access to all patient records or limit access to those that are dated earlier than the late nineteenth or early twentieth century. In yet other cases, records that had been available to researchers have since been restricted.[43]

I do not attempt to determine the "real" nature of historical subjects' mental states, to diagnose them according to modern classifications, or to authorize or discount their religious expressions. I cannot say if Judy

B. had dementia, an underlying psychosis, or special insight into the spiritual world. Judy's attention to the operations of witches and hags in corporeal and spiritual form located her among many African Americans in slavery's wake who interacted with these malevolent spiritual forces, and she may have sought healing and support through other spiritual means.[44] The question for our purposes is how white physicians and medical professionals around her interpreted such activity and the implications of these interpretations. The historian Jonathan Sadowsky helpfully notes from his work on psychiatry in colonial southwest Nigeria that "we must work with what we know—that these people were *considered* mad—rather than speculating about the validity of these considerations."[45] But I am also interested in understanding *who* considered these people mad and, as the religious studies scholar Ira Helderman frames it in his work on conceptions of the secular and religion in Buddhism and psychotherapy, illuminating "what forces support their authority."[46]

In this book, I focus on how constructions of race, religion, and mental normalcy and deviance came together in the work of late nineteenth-century and early twentieth-century psychiatrists and the experiences of their patients. As such, I most often use the terms the historical actors in this study used, such as "lunacy" and "insanity," to explore how they understood these categories and the meanings these terms and their associations assumed in the wider culture. Similarly, I often use the racial terms that were most common in these periods, not to naturalize them but because of the significance of ideas about an essential Black nature to this psychiatric theory about race, religion, and mental illness in the context of American racialization.

As much as I wish to know more and to make this story known, I have chosen to protect the privacy of individuals whose stories I encountered in the archives of the state hospitals by using their first name and the first initial of their last name. In some cases that were publicized in newspapers or other public documents and for which I do not draw on patient records, I use their full names. These conventions reflect the legal requirements of health privacy legislation, particularly the Health Insurance Portability and Accountability Act (HIPPA) of 1996, however variously applied in individual states, and concerns for the stigma and emotional harm accruing to descendants of these patients. The historian Susan Lawrence has raised questions about the broad application of HIPPA with respect to privacy rights of the dead and the problem of historical research and writing under such circumstances.[47] I do not wish my adoption of this practice to imply endorsement of mental illness as worthy of stigma or secrecy. At the same time, I do not wish to reproduce the violence of the histories of medical racism against vulnerable people but recognize that such work takes place on complicated terrain that demands, in the words of the anthropologist Todne Thomas, "naming the violence of white supremacist racial and representational dominance."[48]

I cannot forget that I have seen Judy B.'s photograph, her expression, the staff member's hand on her head. I have wondered what transpired in the years between her admission to St. Elizabeths Hospital and the commencement of institutional recordkeeping about her case. I have read letters her daughter Hattie sent to the hospital from her home in Baltimore in the years immediately following Judy's admission, inquiring why she had received no response from her mother and conveying hope of visiting soon. In one letter she writes of fabric she sent to have a dress made for her mother, perhaps gingham, like what Judy wears in the photograph.[49] I have tried without success to discover what happened to Hattie, with whom the hospital lost touch by the time Judy died and was buried in the hospital's cemetery. Even as this is primarily a history of race and medicine that foregrounds the ideas, voices, and actions of mostly white psychiatrists, I hope readers will see people like Judy B. who appear in this book as individuals in challenge to the racial essentialism and pathologizing of Black spiritualities that dominated the psychiatric and social worlds in which they found themselves.

1

# The Making of Black Religious Fanaticism

In the summer of 1889, hundreds of Black residents of Liberty County, Georgia, congregated in daily worship on rough-hewn benches arranged in a circle beneath the branches of two moss-covered live oak trees near Walthourville. It doubtless did not escape those gathered that they prayed on land where the white Baptist layman George Washington Walthour and his family had enslaved several hundred Black people several decades earlier.[1] In fact, some participants, including one of the group's leaders, bore the Walthour surname. Others had surnames that signaled that their families had been held in bondage by yet other local white families. By 1889, Black residents of Liberty County, including the worshippers, had built lives and livelihoods in slavery's wake. Some were farmers who owned the land they tilled. Others worked as farmhands, seamstresses, teamsters, and hands at the turpentine distillery, as timber cutters, washerwomen, homemakers, and on the railroad. Many Black men in Liberty County were among those registered to vote, some owned property, and many of the children had spent part of the year in school. Some were members of local Baptist, African Methodist, Congregational, and Presbyterian churches. But that summer, many sought communion with God and each other under the canopy of the trees, much like the secret hush harbors in which enslaved Africans had worshipped, and proclaimed a message of deliverance.

Several leaders emerged over the course of the summer's worship, and although the substance of their preaching was not identical, there was a common focus on biblical promises of divine justice for the faithful in this world and in their lifetime, rather than patiently awaiting a reward in heaven. It was a message familiar to Black Christians who had sustained and been sustained by the religious community the enslaved had created, affirming that Christian teachings and scriptures were opposed to the dehumanizing and oppressing religion of their enslavers and finding hope of God's deliverance.[2] According to some reports, worshippers in Liberty County who embraced this message called themselves Children of the Wilderness, a designation that captured how they had stepped out of ordinary time and occupation to gather in anticipation of divine action on their behalf. Perhaps they meant to call to mind the biblical account of the Exodus of the Israelites from bondage in Egypt, where the text tells of God leading "the people through the way of the wilderness of the Red Sea."[3] Perhaps the proclamation that they were of the wilderness also indicated recognition of the spiritual powers of the natural world and the protective capacities of the nature spirits who served as "guardians of the land."[4] They may have thought of the references to the wilderness in the book of Revelation, including as a place of protection prepared by God. Like other Black Christians in slavery's wake, they may have interpreted the text with an urgency born not only of anticipation of the future millennial age of peace but also with the expectation of justice in the face of racial oppression.[5] The time seemed right for them to do their part in God's plan.

Liberty County's Children of the Wilderness brought widespread attention to African American religious life during that summer of 1889 and put on the national agenda an example of the potential dangers of Black religious enthusiasm in the form of what one white newspaper characterized as "a negro fanatical sect."[6] The group attracted notice because the gatherings were spurred by the appearance in June of a man who said his name was Christopher Columbus Jacob Orth Dupont Bell, but people in Liberty County referred to him as Dupont Bell. When reporters first took note of the spiritual excitement, their descriptions of Bell varied widely. He was a decrepit old white man, with long hair parted in the middle and wearing a suit and blouse; a shabbily dressed Black man; or a bearded, long-haired thirty-year-old white man standing six feet tall who resembled "the accepted pictures of our Lord" and carried a staff and a Bible. In what must have been a printer's error, one paper reported that he was almost nine feet tall in an exaggeration that inadvertently pointed to the anxiety in the county about the stranger's increasing power among Black residents.[7] For his part, Bell presented himself consistently as a white man who had been born in Circleville, Ohio, thirty years earlier.[8] The white media's confused presentation of Bell's racial identity highlighted the fact that he preached in a part of the

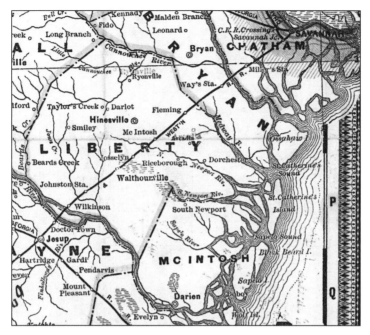

Figure 1.1. Map of Liberty County, Georgia, in detail from George Franklin Cram, *Indexed Railroad and County Map of Georgia* (Chicago, 1883), Library of Congress, Geography and Map Division.

county where Black residents were in the majority and that he "refused to come up to . . . where the white population reside."[9]

Bell reportedly crossed the color line in Liberty to tell its Black residents that the world would end on August 16, 1889, and announced that, although his body was thirty years old, he was actually "Christ in spirit." He said he had come to save them and "lead them through the Land of Canaan to Jerusalem."[10] Bell spread his message by going house to house and eventually gathered hundreds of listeners interested in what the white press claimed was an absurd and dangerous message of racial reversal: Black people would become white, and white people would turn black.[11] Rather than an envy of and desire for whiteness, as white residents imagined, those who took Bell's appearance in the area as an occasion to gather were likely drawn to the promise of disempowerment of former enslavers and white supremacists whose political and social dominance constrained their flourishing. Whether this was a part of Bell's preaching is not clear, but the other elements of the reported message—the need for unity and a divine message of justice and deliverance—had deep roots in Black spirituality in America. Similarly, the aim to journey through Canaan to Jerusalem resonated with an African-Atlantic perspective in which passage through the wilderness enabled spiritual growth and transformation.[12]

While Bell's message amplified existing religious sensibilities among many Black residents of Liberty County, other residents, Black and white, viewed him as a dangerous instigator of religious novelty, labeling him a "false messiah" and a "pseudo Christ."[13] Within two weeks of his appearance in the county, Bell was standing in a courtroom packed with three hundred observers, having been called to account for his sanity before a physician and a jury of twelve white men. The lunacy hearing resulted from a petition filed by William H. Styles, a local Black Baptist minister and politician. In his petition Styles asserted that Bell "declares himself to be Jesus Christ," was "holding public meetings composed exclusively of the colored people" of the county, "preaching to them in an incendiary manner, and . . . leading them off from their homes and work and into vagrancy."[14] With the reported sound of hymn singing from members of a large crowd of Black supporters outside the courthouse in the background, Bell was said to be riveting in his lively responses to questions from T. M. Norwood, a white former judge and US senator, who represented Liberty County at the hearing. Despite Bell's engaging performance in court, the jury declared him to be insane and committed him to the Georgia Lunatic Asylum at Milledgeville, where he was held for a decade before being released as cured.[15] In assessing these unusual events, the press generally concurred with the court's decision, with one account in a Georgia newspaper telling readers, "Bell is of course a hopeless lunatic, having gone crazy, doubtless, during some period of religious excitement."[16]

Had the story ended there, attention would probably have faded quickly, as with other passing religious enthusiasms of the day. This one might have endured a bit longer because of newspapers' ridicule of what white commentators portrayed as credulous Black folk duped by a white lunatic reportedly selling them angelic wings for the journey to Jerusalem at five dollars a pair.[17] But as the summer wore on after Bell's commitment to the asylum, events in Liberty County alarmed

Figure 1.2. Center building at the Georgia Lunatic Asylum at Milledgeville, 1894.
Courtesy, Georgia Archives, Vanishing Georgia Collection, bal-027.

and horrified many Black and white residents and set off a national discussion about race, religion, and insanity that revealed the stakes for African Americans of popular, legal, and medical claims about their religious inclinations. With Bell institutionalized, new religious leaders emerged from among his supporters within Liberty County's Black community and kept the momentum going among this group of devotees who sought religious experience outside of the local Black churches and forged community connections beyond the everyday tasks of labor in the rice fields, sawmills, and turpentine farms and on the railroad. What had come to public attention in June as a curious case of African Americans following a white stranger who claimed to be Christ continued as a Black-led event through which participants enacted spiritual and social freedom. Perhaps Dupont Bell had been attracted to Liberty County in the first place because he was aware of spiritual fervor among its Black residents who may have long gathered as Children of the Wilderness, escaping the notice of white employers, clergy, and political leaders. Perhaps he sought to disrupt the legacy of the county's influential model of Christian slavery. Whatever the case, Black residents of Liberty knew full well that they lived in a society structured by an oppressive racial and religious hierarchy. They hadn't needed Bell to explain that reality to them. Bell's appearance may have interrupted the rhythm of daily life, labor, and worship, but it probably did not alone generate the religious fervor that brought Liberty County to the national spotlight in the summer of 1889.

The intensity of the responses of white and some Black residents and the tone of alarm in the national press coverage signal how much was at stake in the gatherings of the Children of the Wilderness. Reactions to these events among white religious and political authorities focused on the literal geography of Liberty County, Georgia, but they were also a response to Black liberty from slavery and to African Americans' expressions of freedom, including to what historian Nicole Myers Turner characterizes as "soul freedom."[18] White Americans' evaluations of the belief and behavior of what one newspaper derisively called "Liberty's Crazy Negroes" connected Black religion and insanity, and, for many, this connection foretold a worrisome future for Black life in America. Specifically, for many white Americans, the possibility of a link between Black religion and insanity affirmed their conviction that Black people were deficient religiously and incapable of being trustworthy political and social actors. White religious and political leaders used the gatherings to assert dangerous religious excess as a key component of Black culture unrestrained by white oversight. For these commenters, freedom and fanaticism were entangled in post-emancipation Black life. The popular notion of Black religious fanaticism that could disorder the mind, illustrated vividly for white observers in the Children of the Wilderness, shaped the late nineteenth-century American cultural landscape in which white physicians evaluated the relationship of African American religion to mental normalcy. While the medical theories and the terms psychiatrists employed differed from popular discourse about race and sanity, emerging psychiatric theories and popular discourse shared racialized assumptions about the dangers of religious excess and irrationality to American society.

## "An Epidemic of False Christs"

Four Black Liberty County residents assumed leadership in succession of the gatherings that had come to public attention with Dupont Bell's arrival. Coverage of their activities amplified and solidified conceptions of a connection between a racialized innate fanaticism and insanity. It is difficult, given the racism of representations in the white press and the absence of direct accounts from participants, to disentangle the reported content of the leaders' preaching and the group's activities from white Americans' commonplace ideas about Black primitivism. Media accounts suggest that biblical narratives shaped the group's sense of purpose, over against dominant white discourses about Black people's moral, social, and political incapacity in freedom. The reporting also points to the conflicts the theology and practices of the Children of the Wilderness generated among Black residents as they envisioned what freedom meant for their religious futures and considered how religion might aid their practice of freedom. Whatever the nature of these discussions and debates among neighbors, coworkers, and fellow congregants prior to the summer of 1889, the events of that summer entangled Black religious expressions with ideas about mental health and civic and social capacity. With the outsider Bell out of the public eye and the group now composed solely of Black residents of Liberty County, discussions in the white press and among white officials turned from characterizing the group as simple and credulous followers of a white "pseudo Christ" to foregrounding violence, sex, and images of the uncontrolled religious excess of Black fanaticism.

Edward James, a justice of the peace and farmer who reportedly declared himself to possess the spirit of God, abandoned his courtroom to assume leadership of the group. Preaching at the daily gatherings, he became the center of the heightened focus on Black fanaticism.[19] James was said to be naked and wild when he preached, and newspapers reported him as keeping a "harem," which white journalists claimed he argued was the right of all men.[20] Here the press accounts connected dangerous white stereotypes of Black men as sexual brutes to ideas about religious fanaticism. White officials and reporters described the gatherings under James as involving "voodoo practices," a label that, in the imagination of white readers, served to couple some notion of ritual with sex and violence.[21] The white press asserted that, in contrast to the pacifism Bell had exhibited when he reportedly insisted that his followers remain peaceful during his arrest, there was "a bloodthirsty streak in James's makeup" and described him as "preaching revolution and immorality with a boldness that is startling to the whites," who feared they would be massacred.[22]

According to press accounts it was not whites, however, but other Black residents who suffered violence at the hands of the group gathered around James. One article noted that James's brother David and his cousin Sampson Carter, whom the reporter characterized as "intelligent colored men," tried to dissuade James from his preaching. In response, James choked Carter, and the gathered worshippers beat the two men.[23] The press reported that during one gathering, James declared a woman from among his followers to be possessed by evil spirits and ordered others to beat them out of her.[24] Press and local officials also attributed Sarah Roberts's murder of her young nephew to participation in the religious enthusiasm. Roberts was said to have had a history of mental illness, and observers believed she had become deranged again by Bell's and James's preaching. Newspaper accounts claimed that James had demanded human sacrifices and Roberts complied, murdering the boy, who was left in her charge while his parents attended one of James's meetings. Descriptions in the news were gruesome, reporting that the boy's throat had been cut and his forehead marked with a carved cross.[25] Roberts was quickly arrested, and a grand jury declined to indict her for murder on grounds of insanity.[26]

Shortly after this series of violent incidents, the Liberty County sheriff and a group of forty men arrested James in response to a petition his brother William had filed for a lunacy hearing, and he was brought before a judge and jury, who committed him to the Georgia Lunatic Asylum.[27] While in the county jail awaiting transfer, James allegedly continued his preaching, with the press reporting that "his incantations can be heard from the jail at all hours, day and night."[28] He was said to have remained committed to his divinity and mission to lead the people to Canaan on August 16, continuing to declare this even on the journey to the asylum, to the distress of his brother William, who accompanied him.[29] James died in the asylum three years after having been declared insane.[30]

Figure 1.3. Building used to house African Americans at the Georgia Lunatic Asylum at Milledgeville, 1894. Courtesy, Georgia Archives, Vanishing Georgia Collection, bal-030.

Shadrach Walthour, a farmer who presented himself as King Solomon, stepped forward to lead the group.[31] Walthour was said to have preached that God loved his people and that, while they been little more than animals in the past, they were animals no more because the spirit of God was in them. He warned, however, that their faithlessness to God was endangering their freedom and that they were at risk of being reenslaved by whites for four hundred more years.[32] By the time Walthour was at the helm of the gatherings, local officials had committed or jailed numerous participants, but interest did not waver. One newspaper reported in late July that a group of self-appointed "regulators," composed of concerned Black and white men in the area, issued an ultimatum to Walthour to disband the group or they would "surround the camp, capture the ring leaders, tie them to trees and whip them within an inch of their lives" in order to stop "the spread of demoralization and insanity."[33] Authorities arrested Walthour shortly thereafter, and he was murdered while in jail. Several other Black prisoners named the white jailor, Andrew Dean, as the murderer, claiming that he had been upset by Walthour's loud Bible reading. Dean was indicted for murder, tried several years later, and acquitted.[34]

The final local leader to emerge among Liberty County's Black "Wilderness Worshippers" in the summer of 1889 was Queen Mary, whom newspapers identified variously as Laura, Sarah, or Ellen Roberts and described as about fifty years old.[35] She received comparatively less attention than did the men in what some newspapers called "the Christ craze," perhaps because she was a woman and did not claim divinity. From the limited accounts available, it seems her ministry was less focused on apocalyptic prophecy and more on the community of people around her. One reporter described participants as asking to be "crowned" and Queen Mary as "pass[ing] her hands over the heads of the candidates for eternal life, mutter[ing] a little prayer, then bless[ing] them as faithful children." Still, the reporter wondered whether "crazy Ellen Roberts is not at present the greatest factor in this peculiar fallacy" because, the author believed, she exerted the strongest influence over the enthusiasts.[36] By early August, newspapers reported that the fervor was abating and Queen Mary's power diminishing following additional arrests of those deemed to be disturbing the peace, the sheriff's destruction of the camp, and ongoing armed patrols.[37]

But August 16, the day Bell was said to have predicted the world would end and he would lead followers to Canaan, still loomed.[38] When the day passed uneventfully, observers noted that most participants had abandoned their site in the wilderness and turned their attention back to the lives they had deserted in anticipation of the coming of divine justice and transformation of their world.[39] In the days following, the press reported several additional "victims" of the enthusiasm, including forty-five-year-old Spencer Washington, who was found wandering with a plank of wood in his hand with which he said "he intended to build a church in which he would preach the true gospel."[40] Authorities claimed that Washington had become deranged from Bell's preaching, and they held him in jail to await a doctor's evaluation and a lunacy hearing. There were also occasional claims that things had not quieted down as much as had been thought. In March 1890, the *Savannah Morning News* reported that there were some "crazy spirits" among the followers of the "false Christs" who were still desirous of finding a messiah to lead a pilgrimage. "Some of them burn fires of nights to light the way of the expected Savior, should his advent be at night," the reporter claimed.[41]

It is impossible from this distance in time and without access to accounts from participants themselves, unmediated by the racism of the white journalists who reported on the events, to know in depth what motivated those who gathered around Bell, James, and their successors. Accounts in the mainstream white press offered readers racist descriptions of the Black participants, salacious accounts of orgiastic ritual, and innumerable contradictory facts that makes reconstructing what happened and why challenging. The historian Thomas Armstrong has argued that those involved had become alarmed by recent natural events nearby, including an earthquake, lightning strike, flood, drought, and fires, which they took to be omens. These omens, he contends, combined with economic distress created by a decline in agriculture and a rise in timber and turpentine industries, along with increasing political marginalization, predisposed them to be sympathetic to Bell's prophecies.[42] As Armstrong notes, many of the Black men in the county were registered voters in the 1870s and 1880s, but "through a combination of terror, fraud, and apathy, black participation virtually disappeared after 1886."[43] In his view, the events of the summer represent a millenarian response in which participants vested hope in a divine promise that the sacrifice of their jobs, possessions, and money would be rewarded with entrance into the promised land. While any deep sense of what drew people to the benches beneath the live oak trees in Walthourville remains elusive, clearly the group's spiritual and political goals were deeply entangled.

In the events in Liberty County, Georgia, in the summer of 1889 and responses to them, we see the stakes of religious independence as the basis for assertion of Black peoplehood in the wake of slavery. The gatherings of the Children of the Wilderness alarmed local whites, in part, because many had persuaded themselves that white Georgians had established a relationship of custodial Christianity in which they successfully oversaw Black people's religious education and worship and tempered what they evaluated as misguided belief or excess. Indeed, in the early nineteenth century, Liberty County had been a significant site for the crafting of slaveholding Christianity that white enslavers wielded in an effort to contain the revolutionary potential of Christian theology among enslaved Black people.[44] Charles Colcock Jones, a Georgia Presbyterian minister and an enslaver of more than sixty Black people, campaigned vigorously among his fellow white enslavers for them to undertake organized and sustained religious instruction among the enslaved, promising that an emphasis on the scriptural command for servants to obey their masters would enhance enslavers' authority and make Black bondspeople more obedient.[45] Jones established mission stations throughout Liberty County in the 1830s, offered oral instruction on the Bible using illustrated scripture cards, and taught Christian theology with his *Catechism for Colored Persons*, which circulated widely across the enslaving South.[46]

Jones's text was, in many respects, a conventional Christian catechism, but with prominent sections devoted to outlining duties of masters to servants—taking Abraham as the model master who provided food, clothing, and good example—and duties of servants to masters. As the historian of religion Albert J. Raboteau notes, Jones developed and propagated these materials amid activism to abolish slavery and in the wake of several planned and effected insurrections in which Christianity provided inspiration, including Denmark Vesey's plan and Nat Turner's Rebellion.[47] In this context Jones instructed that Christian teaching required servants to please their earthly masters in all things, not to be slow in their work or complain, and not to run away or harbor runaways lest they be justly punished.[48] This section of the catechism concluded with the instruction to the enslaved, "Care not for being a Servant—you are the Lord's free-man, and God will bless you and take you to Heaven as soon as he will a King, if you are a follower of Jesus his Son. But if you are an unfaithful Servant the Lord will be angry with you."[49] Jones also sought to keep tight control over the emotional tenor of worship among the enslaved Black people to whom he preached. He counseled prospective white missionaries to conduct worship "*with reverence and stillness on the part of the congregation*" and warned never to "encourage demonstrations of approbation or disapprobation, or exclamations, or responses, or noises or outcries of any kind during the progress of divine worship; nor boisterous singing immediately at its close." In Jones's view, this approach would promote "intelligence and piety" and substance over feeling.[50]

Even as Jones promoted a Christianity consonant with the institution of chattel slavery that became a model for other white enslavers, Black people in Liberty County rejected it as the substance of Christian teaching. Jones recorded a strong negative reaction when, using the story of the enslaved Onesimus in Paul's letter to Philemon, he preached that it was wicked for enslaved people to run away. Some of the enslaved people present walked out, and one lectured Jones after the service that what he had preached "is not Gospel at all."[51] Enslaved Black people in Liberty County exercised their own religious authority in Christian contexts with preachers Mingo, Jack, and Sharper gathering worshippers outdoors under the auspices of the white Midway Congregational Church and at various sites in the county where Black people were held in bondage.[52] African-Atlantic cultures also shaped Black religious life in Liberty County, with enslaved people crossing space and time to encounter and commune with spirits and ancestors through dreams and visions, and conjurers and rootworkers mobilizing material and spiritual resources to heal, protect, or punish, all contributing to the religious resources available to counter the dehumanizing Christianity of the enslavers.[53]

Avenues for Black spiritual autonomy within church institutions remained fraught in the years following the Civil War, and white clergy's interest in determining the religious futures of the formerly enslaved sometimes enflamed conflict between groups of Black Christians. The Children of the Wilderness emerged following a struggle in Liberty County in the 1870s over control of church property, the allegiance of congregants, and the religious future of the area's Black Christians.[54] In 1868, Black Presbyterians in Liberty leased the Midway Church from the white Congregationalists who had abandoned it during the Civil War, and Joseph Williams, a Black Presbyterian minister, shared leadership of the church with Joseph T. Waite, a white minister from New York and graduate of Georgia's Columbia Theological Seminary. Several members of the group that would gather as the Children of the Wilderness had ties to this congregation, including Edward James, whose marriage Waite had performed just a few years before Dupont Bell's appearance in the county.[55] At the same time, Floyd Grant Snelson, a Georgia-born Black Congregationalist minister, accepted a position as a missionary and teacher in Liberty County through the white-led, northern-based

American Missionary Association (AMA). Over the next several years, the local Black Presbyterians and some Black Congregationalists, led by Snelson, sparred for control of the white-owned Midway Church. Snelson was a polarizing figure whose leadership tapped into local Black impulses for religious autonomy, but whose "sponsorship . . . by the white AMA and the accommodationist tone of his preaching" limited his appeal for some.[56] The struggle for institutional control and the emergence of competing claims to leadership of a segment of the local Black Christian community set the stage for the later conflict generated by the millennialist impulses of the Children of the Wilderness.

The participation of Black clergy from Liberty County in Republican politics and in religious and political work in cooperation with white Georgians also set the backdrop for the events of 1889. Snelson became active in politics, serving in the state legislature and participating in many conventions, and he was a close political ally of Rev. William H. Styles, who would file the petition for the lunacy hearing for Dupont Bell. Styles, who was born around 1839 and enslaved for almost thirty years in Liberty County, served on many committees in the state Republican Party from the 1870s through the first decade of the twentieth century. He was elected to the state senate in 1888, having rallied Black voters around the party as better than the Democrats at serving their interests.[57] While Styles sought to represent Black interests as he understood them, he was also open to accommodating white business, political, and religious leaders he thought would be allies in the gradual process of inclusion in the state's political life. Styles was active in the Baptist Missionary Association of Georgia in the years just before Dupont Bell's appearance and the religious enthusiasm of the summer of 1889.[58] In his capacity as the association's regional Sunday school missionary, Styles reported to the Black Republican *Savannah Tribune* on an 1888 visit he made to a labor camp, where workers made turpentine from pine trees, to speak about the Sunday school efforts. He recounted that he found the residents engaged and hopeful about the prospects for religious work and gave special attention in his report to the white owners, writing that they were "very cordial in many respects and assisted people in this . . . Sunday School rally most heartily. It is pleasing indeed to find that our southern white brother is growing more and more cordial and that we are being recognized almost as a brother."[59] Styles's embrace of gradualism in his satisfaction at being recognized "almost as a brother" no doubt shaped his response to Dupont Bell's appearance and the activities of the Children of the Wilderness. In this view, Sunday school efforts that accommodated workers to industries, such as the production of naval stores like lumber and turpentine, were good for the county's Black residents. For Styles, religious gatherings that inflamed millenarian hopes and took people away from labor, schools, and churches could only hurt the community's political and social futures.

## "Wild Fanaticism"

The range of responses to the 1889 events in Liberty County, Georgia, highlight white cultural fears about Black religious fanaticism unbound in the years after the end of slavery and capture the stakes for African Americans of such interpretations of their religious beliefs and expressions. A key factor shaping the responses of law enforcement officials, court officers, politicians, medical authorities, and the white press to the events in Liberty County was the fact that the gatherings took place in an area in which a majority of residents were Black, which, for many, pointed to the dangers of Black self-governance.[60] As noted earlier, the group worshipped near property that had belonged to George Washington Walthour, an enslaver of three hundred Black people who labored on his lands growing rice and other crops.[61] One reflection on the proceedings published in the *Washington Post* offered an account of an orderly society in Liberty County before the Civil War under the benevolent leadership of white Christian men who were descended from "refugees from political intolerance and religious persecution" and who "possessed all the sturdy qualities of the Scotch race."[62] Moreover, according to the *Post*, Liberty County had much to be proud of because of the religious contributions of its preachers to American religious culture. The article asserted that, under the disciplining influence of white Christians, the institution of slavery had been charitable, and that enslaved Blacks enjoyed an education "up to the highest degree of Christianity." In this account, nowhere was this truer than on "the Walthour plantation," which the *Post* asserted had established "an ideal republic" for the enslaved through the work of "generous and conscientious masters."[63] According to the *Post* reporter, the war disrupted the harmonious society that had long existed in Liberty, and although Black people had always outnumbered whites in the county, they now lived without the oversight of "the missionary temper of the white people."[64]

White commentators on the religious gatherings in Liberty County and the violence some participants perpetrated repeatedly describe them as evidence of "savagery" and "barbarism." In using this language, they mobilized popular racist ideas about African cultures as uncivilized, violent, and brutal and framed African American culture through this image. The notion that the majority Black community of Liberty County would inevitably devolve into savagery and widespread barbarism without the moderating influence of white civilization featured prominently in whites' interpretations. Descriptions like "Incredible Barbarism" and "Barbaric Worship of the Sable Children of the Wilderness" headlining articles about Liberty County reflected much white public opinion.[65] T. M. Norwood, the white former judge who represented the county in court proceedings against Bell, characterized the gatherings as "shocking to civilization and to common decency."[66] Samuel D. Bradwell, a state senator and former Confederate colonel, reflecting on the 1889 events in Liberty, asserted, "The real trouble is that the negroes live more apart from the white people than any in the state. . . . They are out of reach of the white man's influence, and it looks like they have gone back to barbarism."[67]

Such claims of the degradation of the society and culture white Christian enslavers had established by the overwhelming presence of Black people were prominent in reflections on Liberty County. One of the few whites to remain in the area, one local newspaper told readers, was Charles Colcock Jones Jr., the son of the Liberty County Presbyterian enslaver who had promoted a theology of Christian slavery. The report informed that the younger Jones refused to sell his property, and the unnamed author lamented that this territory that could have been "a paradise" was largely left to Black residents because of the swampy terrain that was inhospitable to whites.[68] The author of a history of the region bemoaned the fact that the home of Lyman Hall, a Congregationalist minister, physician, and signer of the Declaration of Independence, was "now occupied by an illiterate negro" and that followers of Bell and James gathered near a church where several governors of the state were buried, which represented a "cradle of liberty in Georgia."[69] The majority of white commentators on the events of 1889 asserted that, given the opportunity for political and religious self-governance, African Americans would become a threat to national well-being. Senator Bradwell expressed alarm at the fact that there were so many Black registered voters in the county and argued that "the crazy ones came from a section of the swamp where there are negro preachers."[70] According to an Alabama newspaper reflecting on the situation in Liberty County, "That the negroes would lapse into barbarism even in this county, where they have had more advantages than anywhere else, does not admit of a doubt, if they and they alone were the inhabitants." The paper argued that it was a sobering lesson for the rest of the country and that African Americans should not be allowed to gain political power.[71]

Many of the responses highlighted gender and sexuality as key signs of what commentators saw as the savagery, barbarism, and fanaticism of the 1889 events. Edward James's purported nudity as he preached provided evidence of savagery for commentators, and headlines and subheadings like "The Wild Orgies of the Blacks" and "Negro Orgies in Georgia" were common.[72] One account claimed that "men, women, and children alike yielded an absolute unquestioning obedience to the bestial whims of their leaders," and other newspaper articles claimed that participants stripped their clothes off during the "orgies."[73] The white press further claimed that women predominated among those around Bell and his successors, with assertions that amplified the claims to base sexuality as central to the gatherings. One white reporter argued that "the women are the more gullible of the negroes and have been led into the most disgraceful concubinages and free love practices."[74] Queen Mary was the subject of particularly harsh racist and misogynist attention from the white press, with newspapers routinely describing her as having an "ugly countenance." Where some saw her as an insignificant addition to the leaders of the Children of the Wilderness, others viewed her as an especially sinister force.[75] Whatever the case, for white observers, bodily excesses of nudity, dancing, and sex, along with the predominance of women, served as signs of a collective disorder that they framed as indicators of a racialized demoralization promoting insanity.

That the religious events in Liberty County were spurred by charismatic individuals who made exalted promises also captured the attention of white commentators as they interpreted the appeal of Bell, James,

and the other leaders. The notion that African Americans were especially liable to be held in thrall to outlandish theologies became a common part of the discourse around the religious enthusiasm. As events in
Liberty County unfolded, however, commentators were forced to admit
that following a "false Christ" was not limited to African Americans because the story of George Jacob Schweinfurth, "the false Christ" of the
Beekmanites, had also been in the news in the spring of 1889. Schweinfurth, a white Methodist minister from Ohio, had joined the Church
of the First Born, which Dora Beekman had founded in 1877 in Illinois
around her claim to have the spirit of Christ in her. After Beekman's
death in 1883, Schweinfurth took up the mantle of the new Christ, and
controversy developed in the church in Rockford, Illinois, as the result
of his relationships with multiple women and a high-profile heresy trial
in the Presbyterian church of a Beekmanite in the spring of 1889, just
before Dupont Bell appeared in Liberty County.[76]

Some press analyses likened the effects of Dupont Bell's preaching on
the community in Liberty County to the "lunacy" Schweinfurth propagated in Illinois.[77] In some cases, the fact that whites embraced Schweinfurth as Christ just as some African Americans had accepted Bell's
preaching served as evidence that anyone could fall under the sway of
"false prophets."[78] Other interpretations of Schweinfurth's success distinguished the nature of such fanaticism in racial terms, insisting that it
was "unremarkable that savages should worship their fetishes, that ignorant negroes should believe in the incantations and orgies of voodooism,
[and] that ignorant men and women should accept the materializa-
tions of cunning charlatans." That supposedly upstanding, intelligent,
white residents of small-town America could be captured by religious
imposture was unfathomable for these white commentators.[79] In one
case when a newspaper castigated white followers of white prophets
as manifesting "a form of insanity" and noted that "violent storm[s] of
religious lunatics" could emerge anywhere, it took pains to insist that
"Georgia still maintains her pre-eminence in respect to grotesqueness
and extravagance" for the "perverted religion" among Black residents of
Liberty County.[80]

Arguments about the susceptibility of Black people to "false prophets" and the framing of Liberty County as the quintessential example

of this problem called forth a strong response on the part of Black religious leaders whose congregations were reportedly empty, and their authority undercut by the power of Bell's promises and the draw of the Children of the Wilderness. Floyd Snelson, a Republican politician and Congregationalist minister, was a major voice among Black clergy opposing the gatherings.[81] In July, a group of Black ministers and officers in local churches, unnamed in the press but likely including Snelson and the Baptist minister William H. Styles, who had petitioned the court to assess Bell's sanity, drafted a set of resolutions to appeal to white authorities to order the "fanatic followers of Dupont Bell, the imposter, to disband."[82] The ministers and church officers characterized the group as "a crazy mob" whose members embraced doctrines and engaged in practices that were "vile and demoralizing" and that had rendered many people insane. The clergy predicted more violence and cases of insanity if the movement was not stopped, and they expressed concern about the damage the "craze" was doing to "the honor and character of our people at home and abroad, misleading the public mind as to the intelligence and piety and honor of our people."[83] Such an appeal calculated the danger to the welfare of Liberty County's Black community the Children of the Wilderness posed as greater than that of calling on white authorities to intervene. Even as they framed the gatherings as harmful, Black ministers insisted that participants represented only a small percentage of residents. Rev. George B. Reid, an African Methodist Episcopal (AME) minister, wrote to the AME paper the *Christian Recorder* to express alarm at the events. "To see many of them act as heathens, yes, worse than heathen in this glorious day of gospel blaze, is marvelous," Reid wrote. "Several of them became perfect lunatics, many families demoralized and all sorts of depredations, not named among heathen, committed."[84] Reid reported that the local AME Church, "with one or two others which was in the midst of the storm, stood almost unshaken," and he assured his readers that the denomination had not contributed to the "ungodly actions" and "abuse of the Christian Church."

Making the case that the members of the Children of the Wilderness represented a small percentage of the county's Black residents was especially pressing for Black religious leaders because of white commentators' emphasis on the fact that educated Black community members like the justice of the peace Edward James were as enthusiastic about what Bell had set in motion as were residents with less formal education.[85] The religious gatherings were, in the words of one white reporter, evidence that the community had "deliberately relapsed into barbarism."[86] One newspaper held, "Every natural tie was forgotten and the most horrible licentiousness prevailed. A noticeable fact in this connection is that the most prominent negroes connected with the outbreak are well-to-do and naturally leaders among their people. The Walthour negroes, the McIvers and the James family have all been noted for their acquired thrift and intelligence. Sam Jones, another leader, is as bright a negro as there is in the county. So with Toney LeCount and a dozen others. The most enlightened have been the most depraved."[87] Moreover, reports in the white press claimed that the enthusiasm had gained "an influence which has thus far paralyzed the advice of the old orthodox colored preachers," including Snelson.[88]

Arguments by white commentators across the nation that even education was no defense against a lapse into savagery, barbarism, and attendant fanaticism and insanity supported calls to prevent African Americans from having access to the vote and to limit their religious autonomy. One newspaper asserted in the context of analyzing the events in Liberty County that "the great crime of the age was the enfranchisement of the negro" and argued that "a people who have shown so little capacity for government should not be considered in the same connection with others of a higher order of intellect."[89] Another warned that Republicans "will have no greater sin to atone for than having forced negro suffrage upon this country."[90] Reflecting back some years later on "traits of the negro race," T. M. Norwood, who had represented Liberty County in the lunacy proceeding against Bell, argued that the events showed the reversion of "our negroes" to "the racial traits of [their] ancestors in Africa" and that this was inevitable after "twenty-five years of freedom and religious instruction by their own race."[91]

The prescription many white commentators offered to quell supposed Black religious fanaticism included renewed emphasis on missionary work and a reconsideration of support for worship separate from whites. James Stacy, a white Presbyterian minister in Liberty County, argued that few participants had come from the local Presbyterian churches, which he believed was due to the enslaver Charles Colcock Jones's insistence on white clerical oversight of Black preachers and the continuation of this practice among the Presbyterians in Georgia. Stacy concluded, "Such proceedings could never have occurred in the days of slavery, when the two races worshipped together" and argued that whites needed to "do more for the religious uplift and training of the colored people" to prevent anything similar from happening.[92] James T. H. Waite, the white Presbyterian pastor of Midway Church in Liberty County at the time of Bell's appearance, offered a similar assessment, characterizing the majority of the community as "Negroes grossly ignorant and dull in the extreme . . . showing no improvement in mind or character or condition since they were freed—mostly members of churches with uneducated ministers."[93] He claimed that very few Black members of the Presbyterian churches attended the meetings of the Children of the Wilderness, even out of mere curiosity, and that his congregants spoke out against the gatherings. In the end, he said, only four from among these congregations "were caught in the craze," and many of the ardent participants emerged "dazed and shamed and looking withered."[94] Waite ended his reflection with a dire warning that of the four million Black people born in America since the end of slavery, only one hundred thousand were in churches. In his view, this situation made another event like that in Liberty County likely, since "all the other dark millions are inclined to the wildest fanaticism."[95]

White observers responding to the Children of the Wilderness embraced and promoted the notion of inherent Black savagery, moderated somewhat by the benevolent influence of Christian slavery but unleashed with emancipation from slavery. For many white commentators on the events of 1889, the group's reported degrading and demoralizing doctrines and ceremonies represented a predictable, if not inevitable, regression to a natural state of barbarism. Commentators on Liberty County characterized the events as involving ignorant people easily duped by religious imposters and marked by religious fanaticism that propagated an infectious insanity against which even education and Christian instruction could not inoculate them. In their published articles in psychiatric journals and addresses at conferences, white psychiatrists, especially those connected to southern hospitals for the insane, promoted similar ideas about Black people's racial propensity for religious excess. In accord with white popular discourse, they argued that African savagery underlay African American religion and had the capacity to foster insanity. Late nineteenth-century white psychiatric theorists of race and mental illness did not necessarily use the popular language of fanaticism, but racial stereotypes of savage and barbaric religion and political and social claims of Black civic incapacity marked their racialization of "religious excitement," understood at the time to be among the possible precipitating causes of insanity.

2

# Black Freedom and the Racialization
of "Religious Excitement"

In December 1896, forty-three-year-old North Carolina–born Charles K. was admitted to the Government Hospital for the Insane in the District of Columbia, also known as St. Elizabeths Hospital. In the synopsis of record that opens his hospital file and that is now housed in the National Archives, Charles is characterized as a "D.C. transient," perhaps an indication that he had arrived recently or had no permanent residence in the city.[1] He was admitted to St. Elizabeths from the almshouse of the Washington Asylum, which also contained a hospital and workhouse, and, although he was listed as married, hospital staff had no information about his relatives or next of kin. It is not clear from his file how he came to be in the almshouse before being transferred to St. Elizabeths, but the Government Hospital for the Insane would be his place of residence until his death from coronary failure in November 1903 and the internment of his remains in the hospital cemetery.[2]

Hospital physicians diagnosed Charles with acute mania—a state of mania of recent onset—and, in response to a question on the form that solicited information about the "supposed cause" of the patient's mental disease, an official recorded "religious excitement." In the years after his admission, the daily ward notes written by nurses assigned to St. Elizabeths' segregated "colored wards" reported that he "imagines that he is God and rules the world" and described him as talking constantly about his "religious delusions," the Bible, and his desire to preach the gospel. The nurses on the ward characterized Charles as obedient and "doing quite well" at times, but at other times as threatening others and experiencing "occasional attacks of violent excitement." Hospital staff responded to his violence by confining him to his room and restraining him with straps.[3] Even as the ward notes describe him as generally noisy, often slamming doors and "throwing up windows," and occasionally hostile to fellow patients, there are also indications that Charles's condition improved. He was moved from Howard Hall, which had been constructed in 1891 to house violent patients and those deemed criminally insane, to the West Lodge, the general building for Black male patients and into a ward in which the men received less oversight than in Howard Hall.[4] Two of his recorded requests during his confinement at St. Elizabeths were to attend chapel services, as he reportedly was "eager to prove that he could behave himself," and to work outdoors because he said it made him feel better to be active. He was sometimes assigned outdoor labor unloading coal at the hospital's boiler house or working on the grounds and eventually was allowed to go to the chapel, where, according to the ward notes, he "conducts himself appropriately."[5] Charles eloped from the hospital early in 1902 but was returned and transferred back to Howard Hall for some time, then back to West Lodge, where his life continued as it had been since his institutionalization, marked by labor, chapel, occasional violent periods, and finally the illness that led to his death.[6]

Charles's world beyond his confinement at St. Elizabeths is difficult to recover. The US census of 1880, the most recent one for which records survive prior to his commitment to the Government Hospital for the Insane, lists several African American men with the same first and last name born in North Carolina and of his approximate age, but it is impossible to identify him with certainty. He is listed in the 1900 US census as an inmate of the hospital, and the enumerator entered "unknown" regarding his parents' places of birth. The only personal information included in the census entry that adds to what is preserved in the hospital record is an indication that he was unable to read or write.[7] As with the others at St. Elizabeths counted in the census that year and listed as inmates, no occupation is recorded. The hospital's ward notes prior to 1900 are not preserved in his case file, and there are no written records about him other than the one-page synopsis of his record, ward notes, and a one-page preliminary autopsy report. Charles's words appear occasionally in his file as reported by the ward nurses, but the textual record as retained focuses on the hospital staff's diagnosis of acute mania, their interpretations of the role his utterances about religion played in his illness, and remarks about his obedience or failure to comply with hospital regulations. His record also features prominent indications of his race. A hospital official wrote "Colored" in parentheses next to his name on the "Synopsis of Record" page in his file, as was done for all

Black patients, and nurses wrote "Colored" at the top of four pages of the preserved ward notes, calling attention to how the white medical staff framed his illness in racialized ways.

One can see something of Charles himself only in a four-by-six-inch black-and-white photograph taken in 1901 when he was about forty-eight and included in the materials preserved in his file. A dark-skinned man with close-cropped hair, a scar below his lower lip on the right side of his face, and a bushy mustache that extends beyond his mouth and onto his cheeks, Charles is seated with his arms resting on his thighs. He is wearing a dark wool jacket that is in good condition but slightly too small for him, and one can tell by the cuffs that peek out from the jacket that he wears a checked shirt underneath. He looks directly into the camera with a confident gaze and a serious, but not severe, expression. Any sense of his personality, comportment, where he took enjoyment in life, what his fears were, or what religious experience and preaching the gospel meant to him cannot be gleaned from the photograph. Within two years of sitting for this photograph, Charles would be dead and buried in the hospital cemetery along with other "friendless" patients who had no one to claim them or whose loved ones had no knowledge of their whereabouts.

Charles's confinement at St. Elizabeths reflected medical and state assessments that he was unable to care for himself and perhaps that he presented a danger to others. As already noted, he had been transferred to the hospital from the almshouse. As a recent arrival to the city who may not have had a permanent residence, he may have been consigned there under the District's vagrancy laws or because the city's lunacy laws required a stay and evaluation at the Washington Asylum prior to transfer to St. Elizabeths for long-term care.[8] Charles may have been unable to find work, or he may have been uninterested in employment or a permanent dwelling in order to devote himself to the religious mission of preaching the gospel he announced to the hospital staff. His reported belief that he was God may have become the primary focus of his attention to the exclusion of all else. Charles may have struggled financially, experienced mental distress, been unruly in public, or all three and more, motivating authorities to declare him insane and to detain him for an extended period. The preserved record makes it difficult to say more than this.

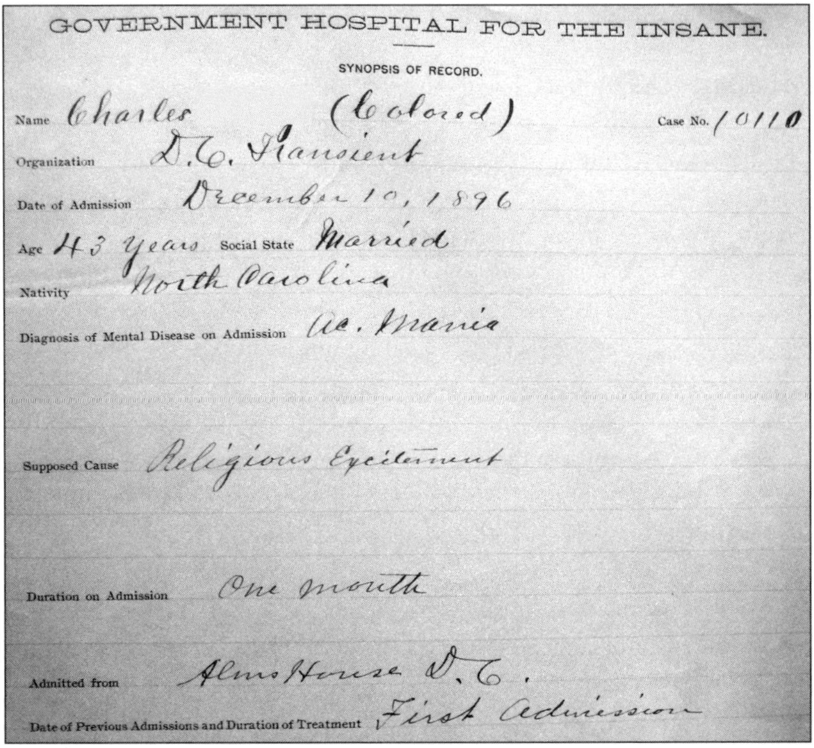

GOVERNMENT HOSPITAL FOR THE INSANE.

SYNOPSIS OF RECORD.

Name Charles (Colored) Case No. 10110

Organization D.C. Transient

Date of Admission December 10, 1896

Age 43 years Social State Married

Nativity North Carolina

Diagnosis of Mental Disease on Admission Ac. Mania

Supposed Cause Religious Excitement

Duration on Admission One month

Admitted from Alms House D.C.

Date of Previous Admissions and Duration of Treatment First admission

Figure 2.1. Detail from St. Elizabeths Hospital Synopsis of Record for Charles K., December 10, 1896, showing "religious excitement" as the supposed cause of his mental disease. Records of St. Elizabeths Hospital, National Archives and Records Administration, National Archives Building, Washington, DC.

What we do know is that Charles was confined in St. Elizabeths at a time when white medical authorities—asylum superintendents, doctors, neurologists, alienists specializing in the psychology of crime, and pathologists—who claimed expertise to define mental normalcy and deviance increasingly understood "religious excitement," the supposed cause of his diagnosed acute mania, in racialized ways and as an agitating cause to which African Americans were particularly susceptible. The claim that religious excitement, a broad category signaling the idea that excessive or disordered religious belief and practice could become overwhelming and produce mental derangement, was not new at this time in the United States and not limited to the United States, nor, as noted earlier, was the diagnosis applied only to Black people. Across American history, medical, religious, and cultural authorities often deemed new theologies and forms of religious expression as having the potential to endanger the sanity of those involved. Such assessments were sometimes aimed at containing the potential social disruption of new religious movements, some of which called on members to reorganize family, economy, and society. But the late nineteenth-century linking of religious excitement and Black religions in a psychiatric context represented a narrowing of the association between religious excess and mental illness from its earlier, broader application.

Throughout the nineteenth century, white religious, medical, and political leaders theorized about the potential negative influence of religion on the mental health of white Americans. The 1860 US Federal Census, for which enumerators were instructed to record information about the prevalence and causes of insanity, provides one snapshot of understandings of religion-related mental illness among whites in the period just prior to the end of slavery.[9] Religious causes were among the options for enumerators to note as they collected data on those deemed by family members or medical authorities to be mentally ill. Enumerators were instructed: "You will in every case inquire into the cause or origin thereof, and write the word—as intemperance, spiritualism, grief, affliction, heredity, misfortune &c. As nearly every case of insanity may be traced to some known cause, it is earnestly desired that you will not fail to make your return in this respect as perfect as possible."[10] In the introduction to the published statistical report of the results of the 1860 census, the unnamed author contended that religious excitement was "among the most frequent generative agents of insanity in the United States." According to the report, such insanity resulted from extended individual or group religious exercises that created "nervous exhaustion," from preaching that "subverts reason" through focus on cultivating fear of divine wrath. It noted that insanity could also result from intense religious study or reading that led to rumination on "personal demerit and its consequent punishment."[11] In addition to these broad characteristics the Census Bureau associated with religious excitement, those investigating connections between religion and mental illness in 1860 considered some religious groups and theologies as more likely to contribute to insanity than others. The instructions for census enumerators offered Spiritualism, a movement popular in the nineteenth century and grounded in belief in the ability to contact and communicate with the dead, as the single example of religion as an exciting cause. But, as the sociologist William Sims Bainbridge shows in a study of the 1860 census and the idea of religious insanity, enumerators offered a range of descriptions in their entries on the census itself, from general religious excitement to indicating specific religious groups.[12]

Thus, the idea that improper religion could precipitate mental illness was not new in the American context when commentators felt moved to reflect on the events in Liberty County, Georgia, in 1889, or in 1896, when Charles K. was among those Black patients committed to St. Elizabeths Hospital and characterized as suffering from insanity caused by "religious excitement." In his discussion of nineteenth-century theories of religious insanity, Bainbridge argues that, although the idea of religious excitement as pathological could be mobilized to contain new groups perceived by some as unruly or dangerous, in general diagnoses of religiously grounded mental illness in the mid-nineteenth century were likely "benevolent" because physicians "saw patients as *individuals* driven mad by very particular circumstances rather than as faceless multitudes swarming in vast herds named by a few diagnostic terms."[13] This may have been the case for white Americans considered to have been made ill by what was perceived as excessive or improper religion, but racialized constructions of both religion and mental illness placed Black patients in a framework that had roots in the era of slavery and alleged that racial traits rather than individual circumstances shaped mental states. As the historian Wendy Gonaver argues in her study of race and early nineteenth-century psychiatry at the Eastern Lunatic Asylum in Virginia, "the only U.S. institution to accept slaves and free blacks as patients and to employ slaves as caregivers," for white physicians, "excessive enthusiasm, evidenced by religious passion or sexual ardor, was associated with black patients; white patients were encouraged to suppress enthusiasm because of its supposed deleterious effects."[14]

By the time Charles K. was consigned to the Government Hospital for the Insane in 1896, formerly enslaved Black people and those born in the wake of slavery were being institutionalized in state hospitals in numbers that marked a shift from the antebellum period, when white enslavers generally oversaw the treatment of those they enslaved. In the case of Virginia, the establishment of the Central Lunatic Asylum for Colored Insane in 1870 allowed white officials to protect white patients from the influence of what they viewed as excessive religious enthusiasm and savagery in Black patients. In other southern states, the region where most African Americans deemed insane were institutionalized, racial segregation within hospitals served a similar purpose at a time when white physicians asserted that religious excitement among Black people had become an alarming problem. The racialization as Black of religious excitement as a precipitating cause of insanity lent medical authority to the pathologizing of African American religious life. The impact of the theories white doctors developed to explain a supposed connection between Black religions and mental illness became amplified in the post-Reconstruction period in the context of debates about Black civic, political, and social capacity. Amid these debates and proffering of medical theories about religion, race, and mental normalcy, people like Charles K. continued to be institutionalized, designated officially as having been rendered insane because of "religious excitement."

## "A World of Mental Excitement"

In an address delivered to attendees at the 1895 meeting of the National Conference of Charities and Correction, the Presbyterian physician James Woods Babcock, superintendent of the South Carolina Lunatic Asylum in Columbia, expressed worry. Babcock informed his fellow white social welfare and charity workers, prison officials, and medical professionals from institutions across the country that, since the end of slavery, diagnoses of insanity among southern African Americans had risen rapidly, particularly as compared with whites, and the increase was placing great stress on the ability of institutions to deal with what he characterized as "this constant accumulation of lunatics."[15] Citing federal census data, he charted a national increase from 175 "colored insane" per million inhabitants in 1850 to 886 per million in 1890. He contended that, while these recent statistics represented admissions to hospitals that did not occur under slavery and that the proportion of insane people of African descent to their representation in the population was far higher in northern states in 1890, the rising number in the South was cause for concern. Babcock provided the example of Virginia, where, he told his audience, "It has been claimed the increase of insanity in the colored race has been for twenty-five years at the rate of 100 or more percent every ten years."[16] Virginia may have presented the extreme case in his survey, but it was not alone. Middleton Lee Perry, a Baptist layman and son of a Confederate army captain, concurred with this assessment a few years later from his position as pathologist at the Georgia State Sanitarium at Milledgeville, where Dupont Bell and Edward James had been committed because of their leadership of the Children of the Wilderness in Liberty County.[17] Perry wrote that, "in forty years, the total negro population of the State has been a little more than doubled, while the number of insane has increased twenty-fold. No other such rapid and radical change in the mental stability of a race is recorded in history."[18]

What did these white physicians think had caused this increase? Babcock told his audience that day that he believed Black people could not manage freedom and that this was responsible for the rise in cases of insanity. Babcock argued, and many white physicians in hospitals for those deemed insane concurred, that emancipation had propelled formerly enslaved African Americans into "excitement and general agitation" from which, he insisted, slavery had long shielded them.[19] In publishing a 1900 address to the American Medico-Psychological Association on African American psychology by Virginia medical professor J. Allison Hodges, the *Richmond Times* summarized Hodges's conclusions in the headline "Freedom Fatal for the Negro" and subtitles "Insanity's Ravages" and "The Race Is Degenerating."[20] Hodges, a Presbyterian who grew up in a family that enslaved twenty Black people in 1860, expressed fondness for the "true soul of the trusty slave" and recalled warmly the "sympathy of my old black mammy," but insisted that he was bringing his scientific expertise to bear on pressing social questions.[21]

These early psychiatrists enumerated causes and precipitators of mental illness among Black people in what J. D. Roberts, the superintendent of the Eastern North Carolina Insane Asylum, a Baptist deacon, and the son of an enslaver, described as Black people's "clash with civilization" after the end of slavery.[22] Proposed causes of insanity under the general diagnoses of mania and melancholy included heredity, senility, injury, alcoholism, and syphilis and were not limited to African Americans. The certainty among white medical professionals that along with these, "religious excitement" was a significant precipitator of insanity among

African Americans, is a striking feature of these accounts. In his address, Babcock highlighted "agitating novelties in religion" as chief among the mental excitements facing African Americans by the turn of the twentieth century and contributing to psychological disorder.

In Babcock's review of hospital data from South Carolina and Virginia, he reported that for Black patients, religious excitement was the second most frequently listed cause of insanity in the previous decades, behind "alcoholic dissipation" in Virginia and heredity in South Carolina.[23] Other physicians concurred with Babcock's assessment about the significance of religion to what many saw as a growing problem among African Americans. In 1901, Alonzo B. Richardson, a Methodist and former Union soldier who served as superintendent of the Government Hospital for the Insane in Washington, DC, told the *Washington Post* that there had been a dramatic increase in the number of patients admitted to the institution in recent years, noting that "it is true that religious mania is a symptom of many of those admitted. All classes have increased in the same proportion, with the exception of negroes. They have gained most rapidly."[24]

The attention Babcock and other doctors gave to the increasing diagnoses of insanity among African Americans in this period, with many attributed to religious causes, emerged within the political, social, and religious landscape of the post-Reconstruction period and helped to justify the hardening system of segregation that shaped Charles K.'s young adulthood in North Carolina. During Reconstruction and the decades after, Black southerners fortified Christian churches as sites for spiritual, social, educational, and economic development, as well as political education and activism. Despite theological differences and varied approaches to organization and worship, Black churches came to occupy a central place in Black communities and served as a bulwark against the rising tide of Jim Crow segregation.[25] It was only one year after Babcock's 1895 address before the National Conference of Charities and Correction and the same year as Charles K.'s admission to the hospital that the US Supreme Court issued its opinion in the case of *Plessy v. Ferguson*, affirming the legality of formal structures of racial segregation. In addition to formal segregation, other means of restriction and containment affected African Americans in the late nineteenth and early twentieth centuries, and the potential for incarceration in a variety of institutions, including jails, penitentiaries,

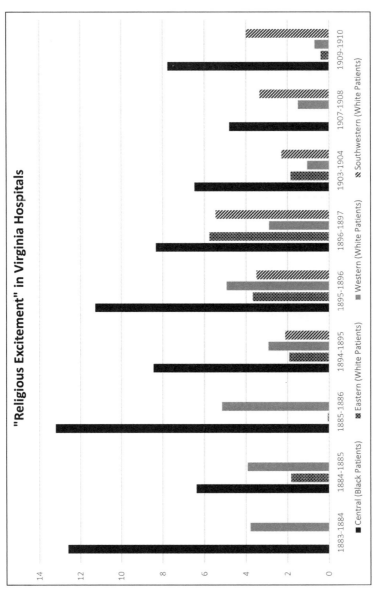

Figure 2.2. Graph showing the percentage of admissions listing religious causes or religious excitement as the supposed cause of insanity in Virginia state hospitals in selected years (1883–1910), drawing on figures from hospital annual reports. Religious causes were listed for a higher percentage of patients admitted to the Central Lunatic Asylum (renamed Central State Hospital in 1893), which housed only Black patients, than for white patients in the state's other hospitals.

almshouses, institutions of reform aimed at curbing prostitution, and insane asylums loomed. Within the context of white doctors' solidifying consensus that there was a connection between freedom and insanity among African Americans, Charles's social and economic struggles as a poor transient in the nation's capital and his turn to religious expression to make meaning of his circumstances could be easily medicalized. He was among many African Americans in this period who were building lives in freedom and came under the scrutiny of psychiatrists, police, and judges applying racialized ideas about religion and mental normalcy.[26]

Late nineteenth-century white physicians' claims of a link between insanity and unfitness for freedom among African Americans amplified antebellum white medical opinion that efforts by enslaved Black people to free themselves constituted a form of mental illness. In 1851, the New Orleans physician Samuel A. Cartwright proposed the diagnosis of drapetomania, a condition he claimed to have identified in the enslaved as "the disease causing Negroes to run away."[27] In proposing this disease, he brought together his experience as an enslaver of six Black people at the time this work was published, his own religious background as a minister's son, and his authority as a physician, although only the latter was made explicit in his writings.[28] Cartwright assured his readers that drapetomania could be cured through proper management of the enslaved, and he contended that the Bible offered resources to effect the cure. Cartwright called attention to interpretations of the story of Noah's sons as the progenitors of racial groups and affirmed the popular conception that Black people descended from Ham, whose son Canaan Noah cursed to servitude.[29] "To ascertain the true method of governing negroes, so as to cure and prevent the disease under consideration," Cartwright wrote, "we must go back to the Pentateuch, and learn the true meaning of the untranslated term that represents the negro race." God's will for Black people, he argued, could be found in the meaning of the name Canaan: "to submit, to bend the knee." In the belief that names reveal nature, Cartwright asserted, "If the white man attempts to oppose the Deity's will, by trying to make the Negro anything else than 'the submissive knee-bender' (which the Almighty declared he should be)," drapetomania will be the result. He counseled the enslaver not to "abuse the power which God has given him over his fellow-man" but rather to treat enslaved Black people kindly as children to prevent or cure the disease. If, however, "any one or more of them, at any time, are inclined to raise their heads to a level with their master or overseer, humanity and their own good require that they be punished until they fall into that submissive state which it was intended for them to occupy in all after-time, when their progenitor received the name of Canaan or 'submissive knee-bender.'"[30]

In the same article, Cartwright proposed another disease, dysaesthesia Aethiopica, which he claimed was "peculiar to negroes, affecting mind and body" and manifested in disrespect for and destruction of property, stealing, and "rascality." He argued that this disease resulted from allowing enslaved people to "live like free negroes in regard to diet, drinks, exercise, etc.," and without the controlling influence and direction of white people. In short, he asserted, this condition "is the natural offspring of Negro liberty—the liberty to be idle, to wallow in filth, and to indulge in improper food and drinks."[31] Cartwright counseled that physical stimulation of skin and liver was required to arouse the enslaved from the torpor of mind and body that he claimed resulted from dysaesthesia Aethiopica, but he noted that because the disease created "a partial insensibility of the skin," oiling the skin, slapping "the oil in with a broad leather strap," and putting the individual to hard labor would be necessary.[32] Cartwright connected the religious and moral development of Black people to white discipline, insisting that Black people can only "receive moral culture and . . . profit by religious or other instructions, when under the compulsatory authority of the white man." This was so, he claimed, because a natural inclination to sloth inhibited the flow of blood necessary for intellectual and moral development. He contended that "the black blood distributed to the brain chains the mind to ignorance, superstition and barbarism, and bolts the door against civilization, moral culture and religious truth."[33]

In this way, Cartwright contributed to religious arguments for the perpetual subordination of Black people, claiming that their divinely ordained status as servants required it. He further linked religious arguments about Black servitude to the medical claim that Black people's impulse for freedom represented a mental disorder. His creation of these disease categories of drapetomania and dysaesthesia Aethiopica sat in the broader context of white racial science of the day and debates about the origins and nature of races.[34] Moreover, he connected the religious and medical arguments for Black people's fixed status as servants to the American political context, insisting that the Declaration of Independence's assertion of equality was "only intended to apply to white men" and that liberty was "not only unsuitable to the negro race, but actually poisonous to its happiness."[35] These interconnected religious, medical, and political arguments, aimed at authorizing Black servitude and framing Black people's desire for liberty as contrary to God's will and reflective of mental unsoundness, prefigured approaches late nineteenth-century white psychiatrists would take in theorizing about Black religion and mental illness.

In the post-Reconstruction medical literature, white physicians rarely made arguments from the Bible and instead foregrounded characterizations of Black religious propensities through a frame they presented as scientific. As they developed a psychiatric frame to assess the impact of religion on Black mental health, white physicians evaluated Black religion in ways that established norms for what they took to be true, proper, and beneficial religion. In accounting for and responding to what they saw as an emerging medical and social crisis, Babcock and other late nineteenth-century and early twentieth-century white psychiatrists produced theories of religion that became constitutive elements of their racialized understandings of the normal and disordered mind. As a precipitating factor for mental illness, "excessive religious excitement," as E. M. Green, clinical director of the Georgia State Sanitarium from 1907 to 1917, argued characterized Black people's expressions, was not a neutral notion.[36] Like so much about evaluations of religion in American culture, interpretations of religious affect were often racialized and gendered, as were assessments of theologies and religious organization. Mainstream white Protestantism, positioned as rational, restrained, orderly, and contributing to the public good, set the standard for popular and medical assessments of acceptable religion, as opposed to religious expressions characterized as excessive and irrational, including aspects of African American religious life.

In many ways the actual content of African American religious beliefs or the nature of religious practices mattered little in this process, although white psychiatrists would develop elaborate theories about the constituent components of what they imagined Black religion to be. Like the social scientists in this same period about whom the historian of religion Curtis J. Evans writes, white psychiatrists "were desirous of providing a scientific analysis of black religion and explicitly sought to distance themselves from a theological framework. For all their protests to the contrary, however, their works contained implicit theological and moral critiques of black religion" as lacking in ethics and bearing the influence of African "superstitions."[37] Many white psychiatrists in this era had deep connections to Protestant denominations and participated in religiously grounded social reform activities. Their assumptions about spiritual authenticity as indicated in thoughtful and rational religion and their view of appropriate worship as restrained no doubt shaped their work as medical professionals theorizing about and attending to Black patients whose religious ways they found lacking these characteristics.

So, too, did their location in a culture of white supremacy set the broader context of their professional practices.[38] Edwin Melvin Green, the clinical director of the Georgia State Sanitarium, for example, was the grandson of an enslaver and the son of a Presbyterian minister, and himself owned land in Liberty County adjacent to the Walthour property where the Children of the Wilderness held their religious gatherings.[39] James D. Roberts, superintendent of North Carolina's Eastern Insane Asylum in Goldsboro from 1882 to 1888, grew up in a household in which his father, also a doctor, held twelve people in bondage and his grandmother, who lived with the family, enslaved eight people. Roberts was a Baptist deacon and represented Goldsboro at the state Baptist convention meeting in 1883. During his time as a deacon in the First Baptist Church of Goldsboro, Thomas Dixon Jr., the author of the novel *The Clansman* that was the source for D. W. Griffith's infamously racist film *The Birth of a Nation* (1917), served as pastor for a brief period.[40] Many other white physicians who worked in state mental hospitals and contributed to the medical literature theorizing the relation of religion to Black mental health had similar personal histories and religious commitments. Influential white psychiatrists developed their theories and treatment practices with respect to mental illness among African Americans in the context of their own religious, political, and social commitments in addition to the prevailing medical standards.

Indeed, commitment to "churchly" white Protestantism that vested authority in religious institutions and indexed the state of society in relation to the health of churches bridged the perspectives of many

white southern doctors from enslaving families and with other investments in the prevailing southern racial order and those of white doctors from other regions of the country who may not have had direct
experience with Black people, slavery, or southern racial segregation.[41]
As staff in the hospitals to which most African Americans were committed for treatment in the late nineteenth and early twentieth centuries,
white southern physicians dominated the public discourse on theories
about the relationship of Black religion to mental health. They propagated their theories on a national scale through publications in medical
journals like *Alienist and Neurologist*, the *Journal of Nervous and Mental
Disease*, and the *American Journal of Psychiatry*; in the annual reports of
state hospitals for the insane; and through addresses at medical conferences and meetings of social welfare workers and public officials, such
as the National Conference of Charities and Correction, where Babcock
spoke in 1895 about his sense of an increase in insanity among African
Americans. The result was a national discourse stemming from the work
of southern white doctors in whose hospitals most African American
patients in this period were treated.

   Late nineteenth-century and early twentieth-century psychiatric assessments of African American religion conveyed a host of racialized
beliefs that rendered a diagnosis of religious mania or religious melancholia, or the identification of religious excitement as a precipitating
cause of mental disturbance for a Black patient qualitatively different
from the invocation of mental disturbance grounded in religious sensibilities for white people. Psychiatrists, charity workers, and religious
leaders offered a standard set of explanations for the apparent rise in
insanity among African Americans. Their approaches revolved around
the relationship of ideas about "savagery," by which they assessed African and African American culture as primitive, to "civilization," as typified in white American culture. White psychiatric theory further traced
Black people's movement from slavery, during which time they supposedly benefited from the custodial care of civilized whites, to freedom that
they were ill-equipped to manage, these doctors held. In this view, Black
people's propensity for religious excess and fanaticism contributed to the
increase in mental illness, and the form of their religious expression in a
state of insanity, most often characterized in the medical context as religious excitement, revealed their underlying racialized mental limitations.

## "The Clash with Civilization"

It was routine for white psychiatrists in the late nineteenth and early twentieth centuries to frame their addresses and published studies about the Black mind by constructing and rehearsing a trajectory from "savagery" as a cultural, moral, and racial state; through benevolent enslavement in the United States; to recent emancipation, a social change that produced overwhelming stress in "the clash with civilization."[42] The historian Martin Summers writes about this body of literature as reflecting "an a priori belief in a distinctive black psyche" and working to "reaffirm the white psyche as the norm." The consistency of the arguments and circulation of tropes about the Black mind, Summers writes, suggests that "we might consider the published work as rising to the level of genre."[43] We can see the components of the genre in a multipart series in 1885 and 1886 titled "Race and Insanity," published in the *Journal of Nervous and Mental Disease*. James G. Kiernan, a New Yorker serving as the medical director of Chicago's Cook County Hospital for the Insane, prefaced his "Ethnological Psychiatry" study of twenty-eight Black patients with broad, essentialist claims about the race's "peculiar relation to the civilization pervading the country" as a result of having been "transported under the most unfavorable circumstances from the depths of the lowest barbarism to the height of civilization." This sudden change produced "but a caricature of civilization," Kiernan asserted.[44]

Such a claim about the mental disruption caused by what white doctors described as barely civilized savages thrust into modernity was widespread in the early psychiatric literature on race and insanity throughout the late nineteenth century and well into the twentieth century, even as many aspects of theories about causes and diagnosis of mental illness changed over time. Studies published by psychiatrists at St. Elizabeths Hospital, which, as the Government Hospital for the Insane, was a leading research institution in the early twentieth century, reflect the enduring impact of this perspective. One St. Elizabeths psychiatrist, Mary O'Malley, daughter of Irish immigrants who grew up in Buffalo and graduated from a Catholic medical university, began her 1914 study of psychoses among black patients with the assertion that "only 300 years ago the Negro ancestors of this race were naked dwellers on the west coast of Africa, whither they had been driven by superior

Negro tribes. . . . Here these outcasts, unfit even to compete with these other uncivilized races, were found by the slave traders in the depths of savagery and suddenly transplanted to an environment of the highest civilization, and 250 years later had all the responsibilities of this higher race thrust upon them."[45] In 1921, her colleague William M. Bevis, a Floridian and grandson of Confederate and Union veterans, began his observations on Negro psychoses with a similar historical frame, writing, "Less than three hundred years ago the alien ancestors of most of the families of this race were savages or cannibals in the jungles of Central Africa. From this very primitive level they were unwillingly brought to these shores and into an environment of higher civilization for which the biological development of the race had not made adequate preparation."[46] And, as late as 1938, Philip Sigmund Wagner, a Cincinnati psychiatrist, framed his comparative study of white and Black psychiatric patients with the assertion that "the Negro is only four generations from 'savage life,' and only two generations from rural life," a state he located on a trajectory of progress and clearly viewed as less advanced than urban life.[47]

While the many similar accounts in the literature marked change over time from Black people's circumstances in Africa to those in the United States, white doctors routinely insisted on the lack of civilizational development or progress on the part of African Americans as a factor in the growth in cases of insanity. John E. Lind, O'Malley's colleague at St. Elizabeths, asserted, "Because he [the Negro] wears a Palm Beach suit instead of a string of cowries, carries a gold-headed cane instead of a spear, uses a telephone instead of beating the drum from hill to hill and for the jungle path has substituted the pay-as-you-enter street-car, his psychology is no less that of the African."[48] As with white missionary and political assessments of what the historian Kathryn Gin Lum calls "the historyless heathen," these psychiatric evaluations of African and African American culture claimed stunted growth because of cultural immaturity deriving from what many white psychiatrists characterized as essential "race traits."[49]

Another grounding assumption in white physicians' discussions about the relationship of race to mental illness for Black people was that insanity did not exist among Africans in Africa because "civilization" was a prerequisite for such mental disturbance. Many argued that, be-

cause of what they believed was the inherent savagery and backwardness of African people, African social life was too simple to produce the
stresses of civilized life. George M. Beard, an American neurologist who
in 1869 described a condition he called neurasthenia as a disease of "nervous exhaustion," built his theory, in part, on the idea that Africans and
Native Americans did not experience mental illnesses. Beard, the son of
a Congregationalist minister, asserted in his book *American Nervousness* (1881) that "where there is no civilization there is no nervousness,
no matter what the personal habits may be, even though the experiment
be made, as in Africa, for centuries."[50] Similarly, at the National Conference of Charities and Correction in 1899, General Roeliff Brinkerhoff of
the Ohio Board, who had served as president of the national conference
in 1880, claimed that "when David Livingstone went to Africa, he never
found a black man insane."[51] In his study of "insanity in the colored
race," Abraham H. Witmer, from a Pennsylvania Mennonite family and
a psychiatrist at St. Elizabeths in DC, justified his focus on the United
States, writing, "We limit our consideration of insanity in the race to the
United States of North America, since in this country alone, so far as I
know, has the subject received the attention of the statistician, because I
have not been able to discover that the disease has obtained recognition
among the native African negroes."[52]

The evidence these white physicians offered regarding the absence
of insanity in Africa was usually hearsay from travel and missionary
accounts. James M. Buchanan, a Presbyterian and an assistant physician at the Mississippi State Lunatic Asylum whose father held twenty-
three people in slavery during his childhood, asserted in an 1886 piece
in the *New York Medical Journal* that "from information obtained by
travelers in Africa, we learn that insanity among the natives is almost
unknown."[53] Babcock prefaced his 1895 address at the National Conference of Charities and Correction in which he presented statistics indicating a dramatic increase in insanity among African Americans with a
similar claim that "according to the testimony of travelers and natives,
mental disease is almost unknown among the savage tribes of Africa."[54]
Regardless of the vagueness of the sources and despite occasional claims
to the contrary, late nineteenth-century white psychiatrists routinely asserted the rarity of insanity in Africa as the opening to discussions of
their conceptions of the Black psyche.[55] Indeed, Beard presented it as

an obvious fact not requiring proof, writing, "It is not necessary to read books of travel in order to know that nervous diseases do not exist, or exist but very rarely among savages or semi-savages, or even among bar-barians."[56] For these psychiatric theorists and medical practitioners, the idea that mental illness was largely absent in Africa did not serve as an argument for the hardiness or superiority of Africans' psychology but simply as a backdrop to justify claims of Black people's essential unfit-ness for civilization as typified in American society.

The notion that slavery had provided a protective environment for Black people who in freedom found themselves adrift in the unknown of "advancing civilization" forms a major theme in early psychiatric lit-erature about African Americans and mental health. J. D. Roberts of North Carolina's Eastern Insane Asylum summarized the view of many medical and charity commentators in writing, "Generally well fed and well clothed he [the enslaved Black person] had but little thought for the morrow, knowing that his master would provide for him, he did not burden his mind with a thought as to any provision for self or family. After emancipation he found himself called upon to provide for those around him."[57] In a discussion among attendees at the 1896 Charities and Correction national conference of approaches to social problems, the minutes record North Carolinian Claudius B. Denson drawing con-nections among various strands of argument in this period about what accounted for the increase in cases of insanity among African Ameri-cans. He contended that, prior to the war, "the spectacle of an hysterical, insane negro was very rare in the South" and that care in hospitals was easily managed. "Circumstances have changed the environments of the negro," he continued. "He is fighting his own battle of life, and is in a hard struggle. . . . He has the care of his own little children, of which he had little before, and the care of himself; and he goes down in the struggle, and very rapidly, and the number of insane has increased."[58] In a paper read at the 1896 meeting of the Southern Medico-Psychological Association and later circulated as a pamphlet, Southern Methodist John Fulenwider Miller, son of an enslaver, former Confederate army surgeon, and superintendent of North Carolina's Eastern Hospital from 1888 to 1906, concluded, "from close personal observation, embracing professional life of nearly forty years among the negroes and from data obtained from professional brethren in different sections of the South," that slavery had been a beneficial environment for Black people's well-being. He asserted, "It is an undisputed fact, known to our Southern people, that no race of men ever lived under better hygienic restraint or had governing their lives rules and regulations more conducive to physical health and mental repose. . . . Freedom came to him and a change came over his entire life."[59]

Other presenters at meetings of the National Conference of Charities and Correction couched similar opinions grounded in personal investments in slavery in scientific cover. William F. Drewry, a southern Methodist and the Superintendent of Virginia's Central State Hospital for the Insane, which housed only Black patients, informed those gathered at the 1908 conference in Richmond, Virginia, that "the old inhabitants tell us that before the '60s an insane negro was a rarity, and the facts all go to show that the disease was by no means prevalent among the race. The regular, simple life, the hygienic conditions, the freedom from dissipation and excitement, steady and healthful employment, enforced self-restraint, the freedom from care and responsibility, the plain, wholesome, nourishing food, comfortable clothing, the open-air life upon the plantation, the kindly care and treatment when sick, in those days, all acted as preventive measures against mental breakdown in the negro."[60] Predictably, given his family's status as enslavers, Drewry argued that "after the war there was a great change in conditions. The negro, as a race, was not prepared to care for himself, to combat the new problems in his life. His weak points were no longer protected."[61] Drewry claimed that "the greater number of insane negroes come from the uneducated, thriftless classes and from the old and decrepit"; he saw some resistance to mental illness among African Americans with more education and financial stability, although he believed they were still more likely than whites to become insane under similar conditions of life.[62]

Some psychiatrists drew connections between the notion that slavery had protected Black people's minds from worry and arguments about the moral benefits of bondage. Abram H. Witmer, a physician at St. Elizabeths, argued in his article "Insanity in the Colored Race in the United States" (1891) that "previous to emancipation, the health and morals of the slaves were carefully preserved, and inebriety, excessive venery, and venereal diseases were closely guarded against; since their liberation, through overindulgence, exposure and ignorance to the laws of health, many have suffered from the effects of these fruitful causes of insanity."[63] Witmer, like many other physicians, highlighted the connection between deteriorating physical conditions in freedom—poverty, unhealthy living conditions, and disease—and the rise in mental disorders. Whereas these conditions could be understood to stem from racism and lack of access to resources and addressed through expansion of economic, political, social, and educational opportunity, Witmer turned to arguments much more common among white psychiatrists about innate, racialized mental and emotional capacity as shaping the response of Black people to the disciplining benefits of slavery. "Untutored in a knowledge of the world," he argued, "and without a sound philosophy or a religion deeper seated than the emotions to sustain them in adversity, many minds have failed under the constant strain of their advancing civilization."[64]

Arguments about geography, race, and culture figured into late nineteenth-century and early twentieth-century psychiatric theories about African Americans, freedom, and an increase in cases of insanity. Some physicians pointed to locations within the United States where they believed African cultures and religions were preserved and that provided unique access to explore the effect of "the clash with civilization" in the years after the end of slavery. In *American Nervousness*, George Beard extended his argument that Africans did not suffer from mental illness into a discussion of what he characterized as "Africa in America" on the Sea Islands off the coasts of South Carolina and Georgia. He asserted that, in this region, Black people "at no time have been brought into relation with our civilization, except so far as it is exhibited in a very few white inhabitants in the vicinity. Intellectually, they can be not very much in advance of their African ancestors."[65] Despite the work of philanthropists to teach formerly enslaved Black people to read and to promote "civilization," he claimed they cared little for it and remained "a bit of barbarism at our door-step." Beard continued to argue that the end of slavery had brought Sea Islanders into a life of stress for which they were unprepared and for which they had little focus or energy. "The anxieties about the future, family, property, etc.," he argued (without evidence), "are certainly so wearing on the negro, that some of them without doubt, have expressed a wish to return to slavery."[66]

White psychiatrists' curiosity about the mental states of Black people in what they framed as the exceptional context of "Africa in America" arose only partly from cultural concerns about how Black "savages" fared in white Christian "civilization." Some white psychiatrists also drew conclusions about racial categories and change, noting that most of their patients classified as racially Negro were not "pure" Africans but rather represented the "colored race" that resulted from the mixing of Europeans and Africans in America. These physicians sought to determine the influence of racial mixture and whiteness on African Americans' mental stability, building on antebellum race science that embraced race as a biological fact; took racial groups to be distinct from one another; and asserted the physical, mental, and moral weakness of the "mulatto."[67] As the psychologist G. Stanley Hall wrote on this question, "The chief event in the history of the Southern Negro in the new world is the infiltration of white blood. . . . The most serious aspect of the Negro question, thus, is found in the fact that the most important portion of the race, whatever its size, inherits more or less of the best Anglo-Saxon cavalier blood, brain, and temper. Thus all the vast psychophysical differences between the two races are bridged, and they possibly fuse with each other by all imperceptible gradations. We know too little of the laws of heredity to evaluate the profit and loss of this blood mixture."[68] In a study of "psychoses of the colored race," St. Elizabeths' Mary O'Malley was willing to offer a more substantive opinion on the impact of racial mixture on moral capacity. "This miscegenation appears to have affected the longevity of the race," she wrote, "and the changed social environment has brought about a moral and mental deterioration, together with a diminished power of vital resistance. Information has been brought out by some writers that the mulatto more nearly approaches the white in the contour and shape of the cranium . . . ; that the race may have gained in an intellectual way but not in a moral."[69]

Several asylum physicians insisted that racial mixture in people of African descent resulted in a higher incidence of mental illness than in "pure" Black or white people. North Carolina's John Fulenwider Miller claimed at the 1893 annual meeting of the American Medico-Psychological Association that, in his hospital, "we have more mulattoes insane in proportion to the mulatto population of the State than we have of the negro proper." J. Allison Hodges of Virginia made a similar assertion in a speech before the same association in 1900, saying that he accepted the opinion of "many intelligent people of competent authority and of full acquaintance with the negro who unhesitatingly state that they never saw a consumptive or insane negro of unmixed blood in the South prior to emancipation."[70] William M. Bevis of St. Elizabeths Hospital may have accepted the idea that "mulattoes" became insane at a greater rate than "pure" Blacks, but he rejected claims of widespread racial mixture in the South, arguing instead that "the pure black African stock" made up the majority of the population. Bevis did so largely on belief in the superiority of white people, asserting that, had there been racial mixing, "the hereditary effect upon the more or less mulatto off-spring would naturally be that of improvement of the traits and mentality of the colored race," of which he said he saw no evidence.[71]

White psychiatrists who discussed the impact of racial mixture on the psychological state of people of African descent in the United States generally avoided noting that white male enslavers' forced sexual relations with enslaved Black women had produced "the mulatto population" of the South, and they failed to attend to the psychological impact on Black women of rape and sexual exploitation under slavery. Some, like St. Elizabeths' William Bevis, claimed that Black women were sexually promiscuous and craved relationships with white men with the goal of producing lighter-skinned children.[72] He went ever further to argue that a core element of the psychological profile of African Americans was the "conscious or unconscious wish . . . to be white. This is brought out in his dreams, the hope of being white and snowy being [sic] in the eternal life and in psychoses in which he *is* or *was* white."[73] Whether or not they incorporated discussion of racial mixing into their theories, white psychiatrists were generally unified in arguing that essential Black racial traits underlay the increase in mental illness, including those spurred by religion.

Late nineteenth-century and early twentieth-century medical literature also highlighted regional comparisons between the US South and North in support of white psychiatrists' claim that southern slavery had protected Black people from the stress of caring for themselves and their families and, thus, had preserved their mental and moral health. In the early nineteenth century, white doctors and demographers put forth statistics indicating a strikingly high rate of insanity among people of African descent in northern states.[74] The results of the 1840 federal census were influential and circulated widely, particularly the count of 1 in 1,558 insane people of African descent in the South and 1 in 145 in the

North. Albert Deutsch, an early twentieth-century historian of medicine, summarized the statistics, writing, "Thus, according to the census of 1840, the rate of mental disease and defect among free Negroes was about 11 times higher than it was among enslaved Negroes."[75] Deutsch notes how quickly proponents of racial slavery seized upon the census data to characterize the institution as a benefit to enslaved people. For example, Secretary of State John C. Calhoun of South Carolina wrote to the British secretary of foreign affairs in 1844, "The census and other authentic documents show that in all instances in which the states have changed the former relation between the two races, the condition of the African, instead of being improved, has become worse. They have been invariably sunk into vice and pauperism, accompanied by the bodily and mental inflictions incident thereto—deafness, blindness, insanity, and idiocy—to a degree without example."[76] This early nineteenth-century data purporting to indicate that enslavement in the South protected Black mental, moral, and physical health and that freedom in the North was damaging supported late nineteenth-century arguments about Black people's incapacity for freedom.

There were a few prominent dissenting voices concerning the claims of a higher incidence of insanity among Black people in the antebellum North. In the wake of the interpretations drawn from the 1840 census about race, freedom, and insanity, Edward Jarvis, a white physician in Dorchester, Massachusetts, and the son of a Congregationalist deacon, challenged these conclusions in detail, emphasizing flaws in the source data. Jarvis argued that the census contained serious errors, resulting in reports of Black mentally ill inhabitants in places where no Black people lived.[77] Writing in *The Liberator*, the New York–born African American physician and Episcopalian James McCune Smith also disputed the data and conclusions about race and insanity drawn from the 1840 census, insisting finally that "freedom has not made us mad; it has strengthened our minds by throwing us upon our own resources and has bound us to American institutions with a tenacity which nothing but death can overcome."[78]

Despite refutations of such statistics and the absence of other corroborating evidence, the regional argument for Black people's unfitness for freedom and the deleterious effect on Black mental health of emancipation held steady among white psychiatrists long after the end of slavery.[79] William A. White, who in 1903 succeeded A. B. Richardson as superintendent of St. Elizabeths Hospital in Washington, D. C., told the *Medical Record* that year that "the negro . . . remains sane despite his unhygienic surroundings so long as he remains in the country, his 'natural home,' but fails when, thrown upon his own physical and mental resources, he enters the strife for existence in Northern cities. As soon as the negro goes North and enters into active competition with the white, who is mentally his superior, he succumbs to the unequal struggle."[80] According to many white southern physicians, the end of slavery produced similarly challenging social circumstances that they argued Black people were unequipped to manage.

White physicians whose work focused on mental illness developed their theories and practices about the nature of the Black mind in the context of broader social, political, and religious interpretations of life in Black communities, particularly among those people building lives in freedom. Some connected what they claimed were the negative mental effects of religious excitement unleashed in the years following slavery to evaluations of Black political and social futures. The 1886 assessment by James M. Buchanan, an assistant physician at the Mississippi State Lunatic Asylum, encapsulates the core elements of the dominant psychiatric frame interpreting mental health among African Americans in this period. Like many other white physicians at the time, Buchanan, a Presbyterian whose family enslaved twenty-three Black people in Chickasaw County, Mississippi, during his childhood, contended that slavery had relieved Black people of the need to think or care for themselves and that conditions after the end of slavery had caused a stressful social transformation. "From a quiet, peaceable being," Buchanan wrote, "he soon became a religious fanatic or a turbulent politician, often both combined, and, whirling in this vortex, night was turned into day with him; his nightly meetings continued after midnight, and at these meetings all restraint was laid aside and his nervous organism strained to its utmost tension."[81] Buchanan argued for expanded access to treatment in hospitals on the grounds that Black people paid taxes and were entitled to this support, but he also recommended that this be done in racially segregated hospitals to ensure the comfort of white patients who might object to Black patients' presence. Even as he endorsed treatment, Buchanan lent medical authority to the notion of a link between religious excitement and political fanaticism, contributing to white politicians' efforts to disenfranchise and marginalize the formerly enslaved and their descendants. The political and social were never far out of view in early psychiatric discussions of religious excitement and African Americans' post-emancipation mental states.

## Equal in Morals and Mental Possibilities

Black religious, political, and medical leaders were cognizant of the stakes of the medical theories white physicians propagated framing "religious excitement" as a precipitating factor in the increasing diagnoses of insanity among African Americans in the late nineteenth-century South. Buchanan's linking of religious and political excess made explicit the claim of some white physicians in this period that African Americans' minds had become disordered because of incapacity for self-governance and the stress of freedom in the advanced civilization of the United States. African Americans' responses to arguments that their civilizational immaturity and supposed incapacity for freedom had caused an increase in insanity generally highlighted Black achievement in the wake of generations of enslavement and emphasized the ongoing impact of racial and social oppression in Black communities. Some commentators, like B. F. Lee, an AME minister and editor of the *Christian Recorder*, argued against viewing the state of Black mental health in the United States as exceptional. Lee wrote in 1887 that "the colored people are about equal to other Americans in morals and in mental possibilities. Recent observations show that many fewer colored persons than white persons become insane or demented."[82] He concluded with a forceful assertion that, rather than hindering national development, "colored men" were contributing to American progress. For religious leaders like Lee, Black churches like his own northern-based AME Church were key institutions for facilitating moral and mental development in Black communities. At the turn of the twentieth century, W. E. B. Du Bois took a social scientific approach to disputing claims of an increase in insanity by questioning statistics from 1903 regarding the incidence of insanity among African Americans. The 1906 Atlanta University Study on African American health noted that most African Americans classified as insane were "in the South Atlantic and South Central states, and in each of those states, except Delaware, West Virginia, and Kentucky, the percentages which the colored constitute of the insane in hospitals are much smaller than the percentages which Negroes form of the general population." The report argued that the numbers indicate only "the extent to which they are cared for in hospitals," rather than anything about the ratio of mentally ill African Americans to the Black population overall.[83]

Many African American leaders who reacted to the claims of increasing cases of insanity turned attention away from the idea of religious excitement as a precipitating factor to the material causes they argued were producing damage and psychic distress in Black communities. The abuse of alcohol was a chief factor in these discussions. Writing in 1885 in the Black Methodist Episcopal newspaper the *Southwestern Christian Advocate*, a Nashville physician, Dr. Robert Fulton Boyd, decried intemperance, offering biblical admonitions and arguing that insane asylums, along with workhouses, penitentiaries, chain gangs, and "many other places of crime and misery," were made necessary by excessive use of alcohol.[84] Boyd called for leaders who could guide the race to "moral emancipation," writing that "our morals need to be lifted from the horrible pits of lewdness and shame to the highest virtuous and religious elevation." Similarly, from his position at the New Orleans Charity Hospital, the physician Dr. J. T. Newman wrote in the *Southwestern Christian Advocate* to implore Black Christians to take on the problem of intemperance, which he declared to be "the cause of insanity."[85] Some years later, the Methodist Episcopal Rev. Daniel W. Shaw advocated total abstinence in a sermon for the Methodist young people's Epworth League, using Romans 14:12–23 as his text. In addition to arguing along religious lines and citing the text's assertion that "the kingdom of God is not a matter of eating and drinking, but of righteousness, peace and joy in the Holy Spirit," Shaw offered social and health reasons for abstaining. Regarding the mental health effects of alcohol, he contended, "The records of the asylums for imbeciles and the insane show that intoxicants are, directly or indirectly, responsible for an alarmingly large per cent of the imbecility and insanity of the country."[86]

African American leaders responded in ways that often trod the line between rejection of claims of a propensity to religious excitement and affirmation of worrisome excess they thought needed to be reformed for the sake of greater respectability and racial uplift. That is, many tried to encourage less enthusiastic worship even as they refused psychiatric arguments about a racial disposition that fostered religious excitement. The Episcopal priest George Freeman Bragg, editor of Virginia's *Afro-American Churchman*, used arguments published in the white press about religious excitement as a cause of mental illness for many Black patients as an opportunity to criticize the culture of worship in Black churches. Responding to a short news item in 1887 featuring the claim "that one eighth of the inmates in the Central Lunatic Asylum located near this city for colored lunatics went crazy on account of religious excitement," Bragg laid the blame on the "large class of ministers who think they are not preaching unless by their emotions and with that familiar moan they have excited their listeners, so that they run up and down the aisles of the church screaming like mad."[87] This was, however, quite different from the approach white physicians took that insisted on religious excitement among African Americans as resulting from innate racial traits.

Another approach was to argue that African Americans were not unique in demonstrating religious excitement. In the article "Characteristics of Negro Christianity" (1886), Ohio-born William Hannibal Thomas rejected a link between Black religion and excessive religious excitement. He wrote, "It is said that, with the negro, physical emotion supplants and is mistaken for an intelligent conception of truth. Religious excitement is as common to many of them as to other classes. I have witnessed as great fanaticism in song and frenzy and shouting among the intelligent whites as I ever saw indulged by the most illiterate blacks; in fact, I have witnessed a greater *abandon* of the properties of life by the former class." In contrast to assertions that African American Christianity lacked ethical or moral components, Thomas claimed a deeper spirituality among Black people, who he saw as naturally inclined to religion, and described that religion as grounded in "ethical piety" and "obedience to morals and deference to law" rather than impiety, as much white popular discourse held.[88] Black religious leaders also pointed to specific cases of religious excitement among prominent whites. In 1889, the Black Methodist *Southwestern Christian Advocate* reprinted a piece from the New Orleans *Crusader*, another African

American newspaper, noting the case of the daughter of a county court judge who had "gone insane on religion" and had been committed to the asylum. The author concluded, "The young lady is refined and well educated and her case is an unfortunate one, but it shows that not only ignorant Negroes go crazy on religion."[89]

Some Black religious leaders who called for more restrained preaching and worship were clear to locate the source of what they considered excessive in the experiences of enslavement and in the immoral nature of white Christianity. Peter Thomas Stanford, a Baptist minister, decried conditions among African Americans in the "Black Belt" of the South, where, he asserted, "wild religious excitement, and a terrible divorce between faith and morals obtains." He insisted that it was the so-called superior race that had sown these seeds in the evils of slavery and that they continued to be cultivated in the convict lease system and efforts "to sustain 'White Supremacy' at any cost of religion or humanity."[90] In an 1893 editorial in the *A.M.E. Church Review*, the editor Rev. Levi J. Coppin criticized the article "The Religious Progress of the Negro" by Henry King Carroll, a white Methodist scholar of religion in the United States and a church statistician. Coppin rejected Carroll's claim that, despite calls by Black clergy like the AME bishop Daniel Alexander Payne for ministers to rid their churches of emotional and loud worship, African Americans remained "intensely religious," but not moral, and engaged in excessive worship. Coppin instead called out the moral hypocrisies of white enslavers who created an environment for "so-called converted slaves" that could "only bring evil results." He continued, "In the face of such facts, it does seem strange indeed that no other reason for religious incongruity on the part of the Negro can be found, other than that it is peculiar to his race."[91] Despite the work Black religious leaders did to refute white popular, political, and medical arguments that essentialized Blackness and linked a pathologized Black religion to increasing cases of insanity, these remained prominent in medical theory and practice. When Black clergy's congregants and other members of their communities came under the jurisdiction of doctors and nurses at state hospitals for the insane, they entered these institutions under the shadow of ideas about religious excitement that located Black religious excess as among the significant causes of mental illness.

Religious Excitement & . . .

Charges of "religious excitement" or agitation fixated on religious subjects were common in the commitment files and patient records of
African Americans admitted to state hospitals in the late nineteenth
century. As we will see in subsequent chapters, in their theoretical literature white psychiatrists elaborated several components of a racialized
religious excitement, including "superstition" and "emotionalism." But
local doctors testifying in commitment hearings and physicians working
in state hospitals for the insane also used the category to paint a broad
brush of pathology, as in the case of a forty-year-old domestic servant,
Maria J. of Prince William County, Virginia, who was committed in 1874
and described by the examining physicians as having "a disposition to
have an undue amount of religion" and suffering from insanity caused
by religious excitement.[92] In many instances, doctors linked "religious
excitement" to a range of other supposed causes or manifestations in
combinations that confuse more than clarify the nature of the patient's
suffering. In some cases, such as that of Eliza K., admitted to Virginia's Central State Hospital in Petersburg in 1903 at the age of forty-one,
those evaluating her associated her religious excitement with political
passions. According to the commitment paperwork, the local constable
had taken her into custody the night before the hearing, possibly at her
husband's urging, because she had suddenly become violent and excited.
The examining physicians testified that the predisposing factors for the
insanity they affirmed were "religious excitement and excitement about
the supposed ex-slave pension bill. Possible menopause has some effect
upon patient."[93] Although the file contains no further details about Eliza's political involvement, she was admitted to the hospital two weeks
after Senator Mark Hanna of Ohio introduced a bill to provide pensions
to the formerly enslaved over the age of fifty or to those charged with
their care. The leaders of the National Council of Ex-Slaves had pressed
President Theodore Roosevelt to pursue this plan, but by the time Eliza
was subjected to a commitment hearing, both the Senate and the president had rejected it.[94]

The notation in Eliza's commitment file pointing to the possibility
that menopause may have contributed to the development of an excessive religious excitement reflects the common association in Black wom-

en's legal and medical files between religious excitement and gendered bodily experiences. One finds postpartum emotional responses, diseases of the uterus, irregular menstruation, and menopause, for example, listed as contributing factors to the development of insanity, sometimes in combination with religion. Sallie W., a thirty-five-year-old married mother of two, was committed to Virginia's Central Lunatic Asylum in 1874, with doctors proposing that ill-health following the birth of a child caused insanity that was manifested in derangement about religion. The loss of a child appears regularly in women's court records and case files in connection with religious fixation. Dolly Ann D., a forty-one-year-old married mother of three, was committed to Central Lunatic Asylum in 1875 because she had become unsettled and occasionally violent. Her husband, Henry, testified that the loss of a child and "mistaken religious ideas" had precipitated her mental illness. Nellie G., a married Methodist admitted to the South Carolina Lunatic Asylum in 1893 at the age of thirty-five, had suffered three stillbirths that, according to doctors, had changed her from cheerful to restless and agitated and combined with religious delusions to cause insanity.[95]

Commitment files and patient records also show many cases in which religious excitement and financial worries were linked. Jacob F. was admitted to Virginia's Central Asylum in 1874, and the examining doctor testified at the commitment hearing that his mental distress was focused on "religion & the ownership of property." Jacob, having been prosperous some time ago, had "lost everything" and become "deranged."[96] Benjamin L., a twenty-five-year-old Methodist who worked as a fireman in Georgetown, South Carolina, was committed to the South Carolina Lunatic Asylum in 1894, diagnosed as suffering from mania. The commitment paperwork indicated several immediate causes such as "religious excitement; interest in Odd Fellows; anxiety about his work" and added "masturbation?" as a possible predisposing cause. According to the testimony of witnesses at the hearing—his mother, wife, brother-in-law, and a friend—the generally quiet and hardworking Benjamin had become violent with his family four days earlier, a state that "began that [sic] he had religion."[97] The judge, J. Jenkins Hucks, a Confederate veteran and former enslaver who oversaw the hearing, affirmed that Benjamin should be committed to the asylum.[98] There was a delay in admitting him to the hospital, likely because of overcrowding, and his conditioned improved enough following the lunacy hearing that the family "begged that his transfer to the Asylum be deferred," and the examining doctors agreed. Several months later, Benjamin's condition deteriorated. The doctors concluded that he would not recover at home and recommended that he be committed. Superintendent J. W. Babcock approved admission in April 1894 but did not list a diagnosis, although the hospital staff described Benjamin as melancholic and refusing to talk upon admission. It is not clear from the hospital records how long Benjamin remained in the hospital, but he was eventually released, and he and his wife moved to Charleston, where their two sons were born.[99]

In cases in which witness testimony and physician reports differed in identifying the precipitating causes for insanity, the mention of religious excitement often became an important factor in the deliberations. Ransom R., a forty-four-year-old Baptist farm laborer in Saluda, South Carolina, was committed to the state hospital in 1901, and his patient record contained no diagnosis or predisposing cause for the agitated condition that had developed over the course of the previous week. Ransom's father-in-law provided information that Ransom was worried about "money matters," "that he imagines he is friendless," and that he had become incoherent and suicidal, to the point of needing to be restrained.[100] While there is little more information available about the nature of Ransom's financial worries, the census from the previous year shows that he and his second wife, Mary, twenty-four when he was committed, had a two-year-old child and an infant, and he may have been struggling to provide for his young children.[101] The doctors who examined him for the commitment hearing did not mention financial worries or depression but focused their testimony on religious excitement, reporting that Ransom had said "that he was specially raised by God to preach" and "that he was in the Spirit" and proceeded to demonstrate preaching in the Spirit to them. This information was copied in full into his hospital patient record, which contained no indication of his other concerns, likely shaping how the hospital's medical staff interpreted his condition.

Few of the surviving records of African Americans who were institutionalized for insanity caused by religious excitement contain more than basic information about the diagnosis, treatment, and the patients' lives and families. Sometimes the simple phrase "acute mania," the most common diagnosis, accompanied by "religious excitement," "religious mania," or simply "religion," is listed as a precipitating cause, are all that remain in the files. The little we know of patients like Francis F., a twenty-nine-year-old woman who was committed to the Central State Hospital in Petersburg, Virginia, in April 1895, illustrates the challenges of this historical research. Francis and her husband, Robert, a farmer, had been married for ten years and had six children when she was evaluated for lunacy. Robert is listed as the petitioner on the commitment paperwork, perhaps an indication of the severity of her condition and his inability to care for her and their children under the circumstances. In addition to Robert's testimony, the justices heard from Grier M. Nickell, a local white doctor from an enslaving family.[102] The testimony indicated that Francis had been agitated and violent for several weeks, presenting a danger to herself and others. Nickell thought that heredity was the primary cause of Francis's mental illness because of a report of an aunt who had been declared insane. The commitment paperwork also indicates that the distress that led to the lunacy hearing "began with a religious mania."[103] The doctor described Francis as "weak, thin in flesh, sleepless, with no appetite." With no other information included on the questionnaire, it is impossible to recover the context for Francis's religious fervor or distress. The federal census taken five years later indicates that she had given birth to seven children and that only six had survived. Perhaps the grief from the loss of a child had caused her agitation and fervent devotion. What we do know is that the testimony persuaded the justices of the peace who evaluated her case to commit Francis and that she was confined by the sheriff in a jail near the Millboro railroad station for two months before being admitted, likely because of overcrowding.[104]

Francis entered the Central State Hospital under the supervision of Superintendent Dr. Randolph Barksdale, an Episcopalian who had enslaved a seventy-five-year-old woman and a thirty-eight-year-old man in 1860 and went on to serve as a surgeon in the Confederate army. Barksdale had inherited money, property, and a major flour mill in Richmond from his father, William, who had enslaved hundreds of Black people in Amelia, Virginia, in the decades before the Civil War, making Barksdale's personal and broader family context one of great investment in the institution of slavery and the control of Black people.[105] Although Barksdale did not publish on the topic of race and insanity in medical journals, his assistant and successor as superintendent, William F. Drewry, described him as "justly regarded as one of the ablest alienists and hospital superintendents of his State and of the South."[106] Indeed, at the 1876 meeting of the Association of Medical Superintendents of American Institutions for the Insane, Charles H. Nichols, the first superintendent of the Government Hospital for the Insane and the group's president, commented to Barksdale, "In view of your experience with the colored people, there is no gentlemen [sic] in the world who has as wide a field of discovery in respect to forms and diagnosis."[107] Nichols could have been referring to Barksdale's experience as an enslaver or as the head of Virginia's Central State Hospital, or both. Whatever the case, Barksdale had established a reputation as an expert on "the colored people" whose "greatest trouble" he diagnosed as "their habits and practices." He lamented the challenge presented by the fact that doctors could find out little about Black patients' life histories ("their age, their parents, whether married or single, whether born in Maryland or Georgia"), something for which he implicitly blamed his patients rather than the social and material violence of the institution of slavery in which he participated, or their desire to keep that information from white medical authorities.[108]

The year Francis was committed to Central, 11.28 percent of the hospital's patients, all of whom were Black, had "religious excitement" listed as the cause of their illness, the second most common, with "unknown" being the most common cause (34.39 percent). This is a significantly higher percentage than for white patients at the state's other asylums: 4.95 percent at the Western State Hospital with religious excitement listed as the cause of illness, 3.68 percent of patients at the Eastern State Hospital, and 3.51 percent at the Southwestern State Hospital that same year.[109] Francis's admission to the hospital took place in the context of heightened attention to the idea that religion was an increasingly common precipitating factor in the rising numbers of mentally ill Black people in the South. These racialized ideas about religious excitement and an incapacity for freedom most certainly shaped the hospital staff's responses to her. Without access to her patient record, we can know nothing more of Francis's individual experience in the hospital or precisely when she was released and under what circumstances. In 1900, the census enumerator found Francis and Robert living in a home they owned in Charlottesville with their six children ranging in age from five to fifteen. Robert worked as a liveryman and Francis as a hotel chambermaid, perhaps at the same hotel, and they continued to live in Charlottesville and raise their children.[110]

Religious excitement served as a broad interpretive frame in late nineteenth-century and early twentieth-century medical discourse, through which white physicians charged with evaluating and treating Black patients produced theories about the effects of freedom on the Black mind and increasingly racialized "religious excitement" as Black. As we will see in the chapters that follow, early American psychiatric theorists held that racialized religious excitement was marked by three characteristics: *superstition*, which they argued represented the persistence of African traditions in African American life; *emotionalism*, which psychiatrists viewed as a natural affective state for Black people that rendered their expressions of Christianity excessive and disordered; and *credulity*, which they deployed to explain the draw of Black new religious movements in the early twentieth-century urban North and the psychological damage caused by participation in what they framed as "Negro cults."

# 3

## Pathologizing Black Supernaturalism

As the year 1885 began, Mary J., then in her twenties, was confined in the Richmond city jail. This was not her first arrest, but it would turn out to have far different consequences than had her previous encounter with white police, jailers, and judges. Two years earlier, police had arrested her for "being disorderly and using profane language on the street," an offense for which she was fined $2.50 and released.[1] While held in jail in January 1885 after her second arrest, Mary awaited a lunacy hearing before three City of Richmond justices of the peace. Although it is unclear what led to her arrest, reports of her behavior convinced a justice to issue a warrant for her to be examined by a physician and for any other relevant witnesses to appear in court to offer testimony as to whether she was of "unsound mind," the vague terms in which the state defined lunacy. Seventy-eight-year-old James Beale, who served as a physician at the city jail, examined her. Beale was a prominent white Richmonder, a member of the Odd Fellows, and a Presbyterian whose marriage to Isabella Pallen drew him into involvement with Beth Shalome, a Sephardic synagogue and the city's oldest, where she was a member.[2] He was well regarded as a doctor but was nearing the end of his life when he encountered Mary, having had to reduce his work in private practice because of diminishing sight, but he continued to serve as the city jail's doctor for some years.[3]

The scope and content of Beale's examination was determined by the state's legal code for the conduct of proceedings to determine sanity and were like those in most states in this period.[4] Any justice could issue a warrant on suspicion of lunacy—a legal concept having to do with one's ability to manage civil affairs—and, together with two other justices, conduct the inquiry. Beale's deposition, with the clerk's record of his answers penned on a printed sheet of twenty-two questions, reveals that he did not know Mary well, if at all.[5] He reported that she was twenty-one, not married, and had no children, and that he had no information regarding her "habits, occupation and reputed property." She appeared to him to be in good health and not to have experienced any bodily changes, such as loss of weight, because of this episode of mental disturbance that had begun four days earlier and that he believed was worsening. He could not provide answers to questions about a family history of mental illness, whether she had had previous episodes of insanity, or if she had taken any curative remedies. To the final question on the form inquiring if Mary was "noisy, filthy, quarrelsome, detractive," Beale responded, "Yes," but we cannot tell from that one-word answer if he meant to indicate all or only some of these. Finally, he joined the three justices in swearing, "According to the evidence before us, we believe Mary J. to be insane."[6]

A court's pronouncement of lunacy required that individuals be sent to the asylum unless family, friends, or an employer could post a bond and vouch that they would be cared for. Because Mary had no one able or willing to post bond, she was certain to be sent to the Central Lunatic Asylum for Colored Insane in Petersburg, where the board of directors would examine her again to affirm or reject the judgment. If affirmed, the board would admit her as a patient until such time as hospital officials deemed her "restored to sanity" and she could be discharged.[7] The hospital's board and superintendent, indeed, affirmed the court's lunacy determination and admitted her as a patient, but not until three months after the initial hearing. Overcrowding at the asylum often meant that there was no room to admit people whom courts had judged insane, and the burden of care in the interim fell on family, friends, or law enforcement. At the end of 1885, the president of Central's board of directors reported ninety to one hundred African Americans being held in Virginia jails awaiting admission to the hospital, which had reached its capacity of 450 patients, and Mary was probably among these.[8]

Beale's account is the only testimony on record in Mary's case. This was not unusual in lunacy hearings, although family members, neighbors, employers, or law enforcement officials sometimes offered observations about the individual being evaluated. Mary's perspective is filtered through Beale in answer to a question directed to the examining physician about the "indications of insanity." What she said to him while in the Richmond City Jail, or uttered in his presence, or what her jailers reported she said distinguished this arrest from her previous one, result-

Figure 3.1. Central State Hospital, Petersburg, Virginia, 1904. *Thirty-Fourth Annual Report of the Central State Hospital of Virginia for the Fiscal Year Ending September 30, 1904* (Richmond: J. H. O'Bannon, Superintendent of Public Printing, 1904). Courtesy of the Library of Virginia.

ing in her confinement in the asylum. Beale reported that Mary's insanity manifested in "complaints of being tricked or conjured," and he named "religious excitement" as the "supposed cause of the disease." Mary's assertion that she believed someone had conjured or "tricked" her by casting some sort of spell to affect her health or behavior made the difference for her between being fined for disorderly conduct or some other minor offense, as in her first arrest, and commitment to the asylum.

Mary J. was among the approximately 26 percent of patients admitted to the Central Lunatic Asylum for Colored Insane in 1885 for whom medical and judicial evaluators held that religion was a factor in their insanity. She was also one of several patients admitted to Central that year whose assertion that they had been conjured was listed on the commitment deposition as evidence of insanity. Fears of being harmed by others, of harm coming to family members, of plots devised against them, and of poisoning appear regularly in the records of commitment hearings and patient case files in hospitals. Physicians noted such fears of persecution and harm among white patients admitted to asylums and indicated occasionally that a given patient characterized their persecution or fear as the result of "bewitching." White doctors generally interpreted paranoid beliefs in white patients as individual examples, as in the representative case of a woman admitted to the South Carolina Lunatic Asylum in 1882 who a doctor described as "suspicious of being poisoned" and diagnosed as "manic depressive, of a maniacal type."[9] In contrast, white psychiatrists often assessed Black patients' claims of having been harmed by conjure in light of popular and medical ideas that pathologized Black supernaturalism: the modes and means some African Americans used to "interact with unseen powers or spiritual forces," to mobilize these forces on their behalf, or to access spiritual insight through dreams and visions.[10]

As we have seen, claims in American religious and political discourse of fanaticism as a characteristic of African American religion supported white psychiatrists' racialization of religious excitement as a cause or precipitating factor of insanity. As white physicians evaluated the mental states of African Americans in jails, courts, and hospitals and engaged varied expressions of Black religions in these contexts, they produced more detailed theories about the relationship among race, religion, and

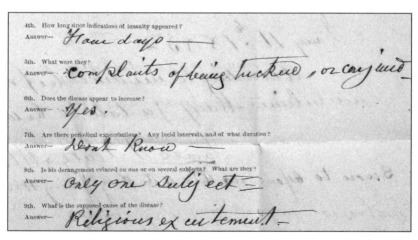

Figure 3.2. Detail from the doctor's deposition in the 1885 hearing to commit Mary J.'s to the Central Lunatic Asylum in which he listed "complaints of being tricked or conjured" as an indication of insanity and "religious excitement" as the cause of her illness. Courtesy of the Library of Virginia.

insanity. These theoretical frames connecting specific modes of Black religious life, real and imagined, to mental illness, and pathologizing them influenced white physicians' assessments of individual cases involving African Americans as they testified in commitment hearings and shaped their treatment of African American patients in hospitals. Mary J.'s case provides insight into early psychiatry's pathologizing of Black supernaturalism. Casting as "superstition" some African Americans' belief in the possibility of engaging and harnessing the power of the spiritual world reduced this spiritual orientation, rooted in West and Central African religious traditions, to irrational and false belief. Moreover, in making medical claims about the nature of what they saw as innate Black superstition, white psychiatrists offered racialized theories of religion grounded in their own personal and professional experience and, in some cases, engaging with the scholarship on the anthropology and history of religions.

Psychiatric claims about the role of superstition in cases of insanity among African Americans were rooted in long-standing European and white American ideas about African beliefs and practices as "fetishism," rather than "religion," with religion understood as characterized by rational devotion directed at the God of the Bible, the only appropriate object of worship. As the religious studies scholar Sylvester Johnson argues, in this view, fetishism represents a confusion of the material and the spiritual, resulting in the worship of false idols, and he shows that European discourses about fetishism developed as part of the process of racial formation and emergent practices of colonialism and racial governance. He writes, "The fetish became not only the established synecdoche for African indigenous religion but also the most potent intellectual category for the colonial enterprise of interpreting and studying religion comparatively."[11] The conviction that African American conjure practices represented the translation of African fetishistic confusion of the spiritual and material to the United States was common in nineteenth-century white American culture. Moreover, the idea that Black people in Africa and the African diaspora lived in illogical terror of unseen spiritual forces acting on them in daily life supported the popular notion of an innate superstitious disposition. As one white newspaper reporter asserted in a lengthy article about African religious practices in the United States, "Fetichism [sic] is the religious worship of material things as the abode of spirits, and is the lowest of unsystematic forms of worship found among uncivilized tribes." In this view, which conformed to broader white public discourse, such "uncivilized" practices undergirded the superstitions the author saw as "peculiar to the African race."[12]

Early nineteenth-century white asylum doctors like John M. Galt of Virginia's Eastern Lunatic Asylum argued that superstitious beliefs could contribute to the development of insanity in anyone but contended that Black people were especially prone to such delusions.[13] A perspective like Galt's, that superstition was not the exclusive province of people of African descent but that Black people were essentially superstitious, was common in white American public culture. White observers and religious opponents may have dubbed movements such as Spiritualism and Christian Science in which white Americans predominated, "superstitious" but they did not see them as manifestations of racial character.[14] In asserting that African Americans were racially predisposed to superstitious beliefs and practices that either precipitated mental illness or served as the sign of mental derangement, early white psychiatrists contributed to discourses that situated Black people outside the realm of authentic religion and that facilitated containment and governance in institutions like mental hospitals.[15] Such a view discounted the role supernaturalism played in Black communities for physical and mental healing and in the management of social relations. Moreover, such psychiatric claims pathologized these practices and the African-Atlantic worldview in which they were situated that provided tools for Black people to wield spiritual power. This is not to say that some patients who invoked conjure as the cause of their mental distress did not sometimes pose a danger to themselves or others or might have needed care. That white doctors and judges evaluated such patients through the lens of racialized views about innate "Negro superstition" is significant, however, for understanding both the role ideas about Black religions played in the history of early psychiatry and the psychiatric pathologizing of Black supernaturalism.

Racialized psychiatric frames stigmatized belief in the close connection of the material and spiritual worlds and a set of practices, referred to as conjure, hoodoo, and rootwork, through which African Americans harnessed supernatural power. By creating bundles with plants, hair, and roots, among other objects, sometimes combined with the recitation of spells, conjurers mobilized this power for physical and mental healing and to shape interpersonal relations through harming, self-defense, and cultivating romantic attraction. As ritual specialists, conjurers were revered and feared by many in Black communities for their ability to wield supernatural power and herbal knowledge for healing, for their aid in resisting white authority, for protection against natural and supernatural forces, and for punishment of adversaries.[16] Despite the cultural power of Black supernaturalism during and after slavery, not all African Americans embraced conjure beliefs or appealed to the system to direct spiritual power. There was sometimes opposition to conjure culture in Black communities among those who, like the African Methodist and novelist Katherine D. Tillman and the African Methodist Episcopal Zion minister, lecturer, and author William H. Ferris, saw it as incompatible with Christianity and impeding collective progress. In 1889, Tillman maintained that while "the labors of Voodooism" were prominent in the era of slavery, cultural change in freedom had diminished the significance of conjure over time.[17] Almost twenty-five years later, Ferris challenged the tendency of white commentators on "the Negro's religion" to locate it "outside of the stream of the general religious development of mankind."[18] He acknowledged the influence of "Negro Voodism [sic], Gopherism, and Conjurism" in Black life but insisted that "the colored man is not constructed psychologically different from other men."[19] Like Tillman, Ferris believed that "the colored man is gradually shuffling off his old superstitions and absorbing from his environment materials for further growth," which, for him would be derived from Christianity.[20]

When white legal and medical authorities evaluated Black supernatural practices in the context of discourses about insanity and fitness for citizenship, the stakes were different than when African Americans lodged critiques of conjure practices within their communities. White Americans' interpretations of conjure framed the value Black supernaturalism placed on engagement with the power and resources of the spiritual world and the practical work of supernatural healing (and, sometimes, harming) as racially innate superstition. The popular white American view of conjure as fetishistic superstition became embedded in emerging psychiatric theory, shaping how jail doctors, public health officials, local court officers, asylum doctors, and psychiatrists evaluated Black patients' descriptions and interpretations of their physical and mental suffering when they invoked conjure and related supernatural beliefs and practices. As we will see, late nineteenth-century white psychiatrists' theories about the influence of an innate superstitious nature on Black mental health proved profoundly influential and durable, persisting even through a major transformation in diagnostic categories in the first decades of the twentieth century that would change American psychiatry.

## "They Are Exceedingly Superstitious"

Emerging psychiatric theories about "Negro superstition" as a cause or symptom of insanity among African Americans overlapped with late nineteenth-century and early twentieth-century white religious, academic, popular, and media discourse to a remarkable degree. Popular public representations formed the broad cultural context that supported the medical stigmatizing of African American conjure and related practices. Newspapers and magazines of the era carried a seemingly endless stream of stories under headlines like "Negro Superstition," "Darky Superstition," "Negro Deviltries," "Curious Negro Superstition," and so on, offering accounts of beliefs and practices the authors cast as ridiculous or barbaric. While reflections on the presence of "Negro superstition" were part of white American culture prior to the Civil War, popular, religious, and medical arguments about Black peoples' innate superstitious disposition intensified in the late nineteenth century. Numerous authors of treatises on the future of the race in the United States mobilized accounts of superstition to argue against extending political and social rights to African Americans. In an 1889 assessment of "the plantation Negro as a freeman," Philip Alexander Bruce, a white Virginia historian, devoted an entire chapter to the subject of superstition, opening with the assertion that "there is no peculiarity of the negro that is more marked in its influence on his conduct than his superstitiousness, and in the individual of no other race is the same trait more fully developed."[21] The notion that superstitiousness was an essential element of Negro character contributed to Bruce's overall pessimistic account of African Americans' civic prospects, a portrait he supposed (white) readers would find "gloomy and repelling in its moral aspects," but that he assured was a scrupulously objective and dispassionate one.[22] "Every circumstance surrounding the negro in the present age seems to point directly to his further moral decadence," Bruce asserted, and he cited Haiti and Jamaica as alarming examples of descent into "the lowest forms of barbarism" under Black self-governance. From this evidence, Bruce concluded that the only possible future for Black people in America involved servitude, supervision, and their "elimination as a political factor."[23]

White American public discourse asserted that pervasive superstition was evidence that, in freedom, Black people were experiencing physical, mental, and moral decline to what white commentators argued was their essential uncivilized state. Only a few years after the Civil War, southern white newspapers began to sound alarms about the degrading quality of Black life, with certain supernatural beliefs and practices serving as powerful signs of trouble. One report from Memphis on the discovery of "hoodoo" practices among African American residents claimed that "these barbarous African superstitions and practices prevail and are increasing among the 'freedmen,' not only of Memphis and Tennessee, but of all the Southern States. It is the clearest proof of the inevitable tendency of the negro to relapse into barbarism when left to control himself."[24] According to some commentators, African American participation in Christian communities only hid an underlying truth. An unnamed writer in the *Atlantic Monthly* asserted in 1891 that, although southern African Americans "seem so readily to have accepted the forms of worship of the dominant race, one finds, on looking closely at the matter, that they cling to some very barbarous beliefs and superstitions, and oftentimes these strange fancies are wrapped about with the garb of religion."[25] In this view, whites' supervision of Black religious life under slavery had been only a temporary check on a racial predisposition for superstition and fetishism that was reemerging in force in freedom and taking on new and greater prominence. A correspondent from Virginia to the *New York Tribune* summarized the white popular view that "many curious traits appear in the negro character, under the influence of the new conditions of his life, or survive as products of the old order not yet outgrown. They are exceedingly superstitious."[26]

White commentators used the term "superstition" to denote several things they saw as related characteristics of Black culture and fundamental elements of African Americans' moral and mental character. White observers evaluated the belief among many African Americans that spirits and ghosts populating the invisible world had the power to act on them in the material world as superstitious, rather than a component of a broader spiritual worldview. The Liberty County, Georgia, resident, politician, and historian Charles Colcock Jones Jr., the son of the Georgia slaveholder, theologian of Christian slavery, and Presbyterian missionary to the enslaved, included a chapter on "Sperits" in his volume *Negro Myths from the Georgia Coast, Told in the Vernacular* (1888). Turning his attention from the animal tales that were the book's main focus to Black folk beliefs, Jones wrote that "belief in the existence of ghosts, 'sperits,' and superhuman influences was very general" in the region and that "comparatively few there were who could lift themselves entirely above the superstitious fears born in Africa and perpetuated by tradition in their new home."[27] He contended that the majority of African Americans he encountered believed that spirits of the dead were all around, and that they had "the ability to intervene in mundane affairs, and to entail harm and misfortune upon those with whom they had not lived amicably while in the flesh."[28] The African-Atlantic religious culture that developed in slavery was, in fact, grounded in a view of the spiritual and material worlds as connected in ways that called for skillful engagement with the powers and dangers this connection has the potential to manifest. White commentators often interpreted this as meaning that African Americans lived in constant terror of these unseen forces acting on them, which resulted in irrational behavior. In the historian Philip Alexander Bruce's assessment, Black people's superstitious disposition derived from the inability to "distinguish [the] incorporeal sphere at all from that in which he breathes and moves," making them constantly attuned to the workings of the invisible and visible worlds on them at once.[29] Psychiatrists would elaborate on this popular idea as they encountered increasing numbers of Black patients in hospitals, some of whom, like Mary J., believed they had been conjured and that someone had mobilized spiritual resources to harm or constrain them.

Black supernaturalism fostered attention to signs and portents in the natural world, as well as in dreams and visions, as a means of protecting one's health and well-being from spiritual malice, from both humans and beings from the spiritual world, such as witches. Popular discourse among white Americans about "negro superstition" asserted that this alertness to signs represented African Americans' belief in a chain of causality that, to white observers, had no apparent logic. A *New York Times* article reprinted in other papers under the headline "Alabama Negroes: Their Superstitions," exemplifies accounts of beliefs white commentators found curious and ridiculous. The author insisted that "nearly all their actions are controlled and influenced by some strange and supernatural belief" and offered as proof a list of beliefs readers were to take as definitive evidence, such as common folk beliefs about lunar influences including that "soap must always be made when the moon is increasing or it will not wash clothes well."[30] White observers also argued that African Americans' investment in the power of signs and portents shaped their behavior in irrational ways. Writing in *Cosmopolitan* in 1888, Eli Shepherd contended that "by dreams this race, as well as all other races in the infancy of their civilization, make augury of coming events."[31] The prominence of "signs of coming death—'death-warnins,'" many related to the appearance of birds and to unusual behavior of animals, captured the attention of white interpreters of Black beliefs.[32] White commentators denigrated the scrupulous care African Americans who believed in the malicious powers of witches took to guard against them. In a piece titled "Negro Superstitions" in *Harper's Bazaar*, the unnamed author described protective strategies like a horseshoe nailed to the door of a cabin and "silver dimes and five-cent pieces with a hole in them strung on a cord and suspended from the neck."[33]

The continued influence of supernaturalism in African American life after emancipation, as indexed in conjure belief and practices, and the fact that some African American Christians also embraced conjure as a source of spiritual power served as an indication for white observers of what many framed as dangerous superstitions.[34] An article titled "Voodooism" (1873) in the *Louisville Courier-Journal* decried "an imported relic of barbarism growing in civilized soil" and warned white residents that there were "thousands whose souls are benighted with the most pernicious species of ignorance, superstition, infidelity and false religion" in their midst.[35] The author described the transformation of what he viewed as base African fetishism into practices of rootwork, "charm doctoring," conjuring, and witchcraft and asserted that such superstition resulted in many genuinely ill people who, "suffering all the tortures of a harassed imagination," attributed their ailments mistakenly to conjure. Among the rootwork practitioners the author profiled was "old Doctor

Joe," who had been born into slavery in Virginia, sold to an enslaver in Kentucky, and then bought his freedom. Joe recounted to the reporter that he had gained the power to heal at a young age, described using roots and herbs as well as healing by touch, and indicated that he was able to cure cases of illness brought on through conjure. In this way, his career exemplified what the author argued was the influence of superstition in Black life. The article's author expressed surprise at hearing that Doctor Joe "had been a Methodist all his life" and that many who sought healing through conjure were also members of Christian churches. Doctor Joe's perspective that Christianity and conjure complemented one another was common, whereas other African Americans viewed these as competing realms of power.

That conjure's tools for harnessing spiritual power included the possibility of using that power to adjudicate social conflict by harming others was of great interest to white commentators on the idea of Black superstition. As the historian of religion Yvonne Chireau explains, conjure as "supernatural harming" could be used for "resistance, revenge, and self-defense" in relation to white American society, but it was also a way African Americans expressed "hostility within their own communities."[36] The popular white press offered numerous stories of African Americans' anxieties about being harmed through supernatural means (referred to as being fixed, tricked, or hoodooed). African Americans who embraced Black supernaturalism were alert for signs of malicious intent in such things as "a devil's powder" placed under the threshold, traps set in the form of "certain arrangements of pulled grass before your door, or of sticks, or of pebbles or feathers" that bring misfortune on those who step over them, and this vigilance became the source of caricature in white popular and press accounts.[37] White observers claimed that fear of harm from conjure preoccupied Black people and could have dramatic physical and social consequences. Mary Helm, a Methodist editor whose enslaver father served terms as governor of Kentucky before and after the Civil War, wrote in an educational text for missionaries, "So great is the effect of the mind upon the body that a man or woman may, without any real ailment, pine away and die because he cannot find a witch strong enough to 'break the spell,' or rebound into sudden health if made to believe he has been released from the power of the enemy."[38] Such accounts reflected some African Americans' belief that the tools of Black supernaturalism could be used to control, harm, or otherwise shape relationships among humans, but popular characterizations like this contributed to the attribution of these beliefs and practices to primitive and pathological sensibilities.

The white press frequently offered sensationalized stories about the combined physical and mental consequences of belief in conjure, as in an 1884 article in the *San Francisco Chronicle* describing Keziah, "a healthy, good-looking mulatto girl" in Little Rock, Arkansas, having been turned into "a raving maniac" by conjuring. The article described her Aunt Mahly's attempt to cure her with a "voodooing" ceremony that involved boiling a mixture consisting of "a piece of an old shoe, rusty nails and spikes, old files and razor handles, a lodestone, a moleskin and a rabbit's foot, also opium and chloroform," which she first applied externally. When that did not work, the article claimed, Mahly had Keziah drink the mixture, but she did not recover and became violent. "She was at length secured and placed in confinement," the reporter concluded, predicting that "a horrible death will likely result."[39] In this and many other such accounts, the press rarely failed to assert in cases of such "peculiar form[s] of insanity" that "the 'conjure' theory . . . is but another instance of the prevailing superstitious credulity of this people."[40]

The accumulation of such accounts that framed Black supernaturalism, including belief in ghosts, spirits, witches, and the practices of conjure and rootwork, as outside the realm of religion and, in fact, submission to illogical causality supported many white Americans' contention that it was in the nation's interest to limit African Americans' access to suffrage and other forms of political participation. Many white commentators on "Negro superstitions" characterized this as an intractable disposition that no amount of education or exposure to white "civilization" would mitigate. Bruce insisted that "[the negro's] retention of this superstition after the lapse of such a great length of time, passed in the midst of different local surroundings and amid the most modifying influences, is one of the strongest proofs of the inherent tenacity of the fundamental qualities of his race."[41] Importantly, such accounts distorted and pathologized modes of interacting with the natural and spiritual worlds that sustained many Black people in slavery and in its wake and rendered both cultural practices and individual spiritual choices as racial traits.

"The Race Superstitions"

Discussions among asylum doctors and early psychiatrists about the relationship of superstition to insanity among African Americans were remarkably consistent in the core elements from the late nineteenth century through the first decades of the twentieth century. Moreover, the early influential psychiatric literature bore much resemblance to contemporaneous white popular and religious commentary. From the early published works on the topic in the late nineteenth century, physicians promoted the idea of the profound significance of innate superstition to African Americans' mental disposition and as a factor shaping the form and presentation of insanity. Although white psychiatrists were not entirely in accord in their assessments of the implications of the claim to innate superstition, the research literature nevertheless perpetuated a set of core ideas about the nature of African religions and their transformations in America, the capacity of Black people to evaluate the world around them through reason rather than emotion and fear, and their capacity for citizenship.

One of the first asylum doctors to elaborate a connection between what he believed was an innate superstition among Black people and an increase in insanity among African Americans after the end of slavery was James D. Roberts. Roberts, a North Carolina native, graduate of New York's Bellevue Hospital Medical College, and Baptist deacon, was the first superintendent of the Eastern North Carolina Insane Asylum in Goldsboro, which opened in 1880 and housed Black patients exclusively. His developing theories reflect racialized understandings of authentic religious belief and practice that privileged white Protestant forms of supposedly rational and true religion that occupied a limited sphere of social life. Roberts argued that Black religious sensibilities revealed a racial character that was "superstitious; fearful of hidden dangers"; he insisted that understanding this was central to addressing the broader question of African Americans' mental health in the late nineteenth century.[42] In an 1883 article, he added his perspective to those of other white physicians who argued that the absence of the stabilizing "fear of the driver's lash" and the stress of "advances in the scale of civilization" combined to result in an increase in insanity.[43] Roberts contended that, after slavery, religious freedom from white oversight was a significant factor in the changed social conditions that caused insanity. "Being now his own master and not having learned to control himself," Roberts wrote, the formerly enslaved African American "is easily carried away by anything of an exciting nature. His superstition is rather cultivated, instead of being suppressed, especially among the more illiterate of the race."[44] James M. Buchanan, an assistant physician at the Mississippi State Lunatic Asylum, argued similarly that "Vodouism," commonly conflated with Black supernaturalism, "plays an important part in their religious worship, and they are victims of superstition to the utmost degree."[45]

Roberts refused to accord the status of religion to the Black supernatural beliefs and practices he classified as superstition, but he also characterized African American Christianity as suspect, marked by unrestrained emotional excitement. He maintained that the incidence of true religious causes of insanity among African Americans was lower than the numbers indicated on commitment papers because testifying physicians and courts failed to understand the influence of underlying "fanaticism" and "superstition" on the state of the Black mind.[46] Thus, he suggested, what appeared to be cases of newly developed religious excitement may actually have been simply amplifications of what he believed was Black people's essential irrationality and mystical bent. Several years later, in an 1890 address at a conference in Berlin that was later published in the *Alienist and Neurologist*, the St. Elizabeths physician Abram H. Witmer also proposed that accounting for "the race superstitions" was key to diagnosis and treatment of insanity among African Americans. Based on his clinical experience, Witmer argued that physicians were failing to recognize melancholia in Black patients because "the race superstitions lead the friends of persons suffering from this form of disease to conceal the true conditions, and to attribute the mental disturbance to the occult influences of 'voodooism,' 'conjuration,' or evil spirits, the effects of which have to be counteracted by some fetish, charm, or 'mystical spell.'"[47]

Some white doctors, such as J. W. Babcock, superintendent of the South Carolina Lunatic Asylum, raised the specter of a supposed link between Black superstition and mental illness as a threat to white people through the communication of insanity.[48] In an 1895 article on the communicative power of "negro witchcraft" published in the *American Journal of Psychiatry*, Babcock presented the case of B.S., a thirty-seven-year-old white man who had been admitted to his hospital in 1884. Babcock described B.S., a farmer, merchant, and Methodist who was not literate, as having turned to George Darby, an African American root doctor and conjurer, for help in treating a case of rheumatism. Darby, who reportedly told his clients that he healed through the "the medium power of God," sold B.S. a "Little Solomon" of roots and herbs fashioned into a bundle that helped reveal the source of the illness as conjure by enemies who had sent witches to poison him.[49] Babcock reported that B.S.'s belief that he had been the victim of malicious conjure disrupted his family and work life and that "he developed a religious frenzy, singing, 'shouting,' and praying," declaring that he had supernatural powers.[50] Babcock was interested in B.S.'s case as one that spoke to the long-standing medical question of the possibility of "communicated insanity," but his brief study mobilized ideas about the ubiquity of belief in "negro witchcraft" and the malign impact of figures like "Doctor Darby" to argue that Black people's innate superstition posed a public health threat to white Americans.

Within the context of courts and asylums, white doctors routinely declared Black patients' references to supernatural and conjure beliefs and practices as precipitating factors or exciting causes of mania and melancholy, the operative diagnoses of the day. In doing so within the frame of emerging psychiatric theory and practice, these doctors stigmatized an aspect of Black spiritual culture through which African Americans interpreted their physical and mental illnesses and personal suffering. The commitment papers and medical records of Black patients admitted to the South Carolina hospital in the late nineteenth century for whom conjure was listed as a cause or symptom, for example, show how for these patients, conjure and broader supernaturalism served as an interpretive frame for a variety of social, physical, and mental conditions. For some, Black supernaturalism may have provided effective treatment or resolution, but the commitment process most often resulted in the pathologizing of Black spiritual resources, regardless of whether the individual was also suffering from mental illness or some kind of mental distress.

We can see conjure's function as an active means of seeking to manage social relations through the use of love spells or the crafting of "hands" (another term for conjure bags or bundles) meant to harm in patients' focus on relatives or neighbors as the cause of their illness. In the spring of 1892, a judge ordered Lige C., a thirty-year-old Baptist and farmer who lived with his wife, Jane, in Fairfield County, South Carolina, to be examined by physicians on the allegation that he was "insane, and a proper subject for admission into the Lunatic Asylum." Two white physicians, one of whom had the same surname as Lige, testified that they believed him to be a lunatic and a danger to himself and those around him.[51] That Lige C. and one of the examining physicians shared a surname was probably no accident. The doctor's father enslaved ten African Americans in 1860, and several of his siblings who lived nearby were also enslavers.[52] While it is unclear whether the doctor's father had enslaved Lige's father, the two men of roughly the same age grew up near one another in the wake of slavery, war, and Reconstruction and encountered each other in a process that would determine Lige's liberty. The intimacy of these relationships—a shared last name in a small community and relations of profound racial domination—hovers in the background of the white doctor's assessment of Lige's sanity.

Lige's wife, Jane, testified that her husband was temperate and industrious but disposed to melancholy, and that he had become increasingly depressed, restless, and sleepless over the course of the previous four months. According to the commitment paperwork, the family or a physician had treated him with nervine, a bromide sedative, but because he had "threatened to take his own life and attempted to take the life of his father whom he believes is the cause of his being conjured," the physicians and probate judges who oversaw the hearing ordered him committed. The hospital's medical record contains no additional information about Lige's belief that his father had conjured him but lists an official diagnosis of acute melancholia. Lige spent a little more than three months as a patient at the South Carolina Lunatic Asylum in Columbia, living with two hundred other men in the old, unsanitary, and dangerous wooden buildings designated for Black male patients.[53] His treatment probably consisted of labor on the asylum's farm or working to care for the buildings, as well as mandatory walks for exercise.[54] The hospital released him as recovered from his bout of acute melancholia, and he returned home to his family.[55] As with most such cases, the surviving records make it difficult to determine the relationship between the interpersonal conflict Lige experienced with his father and mental illness, but the fact that he expressed his distress in terms of conjure belief underscores the significance of supernatural elements to his understanding of causality.

Claims like Lige C.'s of having been "fixed" or "tricked" by relatives, friends, or neighbors through conjure constitute a noticeable theme in the files of African American patients in southern state hospitals in the late nineteenth century. Physicians who examined Jennie J., a fifty-year-old married mother of three who worked as a washerwoman and was committed to the Central State Hospital in Virginia in 1903, described her as engaging in self-destructive behavior and imagining "she has been 'tricked' by a neighbor." In response to a question about the "exciting and predisposing causes" of her insanity, the doctors testified that they believed she was suffering from "monomania" as a result of menopause.[56] In another case, when Rachel C. was committed to the South Carolina Lunatic Asylum in 1891, witnesses testified that she threatened others, was noisy, and was "constantly going from place to place," and her mother indicated that she had "always been off in her mind."[57] The white physicians who examined her—John Wylie Quillian, a Confederate veteran and an active member of the Methodist Episcopal Church, South, and Burt Mitchell, from a family of South Carolina enslavers—told the court that she was "not a safe person to be at large in any community" and described her delusions as taking the form of a belief that she was "under a spell put upon her by others."[58] Their testimony, which framed Black supernatural beliefs as delusional, persuaded the court to order her committed. Upon her admission to the hospital, Rachel's diagnosis was acute mania, and the hospital staff interpreted her mother's description of being "off" to indicate "feeble-mindedness." She was discharged on a trial basis three months after admission but was returned to the hospital at some later time and died there of tuberculosis in 1901.[59]

The records of commitment hearings show that, for many African Americans who named conjure as the source of their mental distress, their concern was not only for their own physical, mental, and spiritual safety but also for that of their family members. Nineteen-year-old Mary F., a single mother working as a laundress, was arrested in 1888 and held in the Richmond city jail while awaiting a lunacy hearing to determine whether she should be committed to the Central Lunatic Asylum. James Beale, the same jail doctor who examined Mary J., assessed Mary F. and provided testimony to the court. While it is unclear from the minimal information included on the commitment paperwork what led to Mary F.'s arrest, Beale indicated that her mental condition had begun to deteriorate three days earlier as she had expressed increasing fear that "an attempt was being made to poison her and her child," an expression of common association between conjure and poison. Beale identified the cause of the attack as "religious excitement."[60] In another case, Malinda W., who was brought to court for a lunacy evaluation on the petition of a neighbor and committed to the South Carolina State Hospital in 1900 at age forty-five, attributed her family's misfortune—her husband's death and the fact that two of her sons killed a man—to a spell put on her by a woman who had died. The examining physician described her as extremely agitated, disheveled, and incoherent, and the family of jailor John Dennis, where she was the only woman held with seven men in the jail located in Dennis's home, said that she "is noisy and breaks everything given to her (cups, plates, etc.)."[61] In Malinda's interpretation, the effects of the dead woman's conjure had caused her mental distress but also extended beyond her own well-being to destroy her entire family.

Thomas N., a twenty-two-year-old Norfolk resident committed to Virginia's Central State Hospital in 1895, had a specific neighbor in mind who he believed had conjured him and caused his suffering. Thomas was arrested in October of that year for trespassing on his neighbor Jane Bell's property and threatening her. According to the deposition, Bell and several other witnesses testified that Thomas had threatened her, and at the time of his arrest, Bell told a local newspaper that his threats "frighten[ed] her as she was never before frightened."[62] Not married, employed as an oyster opener, and described by his neighbors as temperate, Thomas apparently became overwhelmed by the idea that Bell had "tricked him" and that she "holds some spell over him." L. C. Shepherd, the Norfolk health officer, and Benjamin M. Baker, the jail physician and son of an enslaver, provided an assessment of Thomas's mental state for the justices of the peace in their deliberations.[63] The doctors, both active members of Norfolk's St. Paul's Episcopal Church, ascribed the cause of Thomas's disease to "religious fanaticism" and described him as having "religious hallucinations" in the form of "holding communications with the Lord." Thomas was sent to Central State Hospital, and he appears among the patients listed on the 1900 US census, indicating that he remained there or was sent back after first being committed in 1895.[64]

Whether Thomas and Jane Bell had a relationship beyond that of neighbors is unclear, but in some cases African Americans committed to hospitals spoke of conjure explicitly in relation to romantic relationships. When eighteen-year-old Lee R. was committed to Virginia's Central Lunatic Asylum in 1887, the physician who examined him reported that he had been violent against friends and his parents, and he complained of being "affected by witchcraft" that resulted in "disappointment in love."[65] In 1895, Peggy N., a Methodist and widowed mother of nine children who owned her farm in Colleton County, South Carolina, petitioned to have her twenty-eight-year-old son, Robert, committed on the grounds that he was a danger to himself and to others.[66] On the affidavit, the examining physician described him as quiet, industrious, and temperate but also as melancholic and noted that he "believed himself bewitched." Upon admission to the hospital, Robert reportedly said that "he was in love with a woman but did not marry her because their minds did not run in the same channel, that he had dug a hole in the ground to place himself in to cure his pain and to cool his heart."[67] By 1900, Robert had been released from the hospital and was once again living with his mother and working on the family farm.[68]

African Americans who used conjure or other supernatural means to protect themselves from harm by relatives, neighbors, or spiritual forces were sometimes committed to asylums for religious excitement. In 1890, Edward G., a thirty-eight-year-old Methodist and Maryland native, was arrested in the District of Columbia on charges filed by his wife, Julia, who said that he had threatened to kill her with a stick.[69] In court, Edward admitted that he had hit Julia and had, indeed, planned to kill her because she had tried to poison him with arsenic. When asked what his wife's motive might be, Edward replied, "I suppose she wanted to try my faith. The devil made her do it."[70] He insisted that, ultimately, she could do no real harm to him because God had revealed to him in a vision that he should make a potion of Peter's root and liquor, which he reportedly called "Ruler's Root," to protect him from the poison.[71] Edward was committed to St. Elizabeths Hospital, where he remained for almost two months before being discharged as recovered and relocating to Asbury Park, New Jersey. Several months after his release, he wrote to the hospital superintendent William Godding, a devout Christian from Massachusetts and active in the American Colonization Society, which encouraged African American emigration to Liberia, to provide an update on his condition.[72] Edward reported to his doctor that his health was good, but he struggled to maintain employment. Nevertheless, he proclaimed, "Brethren, I do thank God for Christ sake I am spared to obey His command and to fulfill His law and to worship at His feet."[73] While Edward continued to rely on his Christian faith, and perhaps supernaturalism, to sustain him through financial adversity, the state of his marriage after his release from St. Elizabeths is unclear, and there is no further record of his turn to conjure for protection.

The belief that physical and mental ailments or social disruption caused by conjure could only be cured through conjure was common in Black supernaturalism, and in some cases patients insisted that this was their only hope, while physicians interpreted their appeal to conjure as evidence of mental illness. In 1884, Moses G. Carper, a white doctor in Fairfax County, Virginia, testified before a court that three months earlier he had been called to attend to Nelson T., a married farmer with one child, who was experiencing nervousness and "violent heart palpitations," but Carper found "no organic trouble about the heart."[74] Asked to examine Nelson for the purposes of the commitment hearing, Carper related that he had "been informed that he has been taking medicine from a negro root Doctor or *conjurer* as he is called by the colored people." Carper could not determine the cause of Nelson's distress but was certain that "his mind is damaged." Nelson himself interpreted his physical ailments within a religious and supernatural context, reportedly convinced by "communications from God" that he "has been tricked or poisoned by someone," thus requiring appeal to a conjurer to relieve his symptoms. The justices ordered him committed to the Central Lunatic Asylum.

Similarly, Henrietta M., a twenty-seven-year-old Baptist who was separated from her husband, was committed to the South Carolina State Hospital in 1900 at her mother's request. According to her mother, the usually cheerful and industrious Henrietta had become restless and unable to sleep. The examining physicians reported that "she looks downward all the time," and "she has the belief that she has been conjured, that her insides have been destroyed, that she can never be cured except by the withdrawal of the conjurer's influence." Upon admission to the hospital, Henrietta was diagnosed as melancholic and complained repeatedly that she was afraid "her head was dropping off" and that "her arms and legs will fall off." She died in the hospital several years later, and the medical staff noted that she had had aluminum in her urine and "dropsical" limbs, with edema possibly signaling heart failure.[75] Henrietta M.'s case shows how some patients explained physical ailments through the lens of conjure, leading white physicians and courts to determine they required confinement and turning attention away from other possible treatments that may have saved their lives.

In other cases, patients described their physical suffering in ways that emerged directly from the broader worldview of Black supernaturalism. In 1891, Ed W., a thirty-five-year-old married father of five children and a member of the AME Church, was committed to the South Carolina Lunatic Asylum and diagnosed as suffering from acute mania. The examining physicians testified that his mental disease took the form of "incoherence of speech; in a belief that witches ride him at night," and that his body was debilitated from consumption.[76] Ed's belief that his physical deterioration had been caused by a spiritual entity using his body was common in the religious culture of South Carolina and the lower South, and his friends and family reportedly viewed him as "a religious monomaniac."[77] A doctor had treated Ed's mental agitation with a potassium bromide sedative, but the physical exhaustion of tuberculosis that he attributed to persecution by witches led to his death one month after admission to the hospital.[78] Martha B., who was committed to the South Carolina Lunatic Asylum at the age of twenty-seven in 1899, also viewed her physical condition through the lens of conjure belief. A Baptist who worked as a household laborer, Martha was reported to have said that "she was conjured by a lizard in her body at various places but always in the throat at night so she cannot sleep. Says she sees all kinds of objects when her eyes are closed."[79]

In the late nineteenth century, asylum doctors in southern hospitals who presented theories about the innate superstitious character of African Americans and superstition's contributions to a dramatic increase in insanity operated in a context in which mania, melancholia, and dementia were the operative diagnostic categories. Asylum doctors and local physicians who examined individuals and provided statements for lunacy hearings sometimes listed religion or religious excitement as a supposed cause of insanity when patients named conjure, bewitching, or other forms of supernaturalism in describing their suffering. Following long-standing approaches, white asylum superintendents classified religion as a moral cause of insanity—having to do with emotions and passions—along with other supposed moral causes like "domestic trouble," "overwork," "financial embarrassment," or "disappointment in love," as opposed to the many physical causes, including heredity, epilepsy, drug and alcohol use, various diseases, pregnancy, and menopause, that doctors believed underlay mental illness.[80] In this diagnostic frame, insanity grounded in moral causes could be addressed through changes in the patient's environment to reduce the excesses and disturbances that led to mania and melancholy. The widely accepted idea among white asylum doctors of African Americans' enduring racial propensity for superstition and other sorts of emotional excess promoted the conclusion that all members of the race were liable to become mentally deranged under challenging personal or social circumstances. In this view, Black patients who became insane because of moral causes like religious excitement had less chance of cure because of what white doctors viewed as their essential inability to manage the stresses of freedom and the challenges of civilization.

## "An Integral Part of the Race"

The racializing of mental normalcy and deviance in early American psychiatry became solidified in the transition in the first decade of the twentieth century from the older diagnostic categories of mania and melancholia, with religious excitement sometimes listed as a precipitating cause, to manic-depressive psychosis and dementia praecox.[81] Dementia praecox, or premature dementia, came into widespread use in diagnoses of mental illness in the United States through the work of the German psychiatrist Emil Kraepelin, who in 1896 described this psychosis as deriving from underlying metabolic factors.[82] Kraepelin's conception of dementia praecox, the diagnosis more commonly ascribed to Black patients in the early twentieth-century United States than manic-depressive psychosis, was broad, and he described it as "a series of states, the common characteristic of which is a peculiar destruction of the internal connections of the psychic personality." In the first decades of the twentieth century, the disease concepts of dementia praecox and manic-depressive insanity eclipsed the older diagnostic categories in American psychiatry.[83]

Hospital admissions registers from the late nineteenth century contain entries for newly admitted patients from all backgrounds with diagnoses of acute or chronic mania or melancholy and a host of precipitating factors and supposed causes listed, including religion or religious excitement. By 1905, it was increasingly common to see dementia praecox listed as the "form of disease on admission," often with unknown cause.[84] We can see this transformation in the record of one Black patient over the course of 1905, although the transition in operative diagnostic categories was not limited to African Americans. When Charles D., a laborer born in Maryland, was admitted to St. Elizabeths in the District of Columbia in March of that year, he was diagnosed with acute insanity doctors believed had been caused by "religious excitement and weak intellect" and was discharged one month later. Charles was readmitted six months later, and his diagnosis as listed in the admissions register was dementia praecox with unknown cause.[85]

Kraepelin conjectured that dementia praecox was a metabolic disorder, the cause of which lay not in "race, climate, food, or life circumstances" but in biological processes common to all humans.[86] As such, Kraepelin's theory of mental disease did not have an obvious racial component, but this is not to say that he was not curious about the possible relationship of race to mental illness. The historian Jonathan M. Metzl argues that in the American context, "the Kraepelian emphasis on brain biology fit easily into existing beliefs that 'Negroes' were biologically unfit for freedom."[87] As white American psychiatrists embraced Kraepelin's new disease category in the early twentieth century, they mobilized ideas about race and religion in diagnosing Black patients and used their clinical experiences to theorize more generally about race, religion, and mental illness in ways that linked discourses from the older diagnostic system to the new. Modes of racialization in American psychiatry, in turn, influenced Kraepelin. In studying race and the effects of alcohol and syphilis on mental states, Kraepelin visited St. Elizabeths Hospital in 1925, and he brought to his encounters with Black patients and his analysis the influence of white American psychiatric interpretation of African American history and mental capacities, particularly the 1914 study of "psychosis in the Negro" by E. M. Green of the Georgia State Sanitarium.[88] Kraepelin wrote about African American mental health in terms that echo the generic formula of much of early white American psychiatry, stating, "Negroes, a people protected in slavery, tolerably well-nourished and exposed to no dangers, suddenly had to look after themselves after emancipation, although they were entirely unprepared to do so. The result was poverty, neglect, the outbreak of many diseases, the terrible carnage of tuberculosis, and the massive spread of syphilis, alcoholism, wantonness, and licentiousness."[89] Kraepelin himself would later emphasize conceptions of white racial purity and "psychiatric eugenics" that supported his students' contributions to Nazi extermination programs.[90]

Once Kraepelin's disease categories were in widespread use in American hospitals, white psychiatrists began to explore the question of whether African Americans were more prone than whites to developing dementia praecox, and ideas about Black religion and superstition figured prominently in many analyses of the available data. In his 1914 article, E. M. Green, Georgia State Sanitarium's clinical director, offered a comparative study of psychoses in white and Black patients. Green, whose father was a Presbyterian minister and grandfather an enslaver, began his analysis from what he asserted was the accepted fact "that certain psychoses appear more often in one race than in the other" and an interest in exploring the factors that led to this outcome. Confining his data to what he imagined as "the average negro," rather than "the highest representatives of the race," whom he believed were those of mixed race, and focusing on Georgia hospital patients from 1909 to 1914, Green found a higher percentage of diagnoses of dementia praecox among Black patients than among whites admitted to the hospital. The central factor he proposed to understand the disparity was the African American's "fear of the supernatural, the suspicions of his fellows and the necessity of guarding at all times against the bad luck and machinations of enemies."[91] He elaborated what he believed were the psychic effects of a presumed superstitious disposition in African Americans:

> Toward members of his own class the black is suspicious, fearing not ridicule or contempt, but bodily harm; attributing to them all misfortunes and illnesses, which are supposed to be brought about by the aid of witchcraft. . . . He is superstitious, believes in ghosts, witches, spells,

poisons and conjuring. He has at his fingers' ends the meaning of signs, and is versed in the measures by which ill luck may be warded off. From the cradle the negro lives in the fear of the supernatural. As an infant he is threatened with beasts, spooks and witches. In childhood the chief subjects of conversation which he overhears are witchcraft, spells, ghosts and conjuring. The meaning of signs is instilled into him, and he watches his every act that he may escape bad luck.[92]

In Green's survey of records from his institution, some psychoses, particularly those originating in alcohol or drug abuse or physical conditions like brain tumors, traumas, and diseases, appeared with the same or greater frequency among white patients. In his search for causes for the higher incidence of diagnoses of dementia praecox among Black patients, he foregrounded ideas about Black religious sensibilities and innate superstition.

Not all white psychiatrists came to the same conclusion as Green on the question of the incidence of dementia praecox according to race, but even when their analyses differed, their work often featured discussion of a presumed, innate superstition. In a comparative study of Black and white female patients also published in 1914, Mary O'Malley, a senior assistant physician at St. Elizabeths Hospital, began from the premise that "the enormous difference in evolutional development" between the races was a major factor in mental disease, offering the routine white psychiatric account of African Americans' beginnings in savagery in Africa and their current position ill-equipped to manage life in a higher civilization.[93] In reviewing what she understood to be Black people's "psychological tendencies," O'Malley asserted in accord with the conclusions of late nineteenth-century asylum doctors that "there is no peculiarity more marked in its influence on the colored individual's conduct than his superstition, and in the individuals of this race probably no other trait is more fully developed. They believe supernatural agencies can be compelled to intervene in their behalf and control fate."[94] That O'Malley, a native of upstate New York from a Catholic family and a graduate of a Catholic college, was disturbed by her Black patients' appeal to supernatural agencies for intervention may speak of her disaffection from Catholicism or her efforts to distance Catholic devotion from mere superstition on racial grounds.[95] She emphasized what she took to be African Americans' unconscious blending of the material world and the supernatural as the key mark of their superstition, writing, "Their conception of the unreal world is much more distinct than that which they have of the real because it appeals to them through the emotions which make the deepest impression on the mind."[96]

As for the relative frequency of psychoses by race, she found an equal percentage of white and Black patients diagnosed with dementia praecox in her sample, despite her expectation that it would be more prevalent in African Americans, given what she asserted was "the primitive order of intelligence of the colored race."[97] Still, she allowed that psychiatrists might be failing to diagnose Black patients correctly because theory held that the early symptoms of dementia praecox tended to be vague for all patients and, she claimed, "far more so in the colored race, existing as they do in a world of their own, of ignorance and superstition." Like so many other early psychiatrists, O'Malley found Black supernaturalism to be a diagnostic hinderance. She argued that "the first manifestations are often attributed to 'conjurers' or occult influences placing a 'spell' on the individual, and the victim is often taken to fake doctors for the removal of this 'spell.'"[98]

Several years later, in an address before the Washington, DC, Society of Nervous and Mental Diseases, William M. Bevis, O'Malley's colleague at St. Elizabeths Hospital, offered his own assessment of psychoses in African American patients in southern hospitals. As was common among white psychiatrists of this period, Bevis began his discussion by rehearsing the customary white supremacist narrative of Black savagery and immersion unprepared into the higher civilization of the United States. All Black people were, in his estimation, inferior to whites, sexually promiscuous, lacking in initiative and morals, careless, and unconsciously desirous of being white.[99] Bevis asserted that superstition, manifest primarily as fear of the dark, spirits, and ghosts, was more important in Black life than religion, which he characterized as a failed attempt to approximate the religion of whites with whom they worshiped under slavery. At the same time, he saw religion and superstition as so deeply intertwined in Black life as to make it difficult to distinguish between the two. However one understood the relationship, he concluded, "nothing in the life of the Negro stands out more prominently than his superstition. It influences his thought and conduct more than anything else. In no other trait or peculiarity do we find more plainly the imprint of the primitive African life and customs."[100] Bevis contended that the "psychic weakness" of holding to superstitious ideas was "born of fear, credulity, intellectual poverty, and child-like imagination" and represented something "buried deep in the nature of this people."[101] Conjure beliefs and investment in the power of "Witch Doctors" or "Night Doctors" among African Americans were of particular interest to psychiatrists, he argued, because such beliefs created resistance among patients and their families to accepting a true diagnosis of psychosis.[102] His survey of records of Black patients in southern hospitals revealed that dementia praecox was, by far, the most common diagnosis and more prevalent than among white patients. He concluded, "This is not surprising when their racial make-up and the atmosphere of superstition in which they move are considered," highlighting ideas about innate Black racial traits rather than white psychiatrists' racialized application of the diagnostic category.[103]

Psychiatrists at St. Elizabeths, the Government Hospital for the Insane, were prolific theorists of the relationship of religion and supposedly innate "Negro superstition" to dementia praecox. Arrah B. Evarts, a Methodist from Minnesota who was active in the Woman's Foreign Mission Society, proved among the most interested of the hospital's physicians in this question.[104] When Evarts turned her attention in the 1910s to research on dementia praecox among African Americans, her starting point was the recapitulation theory of human development, which she claimed was "recognized by all that the individual in his development relives the history of the race."[105] In her first study, she characterized the race history of African Americans as marked by having been "hurled headlong into civilization" from savagery and, more recently, set adrift from the bondage that had been "a wonderful aid to the colored man" because it had freed him from the "necessity for mental initiative."[106] A prominent feature of African savagery, she contended, was a religion that was "but a belief in witchcraft" and devoid of ethics. "In the few cases where a religion has progressed beyond this stage," she asserted with no supporting evidence, "it has become the most bestial and revolting of rituals, built upon cruelty and sexual excess."[107]

Evarts concluded that there was no difference in the etiology of dementia praecox in white and Black patients, but she claimed that African Americans were more prone to this "deteriorating psychosis" because of their race history that placed the Black person "upon a plane much lower than his white neighbor."[108] As an illustration of "the primitive character of these people," she offered a case study of a woman born in Maryland who worked in domestic service and migrated to Philadelphia in 1911 for more lucrative employment in household labor. When she became ill with a stomach ailment, she appealed to a West Indian "herb doctor," who "told her there was a snake inside her, and gave her some medicine to enable her to get rid of it."[109] The woman became increasingly agitated and violent, convinced that "the herb doctor had put a spell on her and she read her Bible constantly to exorcise it." Evarts reported that during the woman's confinement at St. Elizabeths, she became somewhat more connected to the world around her, but "her faith in spells in general and her own spell in particular is unshaken."[110] In Evarts's estimation, the woman's manifestation of dementia praecox was consistent with its manifestation in white patients, but she also argued that this patient was mired in profoundly primitive religious sensibilities that would persist in spite of hospitalization and treatment.

Evarts's interest in the impact of what she understood to be Negro superstition and primitive Black religion on dementia praecox led her to publish another study on "psychoses in the colored race" in which she considered the relationship of phylogenetic, or evolutionary, inheritances to ontogenetic influences, "the actual memories of individuals."[111] Seeing phylogenetic inheritances most clearly in remnants of shared human religious expressions, Evarts highlighted the study of religion as the interpretive key for treating Black patients and relied heavily on the social anthropologist James G. Frazer's *The Golden Bough: A Study in Comparative Religion*, first published in 1890, for her analysis. In a later review of Frazer's *Folk-Lore in the Old Testament* published in the *Psychoanalytic Review*, Evarts would laud him for his sympathetic ability to "reconstruct the motives of primitive peoples" so that the reader "unconsciously regresses to the stage of his [Frazer's] actors."[112] In keeping with her conclusion in the earlier study that the nature of dementia praecox did not differ substantially by race, Evarts argued that Black and white patients were also not entirely distinct in terms of the phylogenetic or evolutionary elements of their manifestations of the disease. She gave the example of a white male patient at St. Elizabeths, "out of touch with reality," who "has the mannerism of standing with head bowed and hands folded in a devotional attitude" and with a jerking, shuffling walk. Evarts concluded that, although he was unaware of what he was doing, "we can scarce avoid the conclusion that it is a fragment of religious ritual." She proposed that this man's quiet devotional posture suggested May Day and midsummer celebrations or the parading of mummers.[113]

In contrast to Evarts's characterization of the white male patient's unknowing replication of a benign folkloric practice in his "devotional attitude," her assessment of the mental illness of a Black female patient drew on Frazer to cast the underlying phylogenetic pattern as savage and menacing. She described the woman as similarly detached from reality and noted that she "bends slightly backward with chest elevated, and assumes a facial expression intended to be terrifying."[114] According to Evarts, the woman spits, snorts, stamps her feet, waves her skirt, all the while producing "terrifying grimaces." This, she determined using Frazer as a guide, was also a phylogenetic parallel of ancient rituals and ceremonies but, in this case, of those performed by "savages" and meant to "scare away demons."[115] Significantly, where she saw the white man's manifestation as incomplete, fragmentary, and only suggestive of ancient rituals, she insisted that the Black woman's was much more recognizable and complete because "the colored race is so much nearer its stage of barbarism."[116] Moreover, Evarts asserted that the prominence of "hoodoos, conjures [and] spells" in contemporary Black culture established that insanity among Black people was the product of ancient inheritances and that "this primitive method of thought was an integral part of the race" expressed in "the actual beliefs and practices of [their] everyday lives."[117] Her reading of Frazer on talismans, spells, contagious magic, and sorcery only confirmed this assessment.[118]

One year after the publication of Evarts's study, John E. Lind, a senior assistant physician at St. Elizabeths, engaged the question of "phylogenetic elements in the psychoses of the Negro." In the first decades of the twentieth century, Lind oversaw the treatment of a large percentage of the hospital's Black male patients and drew on many of those cases for his study.[119] Like Evarts, Lind considered interpretations of African American religion to be central to this work and offered a synthetic review of "African theology" based on his reading of works by white missionaries, explorers, and ethnologists. He argued that an understanding of this theology was crucial because, "unlike more civilized races, religion with the African is not a matter outside his daily life, but is interwoven in the texture of his actions so inextricably that there is little that he does without some religious significance."[120] According to Lind, along with polytheism, "a host of beliefs, superstitions, customs, omens, etc." contributed to the African cultures that he believed were "very valuable in studying the psychoses of the American Negro."[121] He was less certain than Evarts that African Americans' symptoms of mental illness could be "correlated with phylogenetic experiences" but nevertheless concluded that "we can only surmise from the nature of some of [the symptoms] that they belong to the race consciousness."[122]

To demonstrate the manifestation of the "race consciousness" in African Americans suffering from psychoses, Lind presented brief synopses of symptoms and behaviors of more than two dozen patients at St. Elizabeths. Among the cases he cited in which he saw a clear "similarity to an African custom" was that of a patient he identified by the initials S.Y., who believed that someone had put sea water in his food. Lind concluded that because members of some African "tribes . . . have a superstitious horror of the sea" and, with the exception of "witch-doctors," fear that they will die if they look at the sea, S.Y.'s concern about sea water was a manifestation of race consciousness.[123] Lind's patient S.Y. was Scipio Y., who was committed to St. Elizabeths in April 1872 at age thirty and diagnosed with acute mania. It appears from the surviving hospital records that Lind first examined him and compiled a patient history in 1913, not long after he joined the medical staff and forty-one years after Scipio's admission. Scipio was agitated and afraid to be examined that day, and Lind wrote that it was difficult to convince him that he would not be harmed as the attendants forced him into the room. Lind questioned him about his sleep, which he reported was poor because "boys and girls plague him" in the night, and asked about auditory and visual hallucinations, which Scipio said he had of his wife and child. Lind also reported that Scipio suffered from "vague delusions of persecution," including that sea water was in his food, a claim Lind characterized in the hospital notes as absurd. In an earlier examination by another physician, Scipio was asked about voices and responded that he sometimes heard voices he thought came from God and angels.[124]

Judging from the surviving material in Scipio's hospital file, Lind and the St. Elizabeths staff recorded manifestations of dementia praecox that were in keeping with Kraepelin's description of the range of "psychic symptoms" of the disease, including hallucinations, paranoia, repetitive actions and thoughts, and incoherence in writing, among others. A note one of his doctors wrote below Scipio's graphic representation of his name and address—a series of loops—interpreted it as evidence of dementia praecox rather than of Scipio not being literate, or as writing in what he might have believed to be divine script.[125] In Lind's analysis for a broader white psychiatric community, he magnified the significance of Scipio's paranoia about sea water in his food and interpreted it through the lens of missionary studies of African religions to racialize it as "Negro superstition." In the article's conclusion, Lind considered the counterargument that white patients with dementia praecox also exhibited parallels to phylogenetic precedents. While he accepted that this might be true, he argued that because, in his view, the Negro was "only one degree removed from extremely primitive levels, [he] reverts very easily under stress."[126]

In another case Lind included in his study, he failed to locate the expressions he claimed were like "African customs" in the broader context of the patient's religious life such that he emphasized "race consciousness" over actual practice. The patient, Charles T., had epilepsy and was admitted to St. Elizabeths in 1886 at the approximate age of thirty, and family and friends visited him there.[127] His condition was severe, and although he was able to visit his wife and brother on occasion, his wife found it difficult to care for him and at least once wrote to the hospital to request that he be readmitted.[128] Lind wrote of Charles that "he hears the spirits of the dead which come back" during his epileptic attacks, which Lind interpreted as reflective of a "practically universal belief" among Africans.[129] The hospital case file and notes, which date from twenty years after Charles's first admission, note his severe epileptic seizures and his physical deterioration over the course of his confinement. One physician described him as "very religious and at times spends his leisure moments in his room reading his Bible and counting his beads." Another entry says that "the patient spends the most of time in prayer" and indicates that he did not hallucinate and had no delusions.[130] By the time Lind published his study in 1917, it was clear to the hospital staff that Charles was a devout Catholic who spent much time in prayer and study and took comfort from saying the Rosary.[131] While Charles began to manifest hallucinations of a religious nature gradually, his religious sensibilities remained within a Catholic vernacular that developed during his childhood when his family was enslaved by the Sisters of the Visitation of Georgetown. Charles's father paid to liberate himself and his family when Charles was fifteen, and many of the family remained Catholic.[132] Indeed, when Charles died in 1940 and the hospital was unable to locate any relatives, Rev. Michael Hyle, the hospital's Catholic chaplain and the future bishop of Wilmington, Delaware, presided at his burial in the hospital cemetery.[133] Whether or not Charles's belief in the presence and power of the spirits of the dead represented enduring African spirituality in African American life, that Lind ignored his patients' Catholic commitments reflects the common focus among white psychiatrists in this period on looking for "race consciousness," in this case manifested in "superstition," over all other factors.

By the 1920s, a substantial psychiatric literature was in place arguing that mental illness continued to be on the rise among African Americans and indicating that dementia praecox was the most common diagnosis among Black patients in state mental hospitals nationwide.[134] According to the historian Jonathan M. Metzl, this diagnostic trend accorded with broader popular culture associations of dementia praecox "with marginalized others," as a manifestation of white "anxieties about 'Negroes,' immigrants, criminals, or 'subnormals.'"[135] The change in classifications during the early twentieth century from mania and melancholia to dementia praecox and manic-depressive psychosis allowed psychiatrists to make stronger claims to clinical rigor, particularly with a new framework that emphasized charting the course of disease and outcomes. At the same time long-standing racialized beliefs about "Negro superstition" as an essential race trait that affected mental stability remained active among white psychiatrists as they treated Black patients in this period. As white psychiatrists elaborated theories about superstition and the evolutionary roots of dementia praecox in African Americans, they produced a framework that became applicable beyond the context of the experiences of Black southerners in the transition from slavery to freedom. The deployment of scholarship in anthropology of religion, like Frazer's The Golden Bough, at once grounded these theories in assertions of common human impulses and racialized them to reaffirm arguments that superstition was rooted deep in the Black psyche.

# 4

## Containing Black Religious Emotions

On October 10, 1905, physicians at St. Elizabeths Hospital, the Government Hospital for the Insane in the District of Columbia, received Daniel H., a forty-five-year-old North Carolina resident who had been arrested the previous day by Secret Service agents at the White House as he tried to deliver a handwritten note to President Theodore Roosevelt's personal secretary, hopeful that this would result in an audience with the president. Daniel told the doctors he had long been convinced that God had given him the ability to interpret dreams and declared that he received visions that helped him to see the future. Attuned to the small signs around him, that he believed portended bigger things, Daniel said he had predicted Spain's downfall in the Spanish-American War. Certain that this all amounted to a call from God to be a prophet, he sought a larger mission. He was clear that the church would not be able to help him fulfill his purpose. In fact, Daniel declared that he had given up on his local Baptist church because his fellow congregants had objected when a man who was not an ordained preacher had wanted to speak in church. The man impressed Daniel as trying to "seek a higher religion," and he could not understand why the Baptists found him objectionable. It was the Baptists who were offensive, Daniel concluded.[1]

God had called him, Daniel declared to anyone who would listen. God had gifted him with prophetic powers, and he found authority in Paul's letter to the Romans for his divine mission to "[prevent] evil and do good to the people at large." He claimed that he could now foretell the weather and knew that a deluge, an "overflowing of the land," was coming as punishment for the people's wickedness, but he could prevent it by warning the nation and calling its people back to righteousness. Daniel wrote to Secretary of Agriculture James Wilson to inform him of the danger and to offer his services to find a solution. He was gratified to receive a response and kept the letter close at hand as he contemplated his next move. Finally, he left his home in North Carolina and set out for

Washington, DC, with an urgent message for the president that led the *Washington Post* to dub him "the weather prophet."[2]

After examination by doctors who reportedly were "familiar with the minds of prognosticators" and who certified him insane, Daniel was admitted to St. Elizabeths with a diagnosis of dementia praecox.[3] The unnamed physician who examined Daniel on admission reported him well oriented to time and place but unreliable in recounting his family history and details about his relatives' health. While lack of information about family was not uncommon among the formerly enslaved, in this case the doctor concluded that Daniel did not comprehend the question. The psychiatrist also concluded that he was not suffering from auditory or visual hallucinations or persecutory delusions but "imagines himself a prophet, gifted with the power of preventing evil and of doing good at large."[4] Daniel spent twenty days confined to St. Elizabeths, placed first in Howard Hall for criminally insane patients, during which time he impressed upon the attendants the urgency of his mission to explain his "new kind of religion" to the president. He was otherwise compliant and four days after admission was transferred to the Annex, another ward for male patients, and was put to work helping to tend to the hospital grounds. He was eventually discharged to the care of the Board of Charity of the District of Columbia.

The connection the doctors drew between Daniel's prophetic activity and the diagnosis of dementia praecox highlights late nineteenth-century and early twentieth-century white psychiatrists' assertions of Black peoples' inherent emotionalism as a key component of a racialized religious excitement. As we have seen in claims of innate superstition as a mode of religious excitement among African Americans, white psychiatrists pathologized Black supernaturalism and contributed to broader discourses that supported the social and political marginalization of African Americans. In addition to a focus on superstition, ideas about inherent Black emotionalism figured prominently in psychiatric theory about African Americans, religion, and mental illness, first within the diagnostic classifications of mania and melancholy and persisting as these were replaced by dementia praecox and manic-depressive psychosis in the early twentieth century. Such views drew from general discourses in white American culture about the "extraordinarily emotional" nature of Black religious life, in the words of Frederick M. Davenport, a Method-

Figure 4.1. A group of Black male patients in a "work gang" outside Howard Hall at St. Elizabeths Hospital in 1897. National Archives, photo 418-G-432.

ist political scientist, and were amplified by the authority of medicine.[5] Where psychiatric arguments about innate "Negro superstition" mobilized ideas about the influence of African religions on African American religious culture, the focus on emotionalism and excess served to distinguish between what white psychiatrists understood to be appropriate or inappropriate and true or distorted expressions of Christianity.

Psychiatric characterizations of an inherent emotional nature that was manifested in excessive religion among African Americans pathologized practices and expressions emerging from late nineteenth-century and early twentieth-century theological and institutional transformations in American Protestantism in which Black Christians played an important role.[6] Holiness and Pentecostal theologies and worship in churches and revivals were chief among these, and even though white Protestants participated in these religious developments, the presence and contributions of African Americans became the focus of special concern. Holiness theology emphasizing what the historian Randall J. Stephens describes as "perfectionism and belief in a cleansing or empowering second work of grace" following the conversion experience began to take hold in the late nineteenth-century South across several denominations, in part through missionary work by northern Holiness advocates.[7] For adherents, this work of grace through the power of the Holy Spirit was available to all, freed sanctified believers from sin, and empowered them to evangelize others to reject worldliness and sin. Holiness worship was enthusiastic and ecstatic, sometimes involving speaking in tongues and falling down while "slain in the spirit," leading some outsiders to deride these worshippers as "Holy Rollers." While there were some shared spaces of Holiness activity across racial lines, Black Holiness advocates like the southern ministers C. P. Jones and Charles H. Mason spread the theology among African Americans in the late nineteenth century, generating conflict within Black Baptist and Methodist churches over doctrines and forms of worship.[8]

In prayer and revivals, like the multiracial Azusa Street revival in Los Angeles from 1906 to 1909 and led by the African American minister William J. Seymour, Pentecostals spoke in tongues (an unknown language to all listeners or a language the speaker had not learned) as the sign of sanctification, prophesied, and performed works of healing.[9] As believers were attracted to the Pentecostal movement, they attuned themselves to signs of Jesus's return and, like Holiness adherents, distanced themselves from the ways of the sinful world.[10] While they believed this outpouring of the Holy Spirit meant that they were nearing the end of days, some also created churches in which to locate their evangelism. Charles H. Mason, who embraced Pentecostalism at Azusa Street, was one of the founders of the Church of God in Christ, which became a significant locus for Black Pentecostal life. As Holiness and Pentecostal believers engaged in religious practices aimed at harnessing the power of the Holy Spirit for healing, prophecy, and connection to God, psychiatric theory about African Americans and excessive emotion raised the stakes of medical scrutiny because of the possibility of commitment to mental hospitals. In addition to pathologizing the ecstatic expressions of these newer enthusiastic varieties of Christianity that were gaining prominence in African American life, psychiatric theory about race and religious emotion shaped the medical evaluations of individuals not necessarily connected to these movements and who claimed prophetic, visionary, or divine power or said they communicated with spiritual beings.

The many state-run hospitals for the insane were the arenas in which white psychiatrists worked to regulate what they deemed excessive religious emotion in Black people courts and families had committed for social exclusion and reform. As historians of architecture and of psychiatry have demonstrated, the physical structure and the location of the asylum were both key components of how doctors formulated treatment for those they declared insane.[11] So-called moral treatment involved locating patients in routines, including labor, which doctors argued would restore them to health and prepare them to be productive outside the asylum. For Black patients in southern asylums where African Americans were most likely to have been committed in the late nineteenth and early twentieth centuries, agricultural labor was a large part of their treatment in what the historian Mab Segrest has characterized as the "asylum-plantation model."[12] Productive labor on behalf of the asylum served as evidence of the ability to control excessive emotion and of readiness to be reintegrated into society. At the same time, prevailing psychiatric theory about Black people's emotional natures, which white doctors believed often manifested in religious excess, suggested the challenges of achieving a permanent cure. In this view, religious activities outside the asylum that medical authorities considered to set the context for the development of insanity provoked suspicion.

## "Peculiarly Emotional Natures and Religious Instincts"

As we have seen, many late nineteenth-century white psychiatrists maintained that, in addition to having been a moral, social, and mental benefit for African Americans, slavery had served as a restraint on Black peoples' emotions. The Georgia Lunatic Asylum superintendent Theophilus O. Powell, an active Methodist from an enslaving family who served as a Confederate army surgeon, contended that slavery subjected African Americans to "the laws of health" and to the example of self-control he believed oversight by white enslavers provided.[13] "It must be remembered," Powell wrote in the hospital's 1886 annual report, "that the negro by nature is emotional, hence his tendency to irregular habits—great emotional excitement, political and religious. Not having the restraining influence of refined and cultivated society, they are very frequently led into excesses which produce insanity."[14] Similarly, J. D.

Roberts, superintendent of the Eastern North Carolina Insane Asylum, claimed in 1883 that the steadying atmosphere of slavery had reduced "the risk of madness." "Under his master's rule," Roberts wrote, tendencies to emotional excess manifested in religious form "were largely under subjection. His life was routine, with but little to excite the emotions. Being now his own master and not having learned to control himself, he is easily carried away by anything of an exciting nature."[15]

In addition to the general argument that the absence of the restraining structure of slavery unbound Black emotion to debilitating ends, white physicians crafting theories about race, religion, and mental health also commonly insisted that Black people were constitutionally carefree—"happy-go-lucky not philosophical"—and contended that the overwhelming worry and anxiety of having to care for themselves in freedom contributed to the rising number of cases of insanity among African Americans.[16] In an 1886 overview of what he believed were the causes of an increase in diagnoses, James M. Buchanan, a physician at the Mississippi State Lunatic Asylum, asserted that African Americans' dramatically transformed circumstances had created overwhelming worry. "While the negro had a master he had no thought of the morrow," Buchanan wrote, "not a single care burdened his mind; there was nothing to disturb his equilibrium, and he was always the same fat, sleek, and contented individual."[17] Buchanan continued to argue that the punishments and "will of his master" kept the "passions and animal instincts" of "the Negro" in check.[18]

Undoubtedly, the individual and social disruptions wrought during the Civil War and in the decades after produced profound stress and anxiety among formerly enslaved African Americans. White psychiatrists used the fact of changing social circumstances to make essentialized claims that a disabling emotionalism characterized Black interiority and public affect, and they often located religion at the core of this emotionalism. In 1881, the *Alienist and Neurologist* noted that Thomas J. Mitchell, superintendent of the Mississippi State Lunatic Asylum, had called for doctors interested in the study and treatment of insanity to attend to questions about "the relative curability and susceptibility of the colored race" in the South, "where the condition of the race has been so revolutionized" in the previous two decades. An Episcopalian and Confederate veteran whose father was an enslaver in Alabama, Mitchell wrote of his suspicion that the prospects of recovery for Black patients were less certain than for whites, largely because of what he believed were African Americans' "peculiarly emotional natures and religious instincts."[19] Abram Witmer, a physician at St. Elizabeths, concurred, claiming that a natural racial emotionalism rendered African Americans especially sensitive to excitements of all kinds because they lacked "a philosophy or a religion deeper seated than the emotions to sustain them."[20] White psychiatrists also often linked religious emotionalism and superstition as supposed racial traits, with superstition manifesting in what they viewed as irrational fear that prevented normal social functioning and emotionalism tied most often to embodied exuberance in worship.

Henry K. Pusey, a Methodist who enslaved two women and four children in Meade County, Kentucky, just prior to the Civil War, theorized from his observations as superintendent of the Central Kentucky Lunatic Asylum in the late 1880s about religion and emotion among African Americans. In accord with most southern white psychiatrists, Pusey claimed that insanity was rare among enslaved Black people prior to emancipation but that in freedom it was increasing at a much faster rate than among white Americans, whose constituent white races had reduced such illnesses by advancing to higher degrees of civilization.[21] From this presumption about white Americans' superior civilizational achievements, he asserted that the subject of any white individual's delusion, including those connected to religion, should not be considered the cause of insanity but a manifestation "determined by the mental culture of the individual."[22] With respect to his evaluation of the increase in insanity among African Americans, however, Pusey asserted racial rather than individual grounds, writing, "The negro is essentially an emotional and superstitious character; liberty is accepted by him in large measure as a license to cultivate his emotions and superstitions. . . . His religious excesses are as unrestrained as are his physical and moral debaucheries."[23] John F. Miller of North Carolina's Eastern Asylum concurred with Pusey on the notion of racially innate emotional natures that manifested in relation to religion and argued that this emotionalism rendered Black people excessive in all aspects of their lives. He wrote in an 1896 assessment of the mental health effects of emancipation on African Americans that "the habits, education and emotions of the negro in his same condition differ as a class from the Caucasian. The negro laughs louder, prays and preaches louder than the Caucasian. . . . He carries these character-istics into his insane condition and is therefore more noisy, more vulgar and beastly in his habits."[24]

Some white physicians elaborated on what they imagined were the "beastly" outcomes of excessive Black religious emotion. In two arti-cles published in the *American Journal of Clinical Medicine* in 1910, the Chicago physician and eugenics advocate G. Frank Lydston pointed to religious excitement as a factor in what he argued was the moral de-generation of Black life and purported rampant sexual assaults of white women by Black men. He wrote, "There is more than an indirect rela-tion between the emotional excitement associated with religious fervor in the blacks, and outrages upon white women. Angels are depicted as white, and their pictured beauty has a very disastrous effect upon the brains of the negro when his emotional centers are in condition of [sex-ual arousal] characteristic of religious excitement. The result, in brief, is an inflamed desire for the possession of females of the superior race, and an increase of what may be termed sexual curiosity." Insisting that capital punishment would be no deterrent, Lydston advocated castra-tion because of what he considered false repentance and his notion that Black people happily embraced death with the expectation of instant transport to heaven. Although he also recommended castration for "the white rapist," he did not present religious excitement as a motivating factor for their actions.[25]

Such claims about innate emotionalism persisted in white psychiat-ric literature through the change in diagnostic classification in the early twentieth century from mania and melancholia to dementia praecox and manic-depressive psychosis. In his 1914 study "Psychoses among Negroes," Georgia State Sanitarium's E. M. Green reported that over the course of the previous five years he had found a higher ratio of both de-mentia praecox and manic-depressive psychosis among Black patients than white. In his assessment of manic-depressive psychosis, Green was representative of many white psychiatrists in his belief that African Americans were not prone to depression because of a natural emotional excess that lacked real depth. He wrote, "The negro race, as has been said, is emotional; in grief, noisy and obtrusive, it is of a superficial char-acter and soon passes."[26] Consequently, Green argued, depressive forms of psychosis were less likely to develop in a race that, in his estimation, lived only in the present.

Green claimed that the emotional nature of Black religion was a major factor in the higher number of dementia praecox diagnoses among "the negro," writing in broad strokes that "his religious convictions are most superficial, and while a great church goer, easily swayed by religious oratory and capable of excessive religious excitement, he has no realization of the basic principles of religion and gives way to all kinds of moral derelictions while professing the deepest piety. Of true morality he has no conception nor does the discrepancy between his profession and practice occasion any conflict in his mind."[27] In her 1914 study of "psychoses in the colored race," St. Elizabeths Hospital senior assistant physician Mary O'Malley likewise alleged excessive religious emotion as a feature of Black religion, asserting that "religion in the negro is a form of emotionalism and in this race it is not confined to sex, for the man is as fervent and devout as the woman, being as much open to religious impressions and as much dominated by his emotions in this direction."[28] Thus, white psychiatrists enshrined the idea of excessive religious emotion alongside superstition as a key factor precipitating insanity in African Americans. Moreover, in arguments like O'Malley's claiming that Black men were as susceptible to excess emotion as Black women, psychiatric theorists contributed to a racialized feminization associated with irrationality that positioned African Americans as unsuited for participation in political and civic life.

## "A Religious Frenzy"

The idea that religious emotionalism, particularly when expressed in group settings, could foster mental disorder was not new in late nineteenth-century American culture, nor was its application in legal and medical contexts limited to African Americans. Amariah Brigham's *Observations on the Influence of Religion upon the Health and Physical Welfare of Mankind* (1835) promoted the view that what he characterized as improper religious expression, especially enthusiastic and excited revivalist practices, could lead to insanity. The Presbyterian Brigham, the first superintendent of the New York State Lunatic Asylum at Utica and the founding editor of the *American Journal of Insanity*, grounded his medical views explicitly in his own religious norms, writing in the book's preface of his hope that the volume would aid in "restoring the worship of Christians to that calm, simple and pure manner recommended by our Savior, and thus prove serviceable to the cause of rational and scriptural piety."[29] He enumerated what he believed were the dangers of "extravagant and objectionable" modern Christian revivals, such as the famed Second Great Awakening revival in Cane Ridge, Kentucky, in 1801, and maintained that his reading of scripture assured him that these revivals could not possibly be the result of the influence of the Holy Spirit. Brigham argued forcefully that such camp meetings, "night meetings," and other lengthy revivals produced insanity and were especially dangerous to women, assumed in his text to be white, whose nervous system he deemed more "delicate and excitable" than those of men, also assumed to be white.[30] Not only did such excitement pose a danger of injury to (white) women, Brigham wrote, but he believed that (white) women so stimulated could "transmit to their offspring a tendency to nervous disease and insanity."[31] This perspective reflected associations between reason and masculinity, on the one hand, and emotion and femininity, on the other, that, as the religious studies scholar Sarah Imhoff writes, "permeated much Enlightenment thought, where it often had a close relationship with conceptions of Christianity."[32] For Brigham and others, white women were most endangered by religious excitement, but by the century's end as psychiatrists racialized religious excitement as Black for women and men, they amplified concerns about excessive emotionalism according to a racial hierarchy that positioned African Americans as both racialized and feminized.

Brigham saw religious sentiment as a human universal and the development of religious ritual as a natural product of this universal sentiment, but he differentiated among forms of worship along a scale of progress, with "the superiority of Christianity" appearing to him evident. Those people he consigned to the category of "savages," including "the colored races," stood outside the possibility of grasping "a pure and spiritual religion," and he argued that "they can only comprehend, and perhaps I may truly say, they can be benefitted only by gross forms of religion, and such as powerfully strike the senses."[33] As we have seen, white psychiatrists tended to deem the mental distress their white patients' developed in connection with religious excitement as an individual affair, and they assumed these patients' capacity for mental normalcy as the default. Consequently, they argued that mental disorder in white patients was the result of environmental factors, such as participation in deviant religious practices, or direct family heredity. In contrast, over the course of the last decades of the nineteenth century and into the twentieth, white social commentators, politicians, religious leaders, and psychiatrists argued for a racially determined emotionalism among African Americans that, when connected to religious excess, could trigger insanity or determine the form of its presentation.

By the end of the nineteenth and into the early twentieth century, the increasing prominence of Holiness and Pentecostal revivals, alongside faith healing, trance, prophecy, and ecstatic experience in American Protestantism, garnered the attention of white medical professionals concerned that white participants' frenzy, caused by what these doctors generally viewed as mental manipulation by hypnotizing, mesmerizing, or insane revivalists, would result in permanent mental instability. Responses of physicians, journalists, and mainstream Protestant leaders to the activities of the white "trance evangelist" Maria B. Woodworth in the 1880s and 1890s capture many Americans' interpretations of the revivals and of participants' claims that they had come under the influence of the Holy Spirit. In 1890, her preaching at large tent revival meetings throughout the Midwest generated grave public concerns, prompting two physicians in St. Louis to pronounce her insane and her revival work as hypnotic and precipitating of insanity among some in attendance. After visiting the revivals and interviewing Woodworth, the Pittsburgh psychiatrist and Episcopalian Theodore Diller concluded that "she undoubtedly has what are known as delusions and hallucinations. She has 'insane ideas' and has heard voices and seen visions which had no reality in fact. Her delusions are what are known as fixed and systematized. She is a case of partial or reasoning insanity—a religious monomania."[34] "True religion" would undoubtedly suffer as a result of her influence, Diller concluded, and he and other concerned doctors focused on warning the public to avoid the revivals.[35] While white commentators and medical professionals may have charged that white revivalists practiced mesmeric control or promoted false religion among white attendees, they did not assert that these excitements were the result of an essential racial quality or characteristic of whiteness.

The fact that some interracial religious activity took place under the banner of revivals generated concern among white physicians about the potential contagious nature of "religious excitement" and the effect on white revival participants of what doctors characterized as an innate Black religious excess. An account of an 1897 revival in St. Louis under the direction of William Worley, a white evangelist and divine healer, highlights white public concern about the mental health of white participants in interracial revivals. In a full-page spread, the *St. Louis Post-Dispatch* questioned whether the power of the Holy Spirit was truly at work in these events where Black participants and white "respectable" Christians were engaged in ecstatic worship, or if Worley might be hypnotizing and mesmerizing those in attendance. The newspaper report betrayed particular concern about the effect of revivalism on white women that recalled Amariah Brigham's theories. The paper solicited comment from a local doctor about the "consequences of hysteric exaltation," who warned that "young girls on the threshold of womanhood" were in danger of experiencing harm to their nervous systems from what he saw as a contagious hysteria.[36] This notion of contagion no doubt amplified readers' alarm when set against the attention the report paid to the participation of the Black female evangelist "Aunt Sally" in the proceedings. Describing her as a racial grotesque—"fat and shapeless, of pure African blood, ugly and illiterate, but full of zeal"—the author emphasized her rhetorical skill and ability to wield "those rising and falling inflections of the voice which stirs [*sic*] the negro to the point of hysteria." The racist characterization of "Aunt Sally" as emotional and not rational, as African and, by implication, superstitious, placed her Christianity outside the bounds of authentic religion, with the potential to create social problems beyond the interracial revival.

In assessing the psychological impact of participation in revivals on Black worshippers, white doctors frequently grounded assertions of revivals' debilitating consequences in claims of Black people's emotional religious nature as much as the skill of the revivalist. In considering the future of "the colored race in the United States" at century's end, Eugene Rollin Corson, a physician in Savannah, Georgia, whose parents were Spiritualists and friends of the Theosophist Helena P. Blavatsky, asserted that the increasing cases of insanity among African Americans were "mostly acute mania, of a religious type" and attributed this to a connection between African American emotion and religion. Corson wrote, "The emotional side of the negro is pronounced; you see it in all their gatherings especially the camp-meetings, where many work themselves up into a religious frenzy."[37] As with psychiatric theory that linked innate "superstition" to the mental disposition of African Americans, white physicians framed the excess of "Negro revivals" as a manifestation of the imagined emotional nature and a cause of mental derangement.

More than two decades after Corson's work, Howard D. King, a prominent white physician at the New Orleans Charity Hospital and a clinical instructor of infectious diseases at Tulane University, argued in the *Journal of the South Carolina Medical Association* that the deleterious social effects of religious revivals among African Americans were an urgent matter of public concern. This was the case, he claimed without evidence, because participants were "often goaded to such frenzy that they become criminally irresponsible," leading to assaults and murders.[38] Rather than serving as a sign of the health and vitality of Black religious life in early twentieth-century America, he insisted, these revivals were "distinctly morbid and injurious phenomena." For him, the physical manifestations of participation in revivals, marked in his account by "the sudden relaxation of muscular power, the prolonged convulsions, the foaming at the mouth, the rolling of the eyeballs, the fixed and glassy stare, the wild dreams and incoherent ravings," were not the product of divine forces but were signs of hysterical seizures "brought on by an overwrought condition of mind due to great religious excitement."[39] He argued that such heightened excitement could not be experienced repeatedly "without giving rise to insanity." King called on "the intelligent of the negro clergy" to suppress such "fanaticism" and for legislation to be enacted to curb revivals among African Americans because of the public significance of "the influence of overpowering appeals to the senses in exciting lunacy."[40]

African Americans reflecting on the state of Black life in the late nineteenth and early twentieth centuries recognized the broader stakes of white commentators' assertions of emotionalism and excess as racially determined characteristics of Black religious expression. For many, the religious enthusiasm they experienced in varied Black Christian contexts was deeply satisfying, serving to connect them to the divine and to each other through oratory, prayer, music, and movement. But some Black religious leaders argued that African American Christianity was too emotional and insufficiently rational to aid the formerly enslaved and African Americans in general in achieving spiritual, social, and economic progress. Those urging reform of Black religious cultures deployed arguments about class and education rather than racial propensity, however, even as some denigrated non-Christian religions. The AME Church Bishop Daniel A. Payne, born to free parents in Charleston, South Carolina, railed against participants in "bush meetings" that, to him, represented "a heathenish way to worship and disgraceful to themselves, the race, and the Christian name." Payne also bemoaned that the exuberance of the ring shout—a protracted ritual of song and circular movement meant to make the Spirit present—"was regarded as the essence of religion."[41]

William Wells Brown, an abolitionist and novelist who had been enslaved in Missouri and emancipated himself in young adulthood by escaping, argued similarly in 1880 that religious forms were damaging African Americans' possibilities for social development. Brown wrote, "The moral and social degradation of the colored population of the Southern States is attributable to two main causes, their mode of living, and their religion."[42] Describing the tenor of religious services among southern African Americans, Brown emphasized frenzy and excitement among ministers and congregants in lengthy meetings that left participants exhausted. He also viewed revival meetings as "injurious to both health and morals," the former because of how long they lasted and the latter because of the dubious credentials of traveling missionaries. He concluded, "It will be difficult to erase from the mind of the negro of the South, the prevailing idea that outward demonstrations, such as shouting, the loud 'amen,' and the most boisterous noise in prayer, are not necessary adjuncts to piety."[43] For Brown, "an educated ministry" was the only solution to the excessive and emotional character of Black Protestant worship, but he doubted whether "the uneducated, superstitious masses," made so by the withholding of education during slavery, would "receive and support an intelligent Christian clergyman." Nevertheless, he noted the great desire and admiration for education in general among the formerly enslaved, which he took as an encouraging sign of potential for progress as he understood it.[44]

Late nineteenth-century and early twentieth-century African American women in social reform and civil rights activism focused attention on emotion in Black worship as a concern for the race's future. Some, like Anna Julia Cooper, an Episcopalian, argued for the benefits of "decorous solemnity" and "instructive and elevating ritual" over against what she characterized as the "rank exuberance and often ludicrous demonstrativeness" of some African American worship.[45] Women like the Presbyterian Ida B. Wells and the Baptist Fannie Barrier Williams who engaged the topic of emotion and religion as a problem often laid the blame at the feet of Black male clergy who, they argued, did little to promote social, political, or religious progress in Black communities. The historian Deborah Gray White argues that these women insisted that "by choosing emotion over reason, ministers both hindered the progress of the black masses and proved an embarrassment to the race."[46]

Such leaders in the Black women's club movement and church organizations emphasized gender and class in their critiques of religious emotion, extending beyond the concern with clergy. The National Association of Colored Women's Clubs, founded in 1896 with the Oberlin graduate and Congregationalist Mary Church Terrell as the first president, promoted "moral elevation" of Black women and communities. For these women, public comportment, including in worship, had implications for African Americans as a whole, and they strove to advance their own standing, as reflected in the organization's motto, "lifting as we climb."[47] But, as the historian Barbara Dianne Savage argues about Nannie Helen Burroughs and other women in the Woman's Convention of the National Baptist Convention, "Many black Baptist women who objected to the emotionalism of Black worship practices were not rejecting the practices themselves, since some of them engaged in similar expressions in their own worship services. Rather, they were criticizing excessive reliance on emotionalism in the absence of any meaningful social program or leadership."[48] These women understood the stakes of the image of Black churches as overly emotional because some Black male clergy rejected the criticism of their leadership and instead linked emotionalism to the preponderance of women in the pews and negative associations with the "feminization" of churches.[49]

African American social scientists like W. E. B. Du Bois were also invested in the possibility of a literate and liturgically moderate "Negro church" serving as a platform for Black political, economic, and social development and sought to distinguish "respectable" from excessive worship.[50] Du Bois, Booker T. Washington, and other Black public figures argued that African American religious life was not static and that progress, for them marked by increasingly restrained worship, had been made and continued to be possible. Washington wrote in 1905 that "it has been said that the trouble with the Negro Church is that it is too emotional" and recommended that churches embrace the teaching that "mere religious emotion that is guided by no definite idea and is devoted to no purpose is vain."[51] Several Black clergymen who reflected on emotion and Black religion placed these questions in a longer historical scope and a wider religious context and, in some cases, argued for the positive contributions of Black religious emotion. In 1913, the Congregationalist minister William H. Ferris, who later became ordained in the AME Church, reflected on the common perception that "the Negro is prone to emotional excitement," but he argued that it was more a matter of degree than kind, given the volume and excitements that also characterized "the camp meetings of the poor whites." In contrast to most evaluations of what commentators viewed as a debilitating and harmful Black religious emotionalism, Ferris held that "the aspiration and longing and sorrow and cravings of the Negro" that were manifest in Black religious music demonstrated that "the Negro race is richer, then, in emotional endowment than any other race in the world."[52] Such arguments that tried to recast the source or effect of Black religious emotion were overwhelmed by white popular and medical discourse about racialized emotional natures and dangerously excessive religious forms.

## "Holy Rollers"

Holiness and Pentecostal revivals and churches organized around enthusiastic, embodied worship, the experience of baptism in the Holy Spirit, faith healing, and often speaking in tongues constituted precisely the sort of "agitating novelties in religion" that South Carolina Lunatic Asylum superintendent J. W. Babcock and other white physicians in the late nineteenth and early twentieth centuries pathologized and contended were likely to precipitate mental illness among African Americans.[53] As Pentecostalism garnered public attention, observers sometimes evaluated the religious energy and the phenomenon of speaking in tongues that Pentecostal baptism in the Holy Spirit facilitated as a form of religious insanity. Indeed, one of the first published newspaper accounts, under the headline "Weird Babel of Tongues," framed the multiracial Azusa Street revival in Los Angeles led by the Black Holiness minister William J. Seymour as an expression of excessive religious excitement. "Breathing strange utterances and mouthing a creed which it would seem no sane mortal could understand, the newest religious sect has started in Los Angeles," the *Los Angeles Times* reported. "Meetings are held in a tumble-down shack . . . and the devotees of the weird doctrine practice the most fanatical rites, preach the wildest theories and work themselves into a state of mad excitement in their peculiar zeal."[54] The report emphasized the predominance of African Americans in the revival, who the reporter characterized as making the night "hideous" through wailing and pandemonium. Other early accounts of the activities of those dubbed pejoratively "Holy Rollers" described "fervor and display of religious emotion [that] totally eclipse[s] the oldtime darkey camp meetings of the south" and emphasized the multiracial character of gatherings, a feature sometimes read as itself a sign of the insanity of participants.[55]

Police and medical authorities in California routinely interpreted religious expressions related to these revivals and the church communities that grew out of them as markers of mental derangement. In October 1906, Los Angeles police arrested Henry Printes of the Azusa Street Pentecostal revival and held him for examination for lunacy because he was praying on the street and, they claimed, used "indecent language," perhaps their interpretation of his speaking in tongues. For his part, Printes insisted that he was mentally sound and that his prayers were inspired by the Holy Spirit.[56] When police arrested L. J. Johnson in Los Angeles in 1907 for setting fires and damaging houses in his neighborhood, they decided to have his sanity assessed because of his insistence that he was "the divine spirit" and "the black angel" with a message from heaven. According to a brief newspaper article about the arrest, the police claimed that Johnson was "a holy roller" and that "through constant attendance at their meetings his reason is said to have become dethroned."[57]

In at least one instance, distress over family members' participation in Holiness or Pentecostal revivals was named in the commitment process as a precipitating factor for insanity. This was the case for Missouri-born Arthur E., who migrated to Oakland around 1910 to join his mother and siblings.[58] In 1915, Arthur's sister May C. petitioned for a lunacy hearing, and Arthur was examined by two white Catholic Californian doctors who sat on the San Francisco County Lunacy Commission and whose testimony contributed to his commitment to the Mendocino State Hospital in Ukiah.[59] The doctors described him as "good natured" and "amiable" but, probably drawing on May's testimony, noted the gradual development over the course of the previous six months of worry over "impending troubles" that made him "act queerly and irrationally." According to the report, Arthur had been experiencing auditory hallucinations and delusions of persecution and had become "depressed and melancholic." The doctors noted, "At present mother and brother have left their family and joined the Holy Rollers."[60] Upon commitment, his diagnosis was melancholia, with "worry about family troubles" as an exciting factor. Doctors revised the diagnosis to dementia praecox upon his death at Mendocino State in 1939, bringing it in line with the prevailing categories of the day. The commitment and hospital paperwork do not provide more information about the group Arthur's mother and brother joined, but several years after Arthur's death his brother Joseph listed Cornelia Jones Robertson, a participant in the Azusa Street revival and founder and pastor of Emmanuel Pentecostal Church in San Francisco, as a contact person. It is uncertain if Arthur's psychiatrists were aware of the details of his family's religious life, but it seems clear that those evaluating him for commitment took his family's Pentecostalism as a possible factor in hereditary transmission of insanity.[61]

For their part, early Pentecostals argued that, rather than causing insanity, their beliefs led to the cure and asserted the benefits of their ability to call on the Holy Spirit's healing power. *The Apostolic Faith*, published by the Los Angeles Azusa Street Mission and reporting on the developing Pentecostal movement, sometimes attributed insanity to religious error embraced because of demonic agency or possession. It also featured accounts of restoration of right mind as evidence of the healing power of God.[62] Although it is not always possible from newspaper accounts in the mainstream press, court documents, or hospital records to determine the theological commitments of those diagnosed as suffering from "religious excitement," early Pentecostals noted instances when they were framed as insane and took the opportunity to highlight, instead, what they believed was God's power working in and through them. *The Apostolic Faith* published a piece in 1906 under the headline "Arrested for Jesus' Sake" by someone who called themselves simply "A Worker." The correspondent recounted having traveled from San Francisco to Los Angeles after the earthquake, hearing about the Pentecostal revivals, and eventually experiencing "baptism with the Holy Ghost and [the ability to] speak with new tongues." The writer reported seeing "two colored police officers with whom I was slightly acquainted" while on the way to a prayer meeting at the Azusa Street Mission and stopping to speak in unknown tongues to them. Believing this to be a manifestation of insanity, the police officers took the worker to the station, where the praying in tongues continued before a transfer to the county hospital for examination in advance of a commitment hearing. The worker reported that, at trial, "the Lord permitted me to speak in the Italian language and one of the judges understood it and I was discharged without having to call a single witness."[63] While those drawn to Holiness and Pentecostal theology, practices, and community invested in the power of the Holy Spirit to heal from illness, including of the mind, the medical perception of participants in these movements routinely pathologized them, building on the long-standing contention that the "Negro revival" represented a threat to the mental stability of participants.

White psychiatric theory highlighted group worship in the form of revivals or Holiness and Pentecostal services in characterizing emotionalism as a racial trait, and this facilitated treatment and discipline of individual expressions of religious emotion within the space of the asylum. Some Black patients were committed to mental hospitals at the urging of their families, friends, or employers, and others came before courts for commitment hearings because of manifestations of mania or depression expressed in religious terms. These often took the form of auditory, visual, and sensory contact with divine and spiritual beings, belief in travel to spiritual realms, prophetic revelations, or directives from God. In most cases it is difficult to determine from the records of commitment hearings or patient records the broader context of these individuals' religious lives that shaped their excited religious expressions. Nevertheless, the attention devoted to the role of religion in their illness, framed through the lens of prevailing psychiatric theories about Black religious emotionalism, is significant.

Violence against strangers or family members or destruction of property was often what led to lunacy hearings in which racialized understandings of religious excitement and emotion emerged as a concern for doctors, other witnesses, and public commentators. We get fleeting glimpses in cases like those of Fannie S., admitted to St. Elizabeths Hospital in April 1896 after becoming violent in her place of work as a domestic servant, an event that received attention in the local press.[64] The members of the District of Columbia's Court of Equity declared her insane, and the hospital's doctors diagnosed her with acute mania caused by religious excitement. She was discharged in July 1896 in improved condition but readmitted in November of the following year with the same diagnosis. The events that led to her readmission became public in a newspaper account of her plans to assault a former coworker. The newspapers described her as being in a religious mania because, in the words of a reporter, upon arriving at the home of her white former employer Fannie pronounced that she "had received a Divine command to kill" her coworker.[65] One newspaper represented her religious declaration in grandiose language, reporting her as standing with her hands folded across her breast and saying, "I have been directed by the Lord Jesus Christ to come to see you." Another paper deployed racist imagery in contending that Fannie, whom its reporter described as "a robust colored woman," hissed as she drew her knife, saying, "De Lawd says I mus' kill her wid dis knife."[66] Police arrested Fannie before she encountered her intended victim. Although both published accounts of what led to her readmission to the hospital highlight religious motivations and the testimony of her former employer supported the diagnosis of the forty-one-year-old Baptist as suffering from religious excitement, the racist tropes the *Washington Evening Times* report mobilized underscore the impact of ideas about Black religious emotionalism and excess on legal and medical interpretations of Fannie's acts of violence.

John T.'s detention in Washington, DC, in 1897 also gained the attention of the media when he was arrested after destroying the altar appointments in a chapel of St. Dominic Catholic Church and threatening a Dominican brother and the women who were cleaning the church. The *Washington Morning Times* described him as "a gigantic negro" who was "crazed by religious enthusiasm" to wreak havoc in the church where he had attended Mass the previous morning.[67] John was deaf and nonverbal, and St. Elizabeths Hospital psychiatrists did not record more about his religious commitments after his admission with a diagnosis of acute mania. Hospital staff described him as "filthy and destructive in his habits, excited and noisy at times," but eventually as mostly quiet and observing others.[68] John's brother William wrote to St. Elizabeths' superintendent William A. White in 1911 on receiving news that John's health was declining and insisted that his brother was "a good boy a good brother a good Son to Mother and Father" and "a good and Faithful Servant to all the White People and neighbors that he worked for." William laid the blame for John's mental deterioration on the white Catholic people for whom he worked, charging that "he was Taught and Lead [sic] by them And There Faith and Religious Belief and Ways was What Caused his mind to become unbalanced." William continued to recount that "after he had confessed to become Religious And believed in the Catholic faith," John became convinced that "the Lord had demanded him to become a Priest. That is What Caused him to Loose his mine and Set him Crazy."[69] William lamented that John's inability to hear had inhibited his recovery, that their parents did not visit him regularly, and that he was unable to do so because he had moved away and was then writing from the US Penitentiary in Leavenworth, Kansas. William thanked White for his care of his brother and prayed that he would be released from prison in time to visit again but promised to put his small savings toward a decent and respectful funeral if John died before then. John died in 1913, probably of tuberculosis, and John E. Lind, one of St. Elizabeths' psychiatrists who propagated theories about Black religious primitivism and dementia praecox, revised the diagnosis to dementia praecox, in line with the newly dominant diagnostic categories.[70]

African Americans diagnosed with religiously grounded mental illness entered institutional settings where ideas about Black emotional religious excess held sway, such that even in cases in which doctors pointed to physical rather than so-called moral causes for mental illness, the invocation of religion shaped institutional responses. When Mariah H., a thirty-three-year-old Methodist farm laborer, was brought before a judge in Chester County, South Carolina, in 1899, for example, William C. Hicklin, a white Presbyterian landowner from a family of enslavers and a Confederate veteran who was probably her employer, testified that she had been cheerful, quiet, and industrious but since suffering typhoid fever had become "noisy and talkative" and "irritable and quarrelsome."[71] He indicated that, although her general health was now sound, she "sings and prays and is noisy all the time."[72] In response to questions about Mariah's behavior, the examining physicians, Robert L. Douglas and George Washington Jordan, both of whose families enslaved Black people in Chester County, described her as physically uncontrollable and unconcerned with her well-being, a state they believed required her to be chained at all times. In interpreting her condition, however, the doctors focused exclusively on Mariah's religious pronouncements, reporting her as saying "that she was sanctified," a claim they classed with "all kind of things that no sane person would think of saying," passing judgment on the growing prominence of Holiness theology in American Protestant life.[73] J. W. Babcock, the hospital's superintendent and a prolific theorist of religion and insanity among African Americans, confirmed the court's determination of insanity and authorized her admission. Babcock's initial diagnosis was acute mania, and the patient record follows Hicklin's testimony in listing typhoid fever as a precipitating cause. In a note in Mariah's record less than a month later, hospital staff reported that she continued to be noisy and "preaches day and night," which led them to restrain her. Within six months, the hospital released her, having declared her to have become "quiet, rational, and industrious." Upon discharge the diagnosis was modified to "post-febrile insanity," a turn away from mania produced by religious excess to a physical cause.

While violence in conjunction with perceived religious excitement often led to lunacy hearings and commitments to institutions for Black patients, sometimes only a publicly displayed claim to visionary power was necessary to gain the attention of authorities. In 1911, officials in Houston, Texas, evaluated the sanity of William Rice, a thirty-nine-year-old brickmason, who came under scrutiny because he had been digging for treasure in his yard at the direction of "the spirit," who had come to him several times in dreams.[74] Neighbors concerned about the size of the hole registered a complaint, and a lunacy hearing was ordered.[75] According to a report in the *Houston Post*, at the hearing Rice claimed that he and his wife, Ella, were in communication with

God and Jesus through the power of "a cross made out of ordinary tree limbs" and a fishing pole they carried.[76] This testimony of communication with the divine was sufficient for the judge to find Rice "guilty of lunacy" and order him committed to a state asylum, a judgment that elicited a cry of despair from Ella at the thought of separation from her husband. The case drew the attention of a reader of the newspaper account, who wrote with astonishment that a complaint of "an unusual religious belief" could result in a lunacy hearing and commitment to an asylum. Writing as "Justice," the author invoked the Texas constitution's protections of freedom of conscience regarding religious worship and sought to differentiate between a religious mania in the "poor, ignorant negro," "doubtless evidenced by the usual exhortations, singing, etc., manifested by his kind," and something that constituted a genuine social menace, of which Justice saw no evidence.[77] Justice's objection pointed to the disciplining work the racialized pathologizing of visionary experiences and modes of connection to spiritual forces such court proceedings could accomplish, particularly combined with commitment to a state hospital for the insane.

## Disciplining Black Religious Emotion

In the late nineteenth and early twentieth centuries, Black patients were most likely to be committed to asylums for the insane in southern states, where the majority of African Americans lived, but were also admitted to hospitals in every region of the country. Some states established separate hospitals for the treatment of Black patients, as was the case with Virginia's Central Lunatic Asylum (1870), North Carolina's Eastern Insane Asylum (1880), Alabama's Mt. Vernon (Searcy) Hospital (1902), West Virginia's Lakin State Hospital (1926), and Oklahoma's Taft State Hospital (1931). Most African Americans committed to mental hospitals in states that practiced racial segregation were housed in separate buildings or sections within state hospitals in which most patients were white. State hospitals were generally large institutions that housed hundreds of inmates diagnosed as suffering from mental illnesses with physical causes, such as epilepsy, paresis resulting from syphilis, and dementia, as well as from so-called moral causes, including religious excitement. These institutions also sometimes housed people with

No. 1.—Eastern Hospital, Goldsboro, N. C.        PUB. BY GOLDSBORO BOOK STORE, GOLDSBORO, N. C.

Figure 4.2. Eastern Hospital, Goldsboro, North Carolina, ca. 1900–1910.
North Carolina Postcard Collection (P052), North Carolina Collection
Photographic Archives, Wilson Library, UNC–Chapel Hill.

cognitive disabilities, characterized at the time with terms like "idiocy"
and "imbecility." Because of lack of financial resources, almost all Black
patients were classed as indigent, and their confinement and treatment
supported by state funds.

White hospital superintendents and state political leaders made a variety of arguments in favor of or against separate institutions for Black
patients. Often questions of space and state funds were significant factors in these discussions. Increasing numbers of African Americans
committed to hospitals and overcrowding in existing institutions motivated most hospital leaders in southern states to call for additional accommodations, whether in separate buildings in a state hospital or new
institutions altogether. In his 1888 annual report on the Mississippi State
Lunatic Asylum, Superintendent Thomas Jefferson Mitchell, an Episcopalian from an enslaving family in Alabama, stressed the health dangers of overcrowding in the two wards with African American patients
and argued that such conditions "decidedly lessen the chances of good
results expected from hospital treatment." He noted that Virginia and
North Carolina had established separate institutions but did not think
such a "radical change" was necessary in Mississippi, particularly considering the state's financial constraints. He recommended additional

"cheap accommodations" within the existing institution.[78] Other superintendents made moral and medical arguments, grounded in white supremacy, about the benefits of keeping Black patients within majority white hospitals. In his 1887 annual report, Henry K. Pusey, superintendent of the Central Kentucky Lunatic Asylum wrote, "The associations and surroundings of a white Institution, and the higher requirements of society in behalf of the dominant race, exert a refining influence upon both the white and black management of colored insane department." Pusey, a former enslaver, continued, "The force of example, the higher moral tone and discipline of all connected with an Institution for the whites, with the sense of justice more or less prevalent in every mind, certainly insures the comfort of the negro more effectually in a combined rather than in a separate Institution under the control of both whites and blacks."[79]

In their physical design, late nineteenth-century mental hospitals generally followed the Kirkbride plan, developed in the mid-nineteenth century by a Pennsylvania hospital superintendent, Thomas Kirkbride, and promoted by the influential asylum reformer Dorothea Dix. As the architectural historian Carla Yanni describes it, the Kirkbride plan consisted of a large building "made up of short but connected pavilions, arrayed in a shallow V" and in which all asylum patients were housed, with indigent patients usually in large open dormitories with rows of adjacent beds. Asylums on the Kirkbride plan also sometimes incorporated additional structures, creating a hybrid form with what was known as the "cottage plan" in which patients were housed in a variety of separate buildings on a single campus.[80] The hybrid Kirkbride-cottage plan made it possible for institutions in states that practiced racial segregation to relegate Black patients to outlying buildings, often repurposed properties not intended for medical care. Both hospitals that housed only Black patients and facilities for Black patients within larger segregated hospitals were invariably inferior and overcrowded when compared with facilities for white patients. In the South Carolina Lunatic Asylum in Columbia in the 1880s, for example, up to two hundred Black male patients lived in old, unsanitary, and dangerous wooden buildings, and the crowding there and in Black wards at other institutions promoted the spread of diseases like tuberculosis that often led to patient deaths.[81] Not surprisingly, racism, segregation, and underfunding led

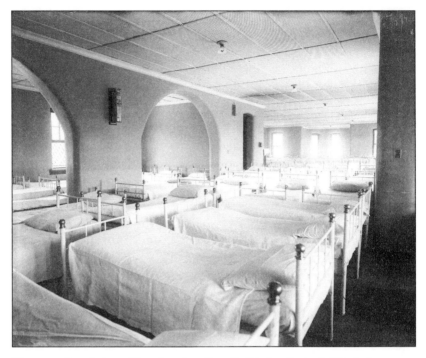

Figure 4.3. Crowded conditions in a dormitory for Black patients, St. Elizabeths Hospital, 1925. National Archives, photo 418-G-344.

to unequal medical care. An 1878 letter to the AME Church's *Christian Recorder* described disparate conditions at the Florida Hospital for the Insane in Chattahoochee, characterizing accommodations for white patients as comfortable and pleasant with nice space for visitors and Black patients' rooms and public spaces as furnished with old, broken furniture, few dishes or cutlery, and no chairs for visitors. The letter's author decried this disparate treatment, emphasizing that Black Floridians paid taxes to support the institution, just as did white residents. "If you want to see differences made between colored and white," the author insisted, "this is the place; for myself it is one of the most God forsaken places that ever blotted the fair soil of the earth."[82]

As we saw earlier, the primary form of treatment for late nineteenth-century and early twentieth-century asylum patients was labor, justified in terms of providing patients with a regular schedule and productive occupation. In 1904, William Francis Drewry, superintendent of Virginia's Central State Hospital for Black patients, wrote in his annual report, "Learning from long experience and from the ablest hospital alienists that the employment and recreation and out-door air are essential factors in the treatment of the chronic insane, and many of the acute class, we keep practically all who are able engaged daily in either some kind of work or suitable recreation."[83] At Central State that year, male patients labored to maintain the hospital, staff, and other patients by working in the boiler, pump, coal, and wood houses, in the carpentry shop, bakery, kitchen, dining rooms, and hospital cemetery, as janitors, and assisting plasterers and plumbers. Female patients also worked in the kitchens, the dining room, and laundry and cleaned the wards in service of maintaining the hospital. Both male and female patients contributed financially through their labor by working in the hospital's farm, dairy, stables, shoe shop, blacksmith shop, and sewing shop.[84] Such labor regimes were in place across the system of state hospitals and, as the historian Mab Segrest has argued in her work on the Georgia Lunatic Asylum that housed

Figure 4.4. Black female patients at St. Elizabeths Hospital doing laundry in the ironing room, 1918. National Archives, photo 418-G-188.

Black and white patients, "patients' work was . . . structured by raced and gendered political economies." In Georgia, for example, Black women were assigned strenuous physical labor on the farm and the laundry, and white women were given work as seamstresses.[85] Similarly, in 1892 in the Alabama Insane Hospital, which housed white and Black patients, white women were the only constituency not represented among the "farm and garden" laborers, and Black women outnumbered all men in that labor arena, in addition to working in the laundry. White women at Alabama's hospital were most likely to be unemployed or to be assigned to labor in the wards and dining room or sewing and knitting.[86]

Central State's Drewry affirmed the racialization of labor in his institution in testimony before Congress in 1906 when he informed representatives that in his hospital, which housed only Black patients, he made inmates engage in more labor than did white patients at the state's three other mental hospitals. Drewry discussed the decision to use old tubs and hand scrubbing rather than newer machines in the hospital's laundry to put more patients to work, and he described hundreds of patients laboring in the fields of the hospital's farm and dairy and building roads. Drewry, a Methodist whose father enslaved dozens of Black people in Southampton County, Virginia, in 1860, justified his different approach to labor from that taken in the hospitals for white patients by asserting that "colored patients can be induced more easily to work than white patients, because all of them have been in the habit of doing manual labor."[87] In his 1910 annual report, Drewry affirmed what he understood to be the treatment benefits of occupation with work— "minds are made contented and the results are better physical and mental conditions"—and reminded the governor of the financial benefits to the institution of inmate labor.[88]

Psychiatrists also acted upon the bodies of patients committed to mental hospitals, sometimes using physical restraints and practices like hydrotherapy, which involved baths at extreme temperatures and wrapping the patient in wet sheets for extended periods. Hospital officials deployed ideas about the hereditary nature of some mental illness to justify surgical interventions like sterilization not to treat patients, they asserted, but to prevent mental disease in future generations. Drewry wrote in Central State's 1912 annual report that among the hospital's exclusively Black patients he found "a rich field for the application by way of eugenics, sterilization, segregation, etc.," and in 1922 he endorsed the state's laws prohibiting "the inter-marriage of the mentally unfit."[89] Virginia's Eugenical Sterilization Act of 1924 empowered the superintendents of the state's mental hospitals to petition for the sterilization of patients they determined were "afflicted with hereditary forms of insanity that are recurrent, idiocy, imbecility, feeble-mindedness or epilepsy." A member of the state's hospital board then reviewed the petition, characterized the patient's condition according to the conditions eligible for sterilization, and decided whether "by the laws of heredity [the patient] is the probable potential parent of socially inadequate offspring likewise afflicted."[90] If so, the state authorized sterilization, which took place within the hospital. In 1929, Central State's superintendent Hugh Carter Henry, the son of a Presbyterian minister, reported that the institution had sterilized thirty-six women, selected because of what he considered "a likelihood of transmitting mental disease or defect to their offspring in the case of pregnancy" and because he deemed them able to be released following sterilization.[91] He concluded, "We have experienced practically no objection to the measure on the part of the patients or their guardians."[92] Two years later, the hospital reported seventy-three sterilizations of male patients and fifty-four sterilizations of female patients.[93] Restrictions on access to patient files related to eugenic sterilization make it impossible to connect commitment to the hospital on the basis of religiously grounded mental illness and the superintendent's decision to sterilize a patient, or to determine whether patients or guardians did, in fact, register objection.[94]

Access to recreation for patients who were not considered violent or at risk of absconding supplemented hospital treatment in the form of labor and medical intervention. In his account of work as a physician at the South Carolina State Hospital, James Lawrence Thompson noted that, in addition to labor, walks for exercise were mandatory for men and segregated by race.[95] Central State superintendent Drewry portrayed recreation at the institution in ways that reveal embedded racialized stereotypes about Black culture and personality. He described the hospital as providing "everything, from a watermelon feast up, I reckon," including "baseball, croquet, dances, cakewalks," and music—in sum, "everything that appeals to a colored man." He also insisted that these were necessarily different from recreation in white institutions, claiming, for instance, Black patients "would not care to play bridge whist," presumably because of his assumption that a game of strategy would not appeal. "They would rather play crap," he claimed, promoting stereotypes of reckless gambling among African Americans.[96] The Crownsville State Hospital in Maryland that housed Black patients reported "dances, motion pictures, and informal social functions" as the main amusements in 1923, in addition to a Christmas minstrel show put on by patients.[97] The Florida State Hospital offered movies for white and Black patients on different nights of the week.[98]

Some hospital superintendents classed the opportunity to attend religious services as part of patient recreation, and others included Christian services as part of the treatments their institution provided for patients. Although these were not religious institutions, a representative of the Eastern Hospital in Goldsboro, North Carolina, told the attendees at the 1896 National Conference of Charities and Correction, "What we are trying to do now in this State is to bring to bear the influences of the Christian religion to elevate them to another and better environment."[99] In 1887, North Carolina Eastern Hospital's superintendent J. D. Roberts, also a Baptist deacon, wrote of the limited facilities for patient recreation and noted that, instead, he gathered some patients "in one of the best wards for reading twice a week," and on Sunday afternoons that reading took the form of "some simple Bible story or a short sermon."[100] Editors of religious periodicals, both local and from other parts of the country, provided free copies for patients at many institutions. Some state hospitals offered Sunday services through the rotation of Protestant and Catholic clergy, and others had Protestant clergy as standing chaplains. At the South Carolina Lunatic Asylum in the late 1880s, the hospital chaplain Rev. Edwin A. Bolles of the Evangelical Lutheran Church and an agent of the Bible Society of the Confederate States conducted Bible readings in the wards and held Sunday services in the chapel within the main building for Black and white patients, reporting with pride that attendees "have conducted themselves with great propriety during the services of the sanctuary."[101] In fact, the hospital's rules required "all patients sufficiently quiet in deportment" to attend chapel services on Sundays.[102]

In some cases, patients found the spiritual care they received inadequate. In 1898, William Dorroh wrote to the AME Church's *Christian*

*Recorder* with an account of a funeral service at the South Carolina State Hospital. Dorroh, who described himself as a member of the AME Church's Columbia, South Carolina Conference and a patient at the hospital, lamented that the young man being buried was "unknown, while living, to every person present," including the chaplain who conducted the service. Not knowing anything about the deceased, Dorroh wondered whether the man had been saved and his soul rested. He reminded all who worked in the asylum that they were responsible for the "protection and care for these unfortunate and helpless inmates."[103] Dorroh's testimony is rare and may represent many more patients who wished for spiritual support during their confinement but found the care lacking or absent.

African American hospital employees also extended spiritual care to Black patients in some instances. After Edwin Bolles left the position of chaplain at South Carolina's hospital, Rev. Charles Jaggers, a well-regarded formerly enslaved preacher and hospital employee, offered nondenominational Christian services. Jaggers, whom white staff and white residents of Columbia called "Uncle Jaggers," was devoted to the support of his Black community, founding a home for care of the elderly, visiting prisoners in the penitentiary, and rendering religious service to hospital inmates.[104] Like Jaggers in South Carolina, W. Banks Wood was a Baptist deacon and employee of Virginia's Central Lunatic Asylum from its founding in 1870 until his death in 1911.[105] In addition to his work as an attendant and laborer on the farm, he conducted services there on Sunday afternoons "attended by all the denominational ministers of the city and of the Normal school," according to a 1901 report in the *Richmond Planet*, the area's Black newspaper. The report noted that these local ministers took pleasure in participating and that the hospital's superintendent supported this work by providing an organ and books for them.[106] African American clergy took general interest in conditions at state hospitals. When Black members of the Methodist Episcopal Church met in 1909 in Jackson, Louisiana, for a district conference, conference officials arranged for them to visit the state asylum there to "see what the State was doing for the unfortunate ones of all races in this State."[107] In 1897 at Virginia's Central State, Superintendent Drewry lauded the local African American ministers who offered religious services "at great personal sacrifice, and without compensation," emphasizing that "the services are always of a simple nature, and devoid of anything likely to produce excitement or emotion."[108] In 1910, a year in which Drewry listed "religious excitement" as the second most common cause of insanity among the hospital's patients, he noted that "colored ministers" from the community were able to offer "religious services of a simple, unemotional character" weekly and on special occasions, a contribution for which he again expressed gratitude.[109]

While African American patients may have encountered Black ministers on occasion within the confines of the asylum, it was rare for them to be treated by Black physicians at state mental hospitals in the late nineteenth and early twentieth centuries. Richard F. Tancil, a Baptist and a graduate of Howard University Medical School, served as an assistant superintendent at Virginia's Central Lunatic Asylum from 1883 to 1885 under the short-lived administration of the Readjuster Party.[110] Constantine Clinton Barnett, also a graduate of Howard University Medical School, was the first superintendent of West Virginia's Lakin State Hospital, opened in 1926 in a newly constructed building on a six-hundred-acre campus near Point Pleasant and housing more than three hundred patients by the early 1930s. This "venture with Negro management," as the historian Carter G. Woodson and Barnett's cousin characterized it, was the only such hospital at the time and served several hundred patients in the state.[111] Barnett's parents had been enslaved in Virginia, and his father, Nelson, was a Baptist minister who served churches in Ohio and West Virginia. Barnett had been on the staff at the West Virginia Hospital for the Insane at Weston before working with his wife, Clara, a nurse, to establish the Barnett Hospital, a general hospital in Huntington. When Barnett moved to take charge of the new State Hospital for Colored Insane, Black physicians nationally took notice of the development, counting it as important not only for patients but because "the state has recognized ability in the colored medical profession to manage this enterprise."[112] Moreover, the *Journal of the National Medical Association*, the publication of the oldest organization of African American physicians, noted that the hospital could also be a site where Black psychiatrists could train under a Black hospital superintendent, supplementing the only other site of the Tuskegee Veterans Hospital. Lakin, as a state hospital with an all-Black staff and superintendent, would be joined in 1934 by the State Hospital for Negro Insane in the all-Black

Figure 4.5. Staff of Lakin State Hospital, West Virginia, in 1930, with Superintendent Constantine Clinton Barnett seated in the front row, third from left. Courtesy of the West Virginia and Regional History Center, WVU Libraries.

town of Taft, Oklahoma, with George I. Lythcott, an ordained Episcopalian from British Guiana, a graduate of Boston University Medical School, and an army veteran, serving as the first superintendent.[113] Lythcott was succeeded as superintendent by E. P. Henry, a Methodist and a graduate of the University of West Tennessee College of Medicine and Surgery, who had served as the hospital's assistant physician.[114]

Lakin and Taft operated as did other state hospitals, with an appropriation from the state and enterprises on site that contributed to the financial maintenance of the institution. At Lakin, patients worked on the farm and in the cannery, dairy, laundry, and kitchen.[115] Reports from the hospitals emphasized the modern equipment and facilities, the result of their founding and construction in the twentieth century and, at Lakin, because of Barnett's commitment to meeting American Medical Association standards from the start, making it the only one in West Virginia at the time to do so.[116] In most respects, practices of care and treatment at Lakin State Hospital were the same as within other hospitals in the United States at the time. Barnett was proud that the hospital was approved by the American Medical Association and characterized it as "not merely a hospital for custodial care." Rather, he contended, "The hospital is a medical institution equipped, ready and anxious to render expert care to its inmates."[117] That care included occupational therapy in the form of labor and recreational therapy such as outdoor exercise, outings, music, sports, and reading. Patients had access to weekly religious services and, at Taft, Lythcott noted that he encouraged local ministers to visit and participate in the services.[118]

Other care and treatment practices reflected changes in broader approaches to hospitalization of people for mental illness in the early twentieth century. Barnett emphasized the need to understand a patient's history, learn about family history and environment, and assess their physical condition. In keeping with current developments in medical treatment, Lakin's facilities included hydrotherapy tubs, which the staff used to administer continuous baths at extreme temperatures over several hours.[119] Lakin's physicians also prescribed sedatives to some patients, and by the 1930s, doctors at both Lakin and Taft employed "shock therapy" using insulin to induce comas or Metrazol to induce seizures, thought to reduce psychotic symptoms.[120] The Black physicians who staffed these hospitals and engaged in invasive practices that often required restraint generally framed them as "all the modern treatment" and reflecting the highest standards of the day.[121] These also included components that were becoming a regular part of patient case histories in early twentieth-century psychiatry, including attention to childhood, educational, and occupational experiences, personality, and habits, as well as "the heredity or stock from which the patient comes."[122]

At the same time, the early Black hospital psychiatrists offered perspectives on hospital care and treatment that diverged from the racial essentialism and interpretations of African American religion that featured so prominently in white psychiatric theory and practice. Barnett argued that, even with the availability of physical interventions and drug treatment, physicians treating mental illness required "familiarity with such topics as religion, mythology, magic, sociology, eugenics." As did white psychiatrists treating Black patients in this period, Barnett found engagement of religious sensibilities to be an important factor in diagnosis and treatment, but he argued for consideration of culture rather than racial traits, albeit in the context of an implicit cultural and religious hierarchy. In his 1932 annual report, Barnett wrote, "The physician often uncovers the clue to the patient's difficulty by virtue of his knowledge of the tenets of some religious cult or mythical practice. Modes of thought in our patient may not seem so strange and unintelligible when we discover that his belief or ritual, at this time quite unusual to us, was indulged or practiced widely many years ago by his primitive brother. A custom in one part of the country, in a certain cultural level, may be considered quite proper, whereas in another part and in a different cultural level, it may suggest a mental disorder."[123] He was also optimistic about the potential results of the care and treatment the hospital could offer, writing, "It should be made distinctly clear that a mental case is by no means always hopeless. Early voluntary treatment or commitment when the patient is unwilling, with a cooperative attitude of relatives toward the hospital by giving a good and thorough history, will go a long way towards understanding the disorder, and finally towards a cure or amelioration."[124] Nevertheless, the practices of management within such institutions of confinement commonly led to incidents of extreme violence against patients, and Lakin was no exception. The 1941 case of two attendants at Lakin who beat a patient to death as they tried to return him to the institution brought calls for an investigation.[125]

Given the rarity of African American psychiatrists and institutions, Black patients and their families navigated a landscape of white public authorities, both legal and medical, whose racialized assessments of emotional religious expressions had the power to shape Black patients' experiences of institutionalization. In 1895, James D., a forty-five-year-old Maryland native, was admitted to St. Elizabeths Hospital, diagnosed as suffering from chronic mania caused by religious excitement.[126] James worked as a janitor in the District of Columbia's high school for Black students and, while hospitalized, was placed on medical leave by a Board of Public Schools that included the famed Black clubwoman Mary Church Terrell.[127] James had been arrested at DC's Asbury Methodist Episcopal Church for assaulting a man newspaper accounts say he "mistook . . . for the devil."[128] Brought before the Equity Court a few days later for a lunacy inquisition, the judge found James to be insane and committed him.

While James was in the hospital, his wife, Lizzie, cared for their young daughter, worked as a seamstress to support them, and advocated for her husband in person and in correspondence with hospital officials, interpreting his emotional state in ways that conflicted with the doctors' evaluations.[129] According to the ward notes, James worked in the hospital's tailor shop, went to chapel every Sunday, and was generally agreeable. He got into conflicts with other patients on occasion, once when one interrupted his morning prayers. Lizzie visited regularly, and James was permitted to visit his family on leave several times. Lizzie desperately wanted her husband released, writing to his doctor, "Sir, I do not want to be annoying or troublesome to you but I am so lonely without my husband and he seemed so well when I saw him last Thursday won't you please let him come and spend Christmas with me."[130] She advocated for him to be moved from the hospital's Howard Hall for criminally insane patients to the West Lodge, the crowded facility that housed Black male patients with less oversight and greater access to the outdoors.[131] "He feels he is well enough to take care of himself," she wrote, "if he is allowed the chance to do so."[132]

In a letter to his wife—the one item in his file that represents his experience directly—James appealed to her to advocate for him, particularly in getting him moved to the West Lodge, which happened finally four years after his commitment. He also expressed joy at a recent visit with Lizzie and their daughter, telling of his sadness at the thought that they might "be broke up forever" and consoling her that he was trying his best and improving and thought he would not have any more "spells." He was hopeful and expressed faith that he would be released "because the Lord knows all about it" and prayed that they would be blessed to be as happy as they were when they were first married. He encouraged her, concluding, "You must not get tired as you tell me not to give up."[133] That the letter remains in his file in the archive indicates that the hospital probably never sent it. James's doctor wrote a note on the back of one of Lizzie's letters: "The sending of this man home has always resulted in an attack of maniacal excitement and once in nearly a homicide."[134] Indeed, when he returned to the hospital from a visit home in October 1902, he was moved back to Howard Hall for the criminally insane for a period but was released in 1903 and died three years later.[135] The surviving records shed only partial light on the discrepancy between James and Lizzie's beliefs about his mental health and his doctors' evaluations of his sanity, but ideas about Blackness and religious excitement certainly shaped his treatment in the court and hospital. St. Elizabeths' staff tracked his chapel attendance and noted his quiet demeanor in that context in evaluating his religious emotion. James understood that a particular representation of religious emotion would be important in persuading doctors that he should be released, and he sought to conform.

Other Black patients resisted the work of disciplining their religious emotion within the world of the asylum. When Thomas G. was admitted to St. Elizabeths in 1898, neither he nor his family and friends conceded that his religious excitement needed to be reformed. Thomas, a twenty-six-year-old who had been born in Arkansas and was employed as a government clerk in Washington, DC, was investigated for lunacy by the District's sanitary officer on the report of friends who were alarmed that he had not left his room for two weeks, except to get food. Brought before the court for a hearing, he was committed.[136] What remains of Thomas's file is incomplete, lacking the hospital's standard "synopsis of record" form that indicates the patient's diagnosis on admission. The daily ward notes date from three years after his admission. In the earliest entry in the ward notes, someone on the hospital's infirmary staff noted that he seemed depressed and had the "idea that he is Jesus Christ he all so says he governs all the people of the world . . . he all so says he has a religious work to be performed but he can't get out to do it he says the authorities here are robing him of his liberty he talks very rational on any other subject but religion."[137] According to the record, Thomas was generally quiet, kept to himself, and took regular walks, but he tried to escape during one walk in 1902.[138]

Thomas's mother, Mary, wrote from Arkansas to St. Elizabeths' superintendent William Godding several times to inquire about her son's condition and express hope that he would be released soon.[139] Thomas's brother-in-law Henry, who, along with his sister Ella, were prominent teachers in Hope, Arkansas, and devoted members of Bethel AME Church, wrote repeatedly to obtain information for the family and to make the case that Thomas's health would be better served by being able to return home.[140] Henry was concerned when Godding affirmed that Thomas remained "absorbed in the peculiar delusions which have so long possessed his mind," but he worked to reframe these as not meriting confinement. "Please allow me to say that he has always been a very singular fellow seemed to prefer to be to himself most of the time and has all of his life been very fond of reading." He also offered to send the manuscript of a book Thomas had been writing, in the hopes that continuing to work on it would be therapeutic.[141]

For his part, Thomas also appealed to be released, writing in 1901 to Godding's successor, Alonzo B. Richardson, who later that same year spoke to the *Washington Post* about the "alarming increase" in cases of religious mania among African Americans.[142] Thomas complained that he had not been adequately examined in court prior to his commitment and that the recent physical transformation of his head to become "as dry and as solid as wood" had "deranged my nervous system to an alarming degree."[143] He asked to be released because he was not receiving any treatment and, like his relatives, felt that he would be restored to "my original health and intelligence" at home. Most important for Thomas was the fact that being institutionalized thwarted achievement of his mission, a "work of such grave importance" to help the world "inherit from the Lord God of heaven and earth the new life which they have been expecting a long while. And there are a few famine and storm stricken places which I intended to relieve many months ago." He asked Richardson to direct him to the proper authorities, insisting, "If I could become acquainted with them, I would persuade them to cease to hold [me]—for humanity's sake. The wretched human family is before us. Being by nature—'the resurrection and life' in this world—I am sure that I can revive the same within a very few days. I am surprised that I have received no cooperation from the friends of humanity. Yours Respt. Christ." Thomas's complaint about not receiving treatment accords with others' accounts of conditions at the hospital in the years of his confinement, a situation that in 1906 led to a congressional investigation into cruelty and neglect at the institution.[144]

Thomas's family's response to his religious mission and their sense in the correspondence with his doctors that his peculiarities did not merit confinement show a refusal to pathologize his visionary and prophetic expressions. Indeed, while his sister and brother-in-law, both well educated and members of a mainstream Black church denomination, might have been expected to argue that his religious emotion was improper or excessive and that it would be better to reform, they considered him harmless and preferred to have him released. Even in the context of a public discourse among some Black Protestants endorsing what they saw as rational, as opposed to emotional, religion, within Black communities such ecstatic religious expression, communication with God, visions, and prophetic calls did not necessarily signal insanity or require discipline and containment.[145]

In psychiatric theory and practice, individual claims to divinity like Thomas's, along with Black patients' assertions of prophetic or visionary powers, ability to communicate with the dead, and exuberant expressions at revivals and church services, served as evidence of the disabling potential of what was characterized as innate Black religious emotionalism. The psychiatric endorsement of certain forms of religious expression as sane and reasonable and the framing of others as abnormal and excessive aided the marginalization of varieties of Black Christianity, such as Holiness and Pentecostal beliefs and practices that were becoming increasingly prominent in the early twentieth century. In this same period, African American migration to northern cities and the emergence of Black new religious movements, often organized around charismatic figures, prompted psychiatrists to focus on what some claimed was an innate credulity and gullibility as a component of African Americans' religious dispositions. At the same time, urbanization and migration set the stage for psychiatrists to engage new questions about how social context affected Black mental health, and Black psychiatrists contributed to changing perspectives about race, religion, and psychiatry.

# 5

## The Social Environment and the "Negro Cult"

Rebecca Isaac found heaven when she entered Father Divine's Peace Mission in Harlem in 1932. The forty-three-year-old migrant from Fulton, South Carolina, had arrived in New York City sometime in the late 1920s, along with her husband, Edward, and their four children. In South Carolina, Rebecca and Edward had been farmers. In New York, Edward worked for a subway company and Rebecca as a maid in a private home. We do not know what motivated them to leave Fulton, but they joined millions of southern African Americans moving from rural to urban contexts in search of employment, safety, and opportunity. In 1930, the Isaacs were sharing an apartment on West Fifty-Ninth Street with two other families from South Carolina.[1] Within two years, the Isaac family's situation changed dramatically, and the new configuration would contribute to growing public concern about the mental health consequences of the rise of Black new religious groups, like Father Divine's, in the urban North.

While it is unclear how Rebecca encountered Father Divine, in 1932 it was hard to avoid news about the religious leader whose followers affirmed him as the God of the Bible in the body of a Black man who came to eradicate race altogether. Divine had been imprisoned for "maintaining a public nuisance" because of enthusiastic interracial banquets at the group's communal home in Sayville, Long Island. When the white judge who sentenced him to a one-year jail term died unexpectedly, Divine was released pending appeal and appeared to take credit for the judge's demise. In response, press and popular attention to the Peace Mission and its leader surged, and when Divine relocated to New York City, the curious multitudes thronged to greet him, hear him speak, and hear testimonies from his followers. Perhaps Rebecca Isaac was among the reported seven thousand attendees at an event for Divine at Harlem's Rockland Palace in June that year, drawn to his promises of eternal bounty.[2] Regardless of how Rebecca was exposed to Father Divine and his teachings, by 1932 she had responded to his call to reject the things of the "mortal world" and had moved to one of the Peace Mission's celibate, sex-segregated communal residences in Harlem, hoping for eternal life in Divine's kingdom. As was the case with many of Divine's followers who left spouses, children, or other family members to live in a Peace Mission "heaven," Rebecca's decision brought profound disruption to her family.

When her fourteen-year-old daughter, Hatty, was found wandering the streets, Rebecca was brought to a hearing at the Domestic Relations court before Judge Jacob Panken, a New Yorker who had been born in Ukraine and was active in the Socialist Party and in Jewish labor and philanthropic organizations in the city.[3] Concerned about the broad social impact of divorce, parental desertion, and juvenile delinquency, Panken made no secret of his dislike of Father Divine's theology that prompted followers to leave their spouses and children. Just as problematic for him were the instances in which parents brought their children with them into Divine's kingdom and yet renounced connections to them, as Divine required. In the Peace Mission's heaven on earth, husbands and wives became as brothers and sisters, and members' children were given over to communal responsibility. Newspapers reported regularly on cases in the late 1930s and early 1940s involving families connected to Father Divine's group, as abandoned men and women sued their spouses for divorce or Divine himself for enticing their spouses away from marriage and family, and the press drew attention to instances when children deserted by parents required state care.[4]

For Panken, the problem of spouses and children left by those who had made new homes in the Peace Mission had social significance beyond the individual cases that came before him. In the context of court hearings, he declared Divine "a menace to the community" and charged him with "undermining the whole family" with a theology that required renouncing what Divine and his followers thought of as mortal ties that limited their spiritual development.[5] That the Peace Mission was organized around belief in the divinity of Father Divine presented broader questions for Panken of the legal and social bounds of conceptions of religion itself. In the case of a boy whose parents left him to follow Father Divine, and who Panken sent to a state training school (likely the Wiltwyck School for Boys), the judge argued that the First Amendment's

Figure 5.1. Father Divine visits Philadelphia in 1939, accompanied by Mother Divine (his wife, Penninah), and is greeted by a large crowd. Philadelphia Evening Bulletin Photograph Collection. Courtesy of the Special Collections Research Center, Temple University Libraries, Philadelphia, Pennsylvania.

guarantee of free exercise of religion did not include disordered religions like the Peace Mission. Panken was reported to have written in his judgment, "To worship a god who is a human, with all the frailties of a human being, with all the possibilities of committing the errors of a human being is not what the Bill of Rights guarantees," no more than it guarantees the right to "worship a god which would justify human sacrifices or a multiplicity of marriages."[6]

In the Isaac family's case, Panken issued a subpoena for Divine himself to appear in court to account for his role in the distress Rebecca's desertion had caused Edward and the children. The event attracted press coverage, in large measure because of Divine's response to Panken's direct question, "Are you or are you not God?" "No, I'm not God," Divine is reported to have said, "but lots of people think I am, and I want them to believe it."[7] While Divine appears to have moderated his claim to divinity when standing before the judge, Rebecca remained steadfast in her belief. A reporter for the *Baltimore Afro-American* described Isaac as having an outburst of commitment to Divine, writing, "Suddenly she thrust her arms high, rolled her eyes to the ceiling and shrieked, 'He is God, he is God, he is God!' She fell writhing and screaming."[8] For Rebecca, her devotion required that she reject parental connection to and responsibility for Hatty. When asked in court whether she was Hatty's mother, Rebecca reportedly replied, "No, God is the mother. Father Divine is God. God is the mother."[9] Her emotional responses to questioning motivated Judge Panken to order that she be admitted to Bellevue Hospital for observation, where her case later became part of a study of psychoses in Father Divine's followers.[10] Rebecca was released after a brief period of observation and likely returned to the Peace Mission "heaven" where she had been living, perhaps adopting a spiritual name that severed her connection to her previous life, as was common among Divine's followers. Edward remarried some years later and moved in with his new wife and her children, while Hatty went to live with her older sister.[11]

Rebecca Isaac was not alone among Father Divine's followers to be evaluated for mental illness because of the dramatic life changes prompted by their belief in his divinity and promise of health and eternal life in his kingdom on earth. Short-term psychiatric evaluations and longer-term commitments of Peace Mission members to city and state hospitals in New York in the 1930s resulted in the publication of several studies in which white psychiatrists sought to understand the individual and social factors contributing to what they interpreted as mental disorder in some of Divine's followers. Intense media, court, and medical attention to Divine and the Peace Mission aligned with broader public discussion of the religious, social, and medical implications of the rise of groups many referred to as "Negro cults." In addition to Divine's Peace Mission, this period saw the founding of several groups, including the Moorish Science Temple, the Nation of Islam, and congregations of Ethiopian Hebrews that rejected classification as Negro and association with Christianity, viewing both race and religion as having been imposed by white people for the purpose of subjugating Black people. These groups presented alternative religio-racial identities that linked race and religion in new ways that members found empowering.[12] In these religio-racial movements in which adherents embraced varieties of Islam and Judaism or followed figures claiming divinity and rejecting racial classification altogether, they also created distinctive social practices marked by the adoption of new names, styles of dress, dietary practices, and family and community formations. Where popular arguments about African Americans' inherent religious fanaticism and the medical racialization of religious excitement as Black represented white Americans' responses to Black people's collective religious world-making in slavery's wake, attention to the psychology of "Negro cults" developed in the context of the migration of southern African Americans to northern cities and to urban religious creativity. Black religious and political leaders also expressed concern about the appeal of these groups, focusing especially on the newly visible leaders who the National Urban League industrial secretary Ira De Augustine Reid classed among the "large number of exploiters and charlatans."[13]

In addition to questions Black religious and political leaders raised about the proliferation of groups many characterized as cults, the appeal these new religious formations held for many migrants prompted social scientific and medical theorization of the effects of participation on members.[14] Psychiatrists' interest in what drew African Americans to these novel groups in the urban North brought questions of social context to the fore as researchers sought to understand how the environment within and outside these groups they framed as cults shaped the psyches of leaders and members. Weighing aspects of social context and the implications of individual adjustment or maladjustment in new environments represented a change from the previous century's psychiatric focus on innate racial traits, but ideas about Black people's inherent religious emotionalism and superstition persisted in some psychiatric theory about the credulity of those drawn to new religious groups. Nevertheless, over the course of the 1930s and 1940s, medical discourse about religion and mental illness among African Americans shifted noticeably from a frame of race to one of environment. In this period, "the Negro cult" emerged as a unique environment through which researchers sought to understand the impact of migration and urbanization on African American religious and social life and assess African Americans' ability to adjust psychologically to a different social world than that of the rural South.

## "The Laboratory of the Social Analyst"

Early twentieth-century psychiatric evaluations of the impact of migration on African American life took place in the context of an increasing focus in social science and medicine on the influence of social context on the development of mental illness and a shift away from arguments about racial traits. Several Black psychiatrists made significant contributions to this turn, emphasizing diversity of experience and psychological makeup among African Americans, in contrast to entrenched arguments about a singular racial nature and mind. In addition, Black social scientists evaluated the impact of psychiatric theory and practice in African American life, and their perspectives supported shifting approaches to the role of race in mental illness. Horace Mann Bond, a graduate of Fisk University with a PhD in sociology from the University of Chicago, published an article titled "Insanity among Negroes: A Symptom of Social Disorganization" in a 1932 issue of *Opportunity*, the National Urban League's journal. Writing from his position in Fisk's Department of Social Sciences, Bond addressed directly a 1921 article in the *American Journal of Insanity* on southern Black psychology, written by William L. Bevis, a physician at St. Elizabeths Hospital. Highlighting as an example Bevis's argument that fear of the dark was a "racial characteristic" of Black people, Bond characterized such work as "pseudoscientific doggerel" and lamented that Bevis's views about the influence of race on individual psychology represented "much of the traditional point of view in psychiatry."[15] In his rejection of Bevis's work, Bond took issue with "the easy explanation of race, and race alone" and the field's focus on "a medico-biological viewpoint which seeks to ascribe all peculiarities of mind and body to inherited structures."

Bond dismissed as worthless the analysis that arose from statistics white psychiatrists gathered in southern asylums, institutions he described as involving "a transmogrified form of jail detention as opposed to scientific treatment" and in which diagnosis was "practically guesswork and characterized by utter carelessness."[16] In formulating this position, Bond was certainly influenced by his brother James P. Bond's experience of institutionalization in the 1930s at the Central State Hospital in Kentucky, diagnosed with dementia praecox.[17] Refusing race as a sufficient explanation for the development of mental illness, Bond underscored the "social definition" of insanity, proposing a focus on individual responses to challenging social situations. He argued that explanations would be found less readily in data from hospitals and more from tools taken from "the laboratory of the social analyst."[18]

While Bond found traditional white psychiatry lacking and sometimes even dangerous for African Americans, he pointed to the Black psychiatrists George S. Moore and Alan P. Smith and the "systematic" nature of their work at the Tuskegee Veterans Hospital as holding potential to show that medical doctors had something to offer.[19] Indeed, for some time, Moore and Smith had been making a similar case from their perspective in psychiatry and in broader Black medical circles about problematic assumptions in the field. In a 1926 introductory "study of neuropsychiatric problems among Negroes," Moore, a graduate of Fisk University and of Northwestern University's medical school, chal-

Figure 5.2. Horace Mann Bond, 1930. Courtesy of Horace Mann Bond Papers, Robert S. Cox Special Collections and University Archives Research Center, UMass Amherst Libraries.

Figure 5.3. Tuskegee Veterans Hospital key staff in 1933, including the psychiatrists George C. Branche, George S. Moore, and Alan P. Smith.

lenged prevailing racialized approaches. From his position as chief of the Tuskegee Veterans Hospital's neuropsychiatric service, Moore cautioned against the field's assumption that all people of African descent are alike, insisting that African Americans had "as varied a psychology, heredity, and environment as the United States contains."[20] From the starting point of foregrounding individual background and experience over ideas about racial characteristics, this group of Black psychiatrists and social scientists argued for the need to attend to social environment as a key factor for understanding Black mental health.[21] Some psychiatrists, like Smith, an associate physician at the Tuskegee Veterans Hospital and a graduate of the University of Iowa medical school, spoke in general rather than racial terms about "some types of mental-makeup or constitution" that, when confronted with stressful events and challenges, cannot adjust or adapt and become disordered.[22] While he was convinced that mental illness was on the rise among African Americans, and at a rate higher than for whites, he concluded that "the etiological factors are largely psychogenic and not organic."[23]

Other contributors to the discussion were more specific about the social factors they considered as contributing to psychological disorders. In a 1924 discussion of African American attitudes toward health, E. Franklin Frazier, a graduate of Howard University who would go on to receive a PhD in sociology from the University of Chicago, emphasized the impact of a climate of fear on the psychological well-being of African Americans. This was not the innate racial fear of the dark proposed by white psychiatrists like Bevis but fear of actual pervasive violence and racial terror aimed at making "the Negro afraid to emerge from the sphere of activities to which [white southern society] has consigned him."[24] Tuskegee's Moore argued that a "conscious disadvantage complex" shaped the emotional lives and reactions of African Americans. According to Moore, the conflict between the social disadvantage enforced through racism and oppression and what he described as African Americans' "conscious self-sufficiencies" had the capacity to lead to "the avoidance of reality." In other words, being aware of both their abilities and the constraints racism placed on their lives could lead to psychological disturbance among African Americans, but Moore also noted that this was a reaction "normal to any oppressed people."[25] He observed that the recent migration trend to northern cities produced additional and new stresses for Black migrants, as well as misinterpretation of their behavior and reactions as abnormal by white psychiatrists unfamiliar with Black history, life, and cultures.[26]

Discussion of religion featured in some works by Black social scientists and psychiatrists who argued for the significance of social context over the traditional white psychiatric focus on race in understanding mental illness among African Americans. Shifting analysis away from ideas about racial traits required engaging long-standing medical arguments that an innate religious character predisposed African Americans to mental illness. In addition, like most of the early white theorists of religion, race, and insanity, this group of Black psychiatrists and social scientists had their own religious commitments and experiences that shaped their discussions of the role of religion in African American life and culture. George S. Moore, chief of the Tuskegee Veterans Hospital's neuropsychiatric service, grew up in a missionary family. His father, the Congregationalist minister George Washington Moore, had been born into slavery in Nashville, attended Fisk University and Oberlin Theological Seminary, and worked as a field missionary for the American Missionary Association in addition to being a professor of biblical history and literature at Howard University for several years. His mother, Ella Sheppard Moore, also born into slavery, was an original member of the Fisk Jubilee singers before marrying Moore and joining him in his work with the AMA.[27] The sociologist Horace Mann Bond was also from Nashville. Bond's father, James Bond, a Congregationalist minister, had been enslaved in Kentucky, graduated from Berea College, and received a divinity degree from Oberlin College. The senior Bond later became the pastor of Howard Congregational Church in Nashville, of which George Washington Moore had been the founding minister.[28] Alan P. Smith, a psychiatrist at Tuskegee Veterans Hospital, was a Catholic from Kansas whose parents had been born in Mississippi and Tennessee, respectively, and whose family members received Catholic educations and were involved with a variety of church organizations.[29] As they engaged older psychiatric research on religion, race, and mental normalcy, these African American psychiatrists and social scientists mobilized their own religious norms. In doing so, they evaluated the diversity of Black religious beliefs and practices that had occupied white psychiatrists—Black supernaturalism and Holiness and Pentecostalism, for example—in a hierarchy that also positioned what they saw as ethical religion and restrained worship as the standard of true and good religion.

Religion functioned in several ways in these Black psychiatrists' and sociologists' discussions of race and mental illness. Moore engaged the topic in greatest depth, addressing long-standing claims in white psychiatric literature that African Americans were innately superstitious, and that this propensity contributed to the development of mental illness in what the white psychiatrist J. D. Roberts had called the "clash with civilization."[30] Moore evaluated Black religious sensibilities through the lenses of class and region in ways that aligned with some elements of white psychiatric theory. He attributed the continuing influence in Black life of what he described as "African traits, customs, superstitions, and traditions" to lack of education.[31] For Moore, ingrained (rather than innate) superstitions deriving from this influence had the capacity to produce compulsions that might be read as delusional in people otherwise functioning normally.[32] He concluded that great care must be taken to distinguish between genuine psychosis, on the one hand, and compulsions and impaired judgment grounded in "superstitious beliefs," on the other.[33] Moore also connected "superstition" to a broader religious environment that he claimed motivated against independent investigation and analysis that might overcome superstition. "Preachers of many and varied cults," as well as "quack and voodoo doctors," took advantage of people and perpetuated superstitious beliefs among all classes of African Americans, Moore contended.[34]

Christianity was what these authors meant most often when using the term "religion," and they discussed what they saw as its largely compensatory functions for African Americans, historically and in the present. "A sense of unworthiness and the acceptance of the belief in his inferior place in this world have led [the Negro] to a sublime faith in a God he trusts to do all things well," Moore wrote.[35] This oft-noted religious character, he suggested, "supplies in large measure the energy and impetus necessary for him to carry on." At the same time, the inability of Christianity, "which he has embraced and devoutly accepted as a panacea for his ills and troubles," to mitigate the power of racial oppression and social stigma "even in the house of God" constituted a significant emotionally destabilizing factor in Moore's estimation.[36] The sociologist E. Franklin Frazier offered an analysis similar to Moore's characterization of the role of Christianity past and present for African Americans. He argued that, in slavery, religion provided a "therapeutic escape from the repressing influences of this world." And while Frazier saw resources for survival in African American Christianity, he concluded that it had developed in a racially repressive environment that produced a "psychology of the sick," shaping both theology and individual sensibilities. For Frazier, this environment of racism "in which yearnings are repressed" directs African Americans' attention from this life to heaven and creates a "religion of death" that he believed was certain to have "pathological results."[37] In accord with the psychiatrist Alan P. Smith's assessment, Frazier claimed that religion was less effective in compensating for social constraints in their contemporary moment than it had been under slavery. For Smith, this was especially true for "the young Negro" who "no longer accepts the Christian religion, like his progenitors, as a panacea for his ills or as a positive assurance of a 'place in Heaven' as adequate compensation for the 'injustices' on earth."[38] For this group of Black psychiatrists and social scientists, useful assessments of the relationship of African American religion to mental health could not be grounded in the traditional psychiatric emphasis on notions of racial propensities. Rather, they called for understanding the history and social functions of religion in Black life and attention to diversity of class, theology, and region.

Questions about the state of Black churches and their social role received sustained attention from Richard A. Billings, a member of the psychiatry faculty of Howard University Medical School and an active member of the AME Church, who published "a psychogenic study" of Black churches in a 1934 issue of the *Psychoanalytic Review*.[39] Like other Black psychiatrists and social scientists in this period, Billings engaged long-standing psychiatric views of the role of religion in African American life, dismissing the presumption that religion's significance is "expressive of [Black people's] inherent emotionalism." He insisted, instead, that "in his religious behavior, the American Negro is guided by general human motives, and rather than being expressive of any specific racial behavior it appears as an adaptive product of particular environmental forces to which he has been subjected since his residence in America."[40] In his analysis, Billings presented a typology of Black churches according to membership, theology, and style of worship, which he grounded in a class and skin-color hierarchy that, in many respects, mapped onto normative white American rankings of religion, race, and class. He characterized upper-class churches (Catholic, Episcopal, Presbyterian, and Congregational churches), frequently pastored by white clergy, as appealing to those light-skinned African Americans who saw themselves as closer to white Americans than to "the darker members of their race."[41] He categorized Methodist and Baptist churches as middle class and having a membership that was "acutely sensitive to privation and humiliation" connected to racial discrimination. For them, he asserted, church served as "free amusement" in segregated contexts and as a means of social escape through the recognition achieved by participating in church organizations and boards.[42]

Billings devoted the most attention to "lower class" churches, of which he described two kinds: small congregations that had split from

Baptist and Methodist churches, and "churches which have been established by some cult leader with a particular doctrine, often based upon some one verse in the Bible."[43] In his estimation, this latter group was large, varied, and difficult to describe, so he took the approach of foregrounding a church he called the House of Prayer, most likely a Holiness or Pentecostal church, as typical of the category.[44] Billings concluded that the members of the congregation he profiled, whom he described as dark-skinned, hardworking, with little access to education, turned to church as a compensatory outlet for opportunities denied them in a racially discriminatory world. He argued that, while the function of church for this group bears similarities to the middle-class churches, the House of Prayer cultivated an intense relationship with a personal God "that seems to be in existence just for the interests of this particular group."[45] The intensity of devotion to God was reflected in the "fervor and enthusiasm" of worship featuring piano, cymbals and tambourines, singing, shouting, and bodily abandon.[46]

Billings proposed that, in addition to functioning as a "mechanism of escape and compensation," such churches were arenas for sexual "sublimation and substitution." For women, he saw the intense religious experience of shouting as producing sexual arousal and suggested that the worship attracted "those who have sexual conflicts," such as homosexual men, who could mask their physical closeness "as the expressions of the ecstasy of religious fervor."[47] In accord with shifts in this period in theories about religion and Black mental health from racial explanations to interest in social context, Billings concluded that "the presumed truthfulness of the oft-repeated statement that Negroes are inherently religious, has of recent been open to considerable doubt; and there is a great deal to suggest that much of the religiosity has developed as an adaptive reaction to definite environmental situations."[48] Such an approach, considering themes of class, opportunity, oppression, sexuality, and environment, would mark psychiatric and social scientific approaches to understanding the functions for members of the "sects and cults" of the urban North.[49]

The impact of migration to northern cities on African American life emerged as a research focus for social scientists and psychiatrists interested in new approaches to understanding the relationship of social environment to mental health. Region, race, and the distribution

of insanity had been a topic in nineteenth-century psychiatric literature in which the idea of a regional disparity between North and South
supported claims about the moral and mental health benefits of slavery.[50] At the turn of the twentieth century, assertions that residence in
northern cities promoted mental illness because African Americans
could not meet the demands of labor competition and self-governance
emerged. In 1903, the year he became the superintendent of the St. Elizabeths Hospital, William A. White argued in the context of an analysis
of the geographic distribution of insanity in the United States that African Americans fared best in their "natural home" of the rural country
and asserted that "as soon as the Negro goes North and enters into active competition with the white, who is mentally his superior, he succumbs to the unequal struggle."[51] White's account of the psychological
destabilization he thought African Americans experienced in the North
predated the substantial migration of southern African Americans that
brought Rebecca Isaac and her family from South Carolina to New York
City. As increasing numbers of African Americans settled in northern
cities, researchers turned their attention to new assessments of the impact of urbanization on Black life and to what the effect of changing
demographics might reveal about race, religion, and mental health.

Comparative studies of rates of hospital admission and diagnoses
among Black and white residents of cities emerged as a common approach to understanding the impact of migration and urban stress on
Black mental health.[52] Several social scientists and statisticians challenged established psychiatric arguments about slavery having been a
beneficial institution for Black physical, mental, and moral health as well
claims about African Americans' inherent inability to cope in northern
urban environments. In analyzing patterns of diagnosis and admission
to mental hospitals, Benjamin Malzberg, a New York State Department
of Mental Hygiene statistician and the child of Eastern European Jewish
immigrants, rejected explanations grounded in ideas about inherent racial characteristics. He concluded that the higher rate of first admission
for treatment among Black New Yorkers when compared with white residents could "be ascribed not so much to racial characteristics, as to the
economic and other social difficulties to which a migratory population
was subject."[53] In a later statistical analysis of data that extended beyond
New York, Malzberg argued directly against the conclusions of "a group

which ascribes the increase in mental disease among Negroes to the removal of the healthy restraining influences of pre–Civil War days, and to the inability of the Negro to live moderately under emancipation." He rejected the analysis of psychiatrists who sought to trace mental disease among African Americans "to the traditions of primitive African Negroes."[54] Malzberg named in this group the most influential figures of the late nineteenth and early twentieth centuries in this field, including J. W. Babcock, Arrah B. Evarts, John E. Lind, Mary O'Malley, T. O. Powell, and Abram Witmer. He called on his readers to "abandon such fanciful notions" of innate racial natures in favor of the statistics that he said provided no evidence of racial factors in mental illness. For him, such an approach offered hope for better mental health with improvement in standards of living among African Americans.[55]

Even as some white researchers and psychiatric practitioners in the era of African American migration and urbanization sought to move the field away from late nineteenth-century stereotypes about healthy and happy slaves, their discussions of religion nevertheless sometimes mobilized nineteenth-century notions of excessive emotionalism. Malzberg puzzled over the higher rate of diagnoses of dementia praecox and manic-depressive psychoses among African Americans admitted to hospitals and pondered the role of environment in this disparity. Despite his resistance to using "racial characteristics" to guide his interpretation, he landed on familiar racialized tropes in suggesting an explanation. Malzberg conjectured, "Here probably is a less stable, more emotional make-up among negroes than whites. Negro music, as seen in spirituals, blues, and jazz, clearly points to such characteristics. Given such emotional instability, it is likely that there is a fruitful ground for functional mental disorders."[56] Philip S. Wagner, a psychiatrist at Cincinnati's General Hospital, drew on hospital admissions data from 1936 and 1937 to determine if white and Black patients had different psychotic reactions in the same environment and to put to the test the "assumption that the colored man is to begin with innately of different composition from that of the white man." Wagner, the son of Eastern European Jewish immigrants who grew up in California, attributed these assumptions to "lay literature and popular opinion" and highlighted ideas about the Negro's "spiritualism and religious fanaticism" as a component of accepted belief about racial difference. He took on the claim that there is "manifested in the negro a greater religiosity," as well as commonplace assertions of hypersexuality, color consciousness, fear, and suspicion and other "qualities the white race has in the past attributed to the negro." Wagner insisted that there "is no definite evidence that negroes are less stable emotionally than white men" and pointed instead to the stressful environment in which poor Black urbanites lived as conducive to the development of mental illness.[57] Still, he mused, "We cannot overlook the observations of men with longer experience who have the impression that the negro psychotic reaction is more apt to be bizarre, religious and transitory," and he regretted that his relatively small sample could not lead to definite conclusions.[58]

Some social scientists and psychiatrists analyzed migration as a general phenomenon, locating the challenges African American newcomers to northern cities faced in broader social context alongside the experiences of other migrants and immigrants. For researchers like Malzberg and Wagner, their own experiences as children of immigrants and as members of a religious minority no doubt shaped their interest in the broad topic and their understanding of the stakes of arguments about groups' adjustment and maladjustment. At the same time, given enduring claims about race and mental illness, analysis of the unique experiences of Black southern migrants and the impact of racial oppression and social, economic, and educational restrictions on their ability to adjust to a new environment required more than a general approach. In proposing a diminishing ability of religion to compensate for African Americans' social marginalization, E. Franklin Frazier drew a connection to migration and urbanization and claims of a higher incidence of mental illness among northern African Americans. He conjectured that the lure of opportunity in the North "raises expectations that cannot be realized"; in this, he saw not the perpetual backwardness of African Americans, as earlier literature asserted, but "an indisputable connection between the social environment and the mental health of the Negro."[59] The psychiatrists George S. Moore and Alan P. Smith made a similar argument, highlighting the limitations Black rural southerners experienced and noting that "the Negro becomes more cognizant of his inability to compete successfully with those who are not similarly handicapped" in the social environment of the urban North.[60] In his study *The Negro Family in Chicago* (1932), E. Franklin Frazier noted disruption in the religious life of Black southern migrants to Chicago as contributing to "disorganization."[61] He wrote of one case of a woman who migrated from Birmingham to Chicago as showing "how the Negro in his aimless wandering from city to city loses the conceptions of life which he acquired in the church, the most important institution in the life of the Negro in the South. He loses his old aims and ambitions, and freed from every form of group control he is the prey of vagrant impulses and lawless desires."[62] Frazier's use of masculine pronouns for "the Negro" to speak to the experiences of Black women leaves unaddressed the predominance of women in Black churches and the appeal of the new religious movements in northern cities to Black women, which would become a focus of some psychiatric analysis of "the Negro cult."

Many white and Black psychiatrists in this period who investigated possible patterns in African American mental health beyond older models of racial traits were influenced by white anthropologists like Franz Boaz, Ruth Benedict, Margaret Mead, and Melville Herskovits, whom Wagner and others cited. In addition, the work of African American scholars appears in the citations and notes in these studies, including the sociologist E. Franklin Frazier and the philosopher Alain Locke.[63] As the historian Ellen Dwyer notes, through the influence of social scientific perspectives, "as World War II approached, psychiatrists increasingly attributed psychiatric disorders to social and economic factors, but a number remained unwilling to abandon altogether the notion of biologically based racial difference. These two very different perspectives would continue to co-exist, albeit uneasily, in mainstream medical writings and practice through the long, hard years of the war and well into the 1950s."[64] Attention to religion would be one area in which ideas about innate racial difference continued to surface in this field. The combination of interest in the social worlds of African American migrants in northern cities and long-standing ideas about race and religion led some researchers to examine early twentieth-century Black "cults" and "sects" as important indicators of the state of Black mental health.

## "The Problem of the Cults"

In early twentieth-century American public culture, discussion of the rise of urban "sects and cults" converged around several themes that recall entrenched psychiatric discourses about Black religions and insanity. In particular, traces of ideas about innate superstition and emotionalism as racial traits that promote mental disorder can be seen in framings of Black new religious movements as cults. In popular, political, and religious discourse in this period, the term "cult" transformed from a neutral descriptor for collective veneration to a characterization signaling a disordered, false, and dangerous religion. As the historian Philip Jenkins shows, this new use of the term reflected increasing contact with "religions in Asia and Africa, which were presented in the West in terms of primitive idolatry and ritual violence."[65] As this new use of "cult," grounded in racialized conceptions of religion, gained traction in the early twentieth-century United States, it facilitated the targeting of a range of groups as having the potential to produce mental illness.[66]

When applied to Black new religious movements, the new uses of the category of cult converged with ideas about African and African American superstition in the image of the "Voodoo cult." This notion became prominent in American popular discourse in the first decades of the twentieth century, extending the deployment of "voodooism" as a general term for ideas about African superstition to a concept that signaled violence committed by people under the sway of a controlling and manipulative leader.[67] In the United States, the media often labeled African American religious practices, particularly conjure and healing work, as "voodoo," linking them to demonizing discourses about Haiti and characterizations of Haitian religion as involving "cannibalism, human sacrifice, and devil worship."[68] As the historian Danielle Boaz shows, by the end of the nineteenth century, white American media raised the alarm that such practices "would likewise permeate African American communities in the United States if white Americans did not step in to provide a 'civilizing influence.'"[69] In a sweeping article in 1913 surveying what it called "the cult of Voudooism" in hemispheric perspective, the New York Tribune characterized "Voudooism" as "rooted firmly in the superstitious mental equipment of the Central American negro and, indeed of the Southern American negro." The article continued to characterize "voudoo" as "a confused medley of snake worship, frenzied sensual dancing and blood sacrifice in its extreme forms, as found among the islands of the Caribbean." The unnamed author argued that, as an organized set of practices, its presence was strongest in the Caribbean and the US South and asserted that "it degenerates to mere selling of herbal remedies and potions, charms and incantations in the negro colonies of Philadelphia, Boston and New York."[70]

The idea of a "voodoo cult," combining African practices indiscriminately with other religious forms and deranging minds to drive a blood lust, was readily available for deployment in relation to Black new religious movements in the early twentieth-century North. In the case of a 1932 murder connected to the Nation of Islam in its early years in Detroit, the police, media, and local African American clergy interpreted the killing through the frame of a "voodoo cult" characterized by disordered beliefs and practices that were the result of mental derangement. The murder brought the Nation of Islam to public attention and generated much speculation about the group. The Nation of Islam's founder, W. D. Fard, began gathering followers in 1930 around the belief that Black people were Allah's original creations and that the earth belonged to them.[71] He said he came from Mecca to return them to knowledge of their true selves and to prepare them for Allah's future destruction of the devilish white people, who he taught were the unnatural creations of a malicious scientist. Joining the Nation of Islam required turn from an invisible "mystery God" of Christianity to Allah and embrace of Islam. Members of the Nation of Islam rejected Negro racial identity, which Fard preached had been imposed on them in slavery, in favor of an understanding of themselves as the original Asiatic Black people.[72] Fard's followers, including Elijah and Clara Poole, migrants from Georgia to Detroit, renounced their "slave names" and requested that he restore their original names. The Pooles became Elijah and Clara Karriem, before eventually receiving the surname of Mohammed or Muhammad, under which Elijah would lead the Nation of Islam from 1933 through his death in 1975.[73]

In late November 1932, Detroit residents, and soon people across the country, learned of Robert Harris's murder of James J. Smith. Harris, whom the press dubbed variously a "Voodoo chief," a "Voodoo King," and the "King of the Order of Islam," killed Smith by hitting him with an automobile axle and stabbing him through the heart on a makeshift altar in Harris's home. Harris reportedly told the police that the sacrifice of someone who was not a member of the order had been foreordained and commanded by the "Gods of Islam."[74] The press reported that upon searching Harris's home the police found "a cheap magazine . . . opened to a story of mysticism in the desert. A clause 'the believer must be stabbed through the heart' was underlined."[75] The murder generated a barrage of media reflections stoking fears of "voodooism's grip" on African Americans in Detroit.[76] As Danielle Boaz notes, because Harris's murder of Smith took place during the US occupation of Haiti, responses to the case reflected broader political concerns and highlighted the power and effects of this demonizing of Black religions. She argues that "this public labeling of black Muslims in the United States as members of a 'voodoo cult' must be understood within the context of dialogues about race and political participation, U.S. imperialism in the Caribbean, and the purported prevalence of ritualized human sacrifice among practitioners of African diaspora religions."[77]

Despite W. D. Fard's insistence when questioned by the police and in a letter published in the *Baltimore Afro-American* that Harris did not belong to the Nation of Islam, many elements of Harris's account of his beliefs bore strong resemblance to the group's teaching.[78] When talking with reporters, Harris spoke of having been converted to Islam through the arrival of a messenger from Asia, presumably Fard.[79] Moreover, there were elements of the Nation of Islam's teachings that, while generic, could be interpreted to support murder if taken literally, which Harris clearly did. Fard had developed a set of catechetical texts for his followers, including "Lost Found Moslem Lessons," that contained the questions, "Why does Mohammed and any Moslem murder the Devil? What is the duty of each Moslem in regard to four devils? What reward does a Moslem receive by presenting the four devils at one time?" The answer provided emphasized the wickedness of the devil and the devil's refusal of Islam. Because of these dangerous and irredeemable qualities, the lesson taught, "all Moslems will murder the devil" and receive the reward of "free transportation to the Holy City of Mecca to see brother Mohammed."[80] Nevertheless, Ugan Ali, an early Nation of Islam leader, insisted to reporters that the group could not be blamed for Harris's actions, that Harris "had no standing in the order, and was not regarded as a leader. Many people avoided him because of the wild things he sometimes said." Edward Harris, Robert's brother, told the press that financial difficulties had caused his brother to "lose his mind. . . . He has been acting queerly in the last few weeks, preaching a lot and stopping people on the streets. Nobody paid much attention to him."[81]

The judge overseeing the case convened a sanity commission composed of three white physicians to decide whether Harris was competent to stand trial. In the interim, Harris was held in the psychopathic ward of the city's Receiving Hospital, along with Ugan Ali and W. D. Fard, who had been taken in for psychiatric evaluation. Reports of these evaluations reveal considerable confusion in the authorities' reasoning on whether mental instability caused people to produce and embrace dangerous, fanatical religious beliefs or whether unconventional beliefs caused mental instability. Regarding Ali, Fard, and Harris, the examining doctors came to different conclusions. The press reported doctors as saying that Ugan Ali's mental processes "are not those of a normal person" and noted that the police blamed his teachings "for the sacrificial murder of James Smith on a voodoo altar more than a week ago." Physicians' reports on Fard characterized him as "not driven into his sinister teachings through insanity."[82] Both Ali and Fard were eventually released, with Ali declaring that he had "realized the danger of his 'teachings' and promising to use his influence to disband the group" and Fard agreeing to leave Detroit.[83] While being held for evaluation, Harris reportedly "alternated between weird mumblings and coma-like trances which lasted sometimes for more than 20 minutes. During his trances he would remain rigid and motionless with wild eyes staring unswerving at the ceiling of his cell."[84] One of the doctors also said that Harris was fixated on events that happened fifteen hundred years ago, possibly describing his preaching of the Nation of Islam's theology of time and history that focused on Black people as God's original creations and Islam as having "inhabited the planet since it has been known to mankind."[85] The members of the sanity commission declared Harris insane, and he was taken to the Ionia State Hospital for the Criminally Insane. The physicians reported that Harris is "subject to mental confusion, delusional thinking, and has hallucinations," and they conjectured that the underlying mental disorder that produced these symptoms may have been the result of an unnamed childhood disease.[86] Harris died in the state hospital in 1935 of heart disease, with dementia praecox listed on his death certificate as a contributing cause of death.[87]

Regardless of the nature of Robert Harris's connection to the Nation of Islam, his murder of James Smith, characterization of him as the head of "the Order of Islam," and his commitment to the Ionia State Hospital having been pronounced insane prompted more general reflections on the appeal of such new groups to African American migrants in Detroit and other cities. Police and media investigations into the Nation of Islam in the wake of the murder highlighted what the press described as startling revelations of many African Americans "enmeshed by the religion" and of "meeting places which for many years had been thought to have been no more than fraternal lodges" found to be "'temples' where susceptible individuals are incited to kill 'devils' in the hope of attaining 'heavenly forgiveness and reward.'"[88] As the local Detroit media expanded its scope of inquiry about such groups, reporters offered accounts dating back several years of what the press characterized as "the amazing growth in recent years of Negro cults with strange Islamic symbols and titles," no doubt including in this the Moorish Science Temple of America, founded by Noble Drew Ali to promote Asiatic Muslim identity for African Americans.[89] Since 1926, the group had been headquartered in Chicago and had branches in many cities, including Detroit. A Detroit Free Press article offered an interpretation of the religious authenticity of members of such "cults," asserting that "it is generally believed that their Mohammedanism [sic] exists only in meaningless, but impressive mixture of Allahs, Mohamets and other Mohammedan incantations."[90] One article raised the alarm about "the effects of the sinister worship upon the gullible and highly emotional members of the cult," and another quoted the AME minister J. D. Howell as among a group of prominent Black clergy decrying Nation of Islam leaders who "preyed upon the more gullible members of their people, and by its force of fanaticism, goaded several Negroes into delusions of divine power which toppled their sanity into homicidal tendencies."[91]

Such assessments of the relationship of so-called cult theologies to insanity as represented in the case of the Nation of Islam were not limited to police, press, and clergy but appeared in medical discourse around the new group. David Clark, a Detroit psychiatrist who oversaw welfare cases at the city's Receiving Hospital, concurred with Detroit media and Black ministers in describing the group as a danger to African Americans' "social stability and welfare." He continued to make a claim that recalled the long history of psychiatric interpretations of African American religion in his reported assertion that "such a religious zeal was not necessarily a form of insanity, but that its effects were often similar to those of insanity" because they promoted a "return to the primal instincts."[92] In the case of the Nation of Islam, observers and city authorities interpreted those "primal instincts" through the lens of stereotypes of "voodoo."

In addition to interpretations of the psychological impact of the "Negro cult" grounded in the notion of the "voodoo cult" as a repository of innate racial superstitions and violent practices derived from these, public discourse about Black new religious movements emphasized the charisma of the leader as preying on African Americans' supposed credulity and innate emotionalism. Father Divine was the subject of much attention in this realm because of his claim to divinity and his followers' devotion. Divine knew well the stakes of legal and medical examination for himself and his followers from early in his career. His arrival in Valdosta, Georgia, in 1914 caused a stir, and the *Valdosta Daily Times* tracked the excitement this "Negro minister of some new faith" had caused in the community. Local Black clergy deemed the content of his preaching at a Holiness church so strange and disturbing that they barred him from speaking again. According to reports, Divine preached that God had appeared on earth "in the form of a Jew," and now "in the form of a Negro" who would usher in the end of the world. The Messenger, as some called him, implored his listeners to follow him, lest they be lost. Despite the opposition of Valdosta clergy, it seemed that the newcomer had attracted a following, "especially among the women, who are usually the first to catch on to new doctrines," the *Times* declared.[93] Local African American men reportedly described their wives and mothers as having become "bereft of reason" and warned that "if something was not done the whole community would be crazed."

Police arrested the Messenger, and a lunacy hearing was called for him and for two women police had also taken into custody and described as "shouting and screaming at the top of their voices." The Messenger was not merely a man, the women were said to have declared, but was "nothing more than God," leading the press to conclude that the Messenger's following represented people who possessed "excessive religious enthusiasm and who believe he really is a persecuted saint."[94] The Messenger himself presented a picture of a certain kind of religious excess to observers. Although appearing neatly dressed in a cutaway suit and impressing the local journalist covering the story as dignified and intelligent, the Messenger was clearly fixed in his unusual beliefs. "His trouble was entirely religion," the reporter concluded, noting that the Messenger responded to the jury's questions about himself with quotations from the Bible. In representing the Messenger, J. B. Copeland, a local white attorney, argued that the strangeness and implausibility of a person's religious beliefs depended on one's perspective and he orchestrated contradictory testimony by two ministers about the nature of true religion. One defended speaking in unknown tongues under the power of the spirit of God and characterized doubters as "spiritually blind and bereft of reason." The other decried speaking in tongues as nothing more than "fanaticism or emotion."[95] That each assessed the other's theological beliefs as indicative of an "unsound mind" made room for the Messenger's claims to be evaluated as something other than legal lunacy. And, indeed, the jury concluded that he was of unsound mind and "unbalanced" on the subject of religion, but not to the degree that he should be committed to the Georgia State Hospital.[96] By the time he arrived in New York, the Messenger had become Father Divine, and his following continued to grow.[97]

Leaders of other Black new religious movements that thrived in the early twentieth-century urban North were evaluated through psychiatric lenses for what outsiders considered their extravagant claims to divine status, prophetic authority, or unique esoteric knowledge. In Philadelphia in 1933, Grand Sheik Joshua Way Bey of the Moorish Science Temple, who rejected the racial category of Negro and asserted Moorish American Muslim identity, was sent for psychiatric evaluation because he had become "excited" during a truancy hearing for the son of a member of the group. The boy's mother had kept him from school because his teacher refused to use the surname members of the group affirmed as their Moorish tribal name, and Way Bey had been in court to explain the Moorish Science Temple's teachings.[98] Charles L. Brown, the white municipal court judge who presided over the case, framed his work overseeing domestic relations and juvenile cases as securing the home in its role as the cornerstone of government. In turn, according to Brown, "those nations thrive and are blest that recognize God and follow His precepts." Counting the United States among these, he was determined to ensure continued divine blessing.[99] Given Brown's religious commitments, Grand Sheik Joshua Way Bey's declaration of Moorish

Muslim identity and claim to represent "the Asiatics of the Northwest" no doubt struck him as unusual, but his decision to send Way Bey for psychiatric evaluation pathologized Black religio-racial difference and intensified the characterization of new religious movements as "cults."[100] Reporters in the Black press, themselves confused, amused, or alarmed about the appeal of these new groups, also routinely labeled them cults. In this case, articles described Way Bey as a leader of "a strange religious cult claiming Moorish descent." After three weeks of evaluation, the examining psychiatrists declared him "a paranoid mystic type" and planned to transfer him to a hospital for treatment.[101]

The characterization of leaders of new religio-racial groups as paranoid extended beyond the Moorish Science Temple in this period. When the Nation of Islam's leader Elijah Muhammad was imprisoned at the Federal Correctional Institution in Milan, Michigan, in 1942 because he refused to register for the draft on the grounds that he was a "citizen of the universe" and "opposed to armed aggression," he was examined by a psychiatrist. The prison psychiatrist diagnosed him with "Dementia Praecox, paranoid type," and described him initially as having "made an adjustment to his psychosis." The physician located Muhammad's paranoid psychosis in what was described as a mental state marked by "a persecutory trend both against himself and his race (Negro)" and the sense that he was being followed and talked about.[102] Here the psychiatrist transformed the Nation of Islam's religious rejection of white supremacy and Muhammad's justified sense of being surveilled—this medical record was later incorporated into his FBI file—into psychopathic paranoia. Almost a year into his imprisonment, Muhammad's record reflected the psychiatric assessment that he had made no improvement "and was continuing in the same schizophrenic [dementia praecox] pattern," including "having visions and communications with Allah in visual and auditory form."[103]

Father Divine himself would not be subject to direct psychiatric evaluation or a court proceeding to assess his mental state after the 1914 lunacy hearing in Valdosta, Georgia. Some white psychiatrists did conjecture about his sanity based on observation of his sermons and Peace Mission worship, and from evaluating and treating his followers. Lauretta Bender, a white psychiatrist at New York City's Bellevue Hospital who specialized in child psychiatry, published several studies in the

1930s based on her assessments of adult members of the Peace Mission and their children, many of whom had been sent for evaluation from Judge Jacob Panken's Domestic Relations courtroom. Bender's experience attending a Methodist church in Los Angeles as a teenager and exposure to works like William James's *Varieties of Religious Experience* while in college shaped her perspective and interest in the impact of different religious expressions on life and culture.[104] In 1938, Bender collaborated with a fellow white Bellevue psychiatrist, Zuleika Yarrell, on an article for the *Journal of Nervous and Mental Diseases* in which they offered an assessment of Divine's mental state based on observation and reports, rather than direct engagement with him.[105] Bender and Yarrell described Divine's sociable personality and his obvious pleasure at the attention he received from his followers, characterizing him as almost believing "in his own omnipotence and immunity." In addition, they conjectured that "in general, he falls into our psychiatric classification of a cyclothymic individual" but cited no evidence of Divine's suffering from a mental disorder characterized by mood swings.[106] James A. Brussel, a New Yorker descended from Jewish immigrants from Germany and a psychiatrist at Pilgrim State Hospital on Long Island, was much less clinical than Bender and Yarrell in characterizing Divine in a 1935 article in the *American Journal of Psychiatry*.[107] Brussel described Divine as a "shrewd, uncanny Ethiopian" who had "enveloped his cult in a shroud of mystery."[108] Like Bender and Yarrell, Brussel was more interested in the effects of Divine, his theology, and the social organization of the Peace Mission on followers than in diagnosing the leader's mental state. From his engagements with Peace Mission members at Pilgrim State Hospital, Brussel concluded, "It seems apparent that the encounter with Father Divine served as a 'strain'—as a precipitating factor in producing well-defined psychotic syndromes."[109]

The psychiatric assessments of religious leaders Father Divine, Joshua Way Bey, and Elijah Muhammad differed in important ways from the many individual cases of religious visionary experiences and prophetic utterances across this period that led to diagnoses of insanity grounded in what psychiatrists viewed as innate emotionalism. White authorities, and many Black religious and political leaders, were concerned that the theologies of the new religio-racial movements had motivated members to reorganize their families, economies, politics, and social lives in socially disruptive ways. Way Bey was in court defending his followers' insistence on their son's use of the name the Moorish Science Temple's prophet taught them was their divine and true name. Elijah Muhammad was sentenced to prison for draft evasion because the Nation of Islam's theology required that he reject the authority of the United States, as representative of the white devil and doomed to Allah's destruction. Although never committed to an institution, the fact that acceptance of Father Divine's assertion of divinity brought psychiatric scrutiny for some of his followers, like Rebecca Isaac, pointed to broader implications for approaches to religion, race, and mental illness. In investigating charismatic religious leaders and the "cult" context, social scientists and psychiatrists addressed a range of questions about the effects of migration and urbanization on the individual health of members of the groups and on Black religious communities more generally.

## In the Kingdom of Father Divine

Father Divine and the Peace Mission received much attention as religious, political, and medical authorities sought to make sense of the appeal and social impact of "Negro cults" and the possible effects of membership on mental health.[110] Some psychiatric researchers who engaged the group located their analysis of the Peace Mission in broader accounts of the character of African American religion that recalled older medical frames. Pilgrim State Hospital's James A. Brussel, who probably did not have firsthand experience of Divine or the Peace Mission, mobilized established white psychiatric interpretations of African American religion along with contemporary reflections by observers to contextualize his analysis of the group. Drawing on a description of Peace Mission worship by Claude McKay, a Jamaican immigrant and Harlem Renaissance writer, in an article in *The Nation*, Brussel offered it as evidence of "a frantic, prancing expression of Black emotionalism in the heart of the great white city."[111] Brussel described the Peace Mission's largely Black membership in ways that hearkened back to the psychiatric discourse of late nineteenth-century white southern asylum doctors. Rehearsing familiar claims, he pronounced Divine's followers as "not far removed from their savage ancestors with their primitive, tribal interest in the unnatural, voodooism, witchcraft, and the more bizarre portions of religion."[112] Similarly, the Bellevue Hospital psychiatrists Lauretta Bender and Zuleika Yarrell turned to W. E. B. Du Bois's assertion in *The Souls of Black Folk* that the religion of the enslaved was marked by "the preacher, the music, and the frenzy" to argue that Father Divine's meetings were "remarkably similar" to "the slavery time church."[113] Supporting this connection, they cited a 1920 description by the white southerner H. Snyder of "a plantation revival service" in which Snyder argued that the music and movement produced "a sort of hypnotic effect, leading to a breakdown of rational inhibitions and to a free display of the emotions."[114] In contrast to those who saw the emergence of "sects and cults" as a new development, Bender and Yarrell argued that "the willingness to follow a new leader and the emotional response to a new religious movement have not changed to any degree during the years" since slavery.[115]

These psychiatrists acknowledged arguments in recent medical and sociological literature emphasizing the effect of environment on psychological states but still included race as a factor in diagnosing psychoses in Father Divine's followers. Brussel asserted that Divine's followers were "maladjusted to a civilized world" and compensated by seeking comfort in the protected environment of the Peace Mission's kingdoms. In these communities, he argued, Divine's followers "are not only enabled, but actually encouraged to openly revert to the frenzied, untamed exhibitions and religious fervor which are characteristic of the voodooism of their ancestors."[116] Brussel's study included only three patients: two African American women and one African American man, all in their thirties or early forties, raised Protestant, married, migrants to New York, and diagnosed with dementia praecox upon admission to Pilgrim State Hospital on Long Island. Although he titled his study "Father Divine: Holy Precipitator of Psychosis," Brussel noted "the striking paucity of references to Father Divine in all three case," and attributed the absence to "the power of the preacher" to "keep the lips of the disciple sealed."[117] In fact, according to the study, in two cases the patients had experienced religious visions or auditory hallucinations before having contact with the Peace Mission and then sought out Divine. In the end, rather than demonstrate that participation in the Peace Mission or contact with Father Divine precipitated psychosis, Brussel's analysis pointed to what he understood to be the characteristics of Divine's followers and the group's social functions for them. According to him, this small sample exemplified those who "fell prey" to Divine's theology: economically and educationally disadvantaged middle-aged Black migrants from the South, "where the colored race is closest to its African ancestry and endowed with simple, gullible and easily molded minds." In his estimation, the "clash with reality," presumably in the challenges of migration and life in northern cities, led them to "eagerly accept the refuge and protection offered by Father Divine."[118] Brussel reported that two of his patients recovered and were released after time at Pilgrim State, and one expected to be released shortly, but he offered no details about the treatment that led to their improvement.

Bender and Yarrell's conclusions relied less clearly on racialized assumptions about the Black psyche than did Brussel's, even as questions about race, culture, and evolution figured in their research.[119] Their study was larger than Brussel's, with eighteen patients ranging in age from twenty-three to seventy-five years old: fifteen women and three men, all Black, except for one white woman. Most were in their thirties and forties, with a variety of family situations—married, formerly married, parents of children—and the few with religious backgrounds identified were Protestant or Catholic. As with Brussel's small sample, direct connection to Father Divine and the Peace Mission was unclear in some of the cases Bender and Yarrell presented. Perry, a forty-year-old man who was brought to Bellevue Hospital from jail after having been charged with disorderly conduct, praised and cursed Father Divine in his "rambling, disconnected" speech. They described him as manic but did not attribute this to participation in the Peace Mission. Similarly, Ada, a thirty-eight-year-old woman, was brought to Bellevue from the mayor's office where she had gone to seek help because she believed Father Divine was persecuting her. The psychiatrists characterized her as suffering from "the paranoid delusions of a schizophrenic," but they presented no evidence that the woman's paranoia was connected to interaction with Divine himself or Peace Mission members.[120]

In the cases of two women, Rebecca and Annie, both of whom were referred for evaluation because of authorities' concern for their children, Bender and Yarrell concluded that they were not psychotic but merely subscribed to "a teaching not recognized by society."[121] They noted that Rebecca, who was almost certainly Rebecca Isaac, Hatty's mother, expressed elation to the point of being "hypomanic" when talking about her belief in Father Divine's divinity. In addition, they interpreted both women's attitudes toward marriage and parenting as having been shaped by the Peace Mission's celibacy and view of children as signs of the sin of sexual intercourse. In Annie's case, they found the children to be happy and cared for despite their mother's embrace of Divine's theology; in Rebecca's case, she had left her child in its father's care after she had moved to a Peace Mission residence. Although Rebecca's husband was clearly distraught about her abandonment, the physicians did not view her actions as a clinical problem. For Bender and Yarrell, these women were simply living as the Peace Mission's theology required, and the fact that others found the beliefs strange was not evidence of psychosis.

Bender and Yarrell characterized half of the patients admitted to Bellevue Hospital "proclaiming the teachings of Father Divine" as showing "manic-like excitements in cyclothymic individuals" and diagnosed eight with manic-depressive psychosis.[122] In several cases they attributed the onset of psychosis to participation in the Peace Mission's ecstatic worship, sometimes combined with social and financial challenges or emotional distress about sex, marriage, or children. A thirty-year-old member of the Peace Mission who had taken the spiritual name of St. John to divest herself of what Divine called mortal connections and remake herself in Father Divine's kingdom on earth, had been preaching on the streets and was brought to the hospital for evaluation because she would not give authorities her "earthly" name or address. Like the two mothers Bender and Yarrell did not diagnose as psychotic, St. John embraced the novel religious beliefs of the Peace Mission, but they deemed her in need of psychiatric care because her devotion created "an uncontrollable urge to tell others." Here Bender and Yarrell argued that participation in Peace Mission worship had the potential to lead to psychosis requiring hospitalization and that this religious excitement, "carried too far," could render the line between "so-called normal participants" and psychotic ones thin.[123] The researchers reported that St. John had been transferred to a state hospital and remained there, still preaching, and refusing to answer to any other name.

In some cases, Bender and Yarrell decided that a patient's prior emotional instability had been exacerbated by engaging Father Divine's theology. Forty-five-year-old Elise had been brought to the hospital by another Peace Mission member who reported that she had appeared at one of the residences a few days earlier and had been acting strangely. Elise told the doctors that she had heard Father Divine's voice months ago, affirmed his divinity, and brought her son to Harlem to see him. She had determined to join the kingdom and leave her son with someone else, but the separation caused her emotional distress. The psychiatrists reported that the case "shows how anxiety and depression were followed by strong and stronger religious feelings until the patient went into a panic when she was unable to find her child." They continued to argue that "this case illustrates the influence of Father Divine on people who are suffering from difficult economic situations."[124]

From their examination of these cases of people they classed as followers of Father Divine and who were admitted to Bellevue Hospital, Bender and Yarrell concluded that, for some, Father Divine's teachings and the practices of the Peace Mission precipitated the onset of psychosis. For other patients, they argued that individual psychogenic factors, such as "emotional, social, and religious conflicts with which the individual was struggling," were at play in the development of mental illness.[125] Even as they considered social factors, these psychiatrists mobilized long-standing racial tropes in their analysis of the susceptibility of their patients to Divine's charisma and the Peace Mission's theology and practices, arguing that as a result of participation in the excitement of Peace Mission worship, "there is a tendency for more primitive features to present themselves."[126] They did not present race as decisive in shaping all these patients' experiences of illness, however. They concluded that, "even when we have a fairly pure experiment in a race which is reputed for its excessibility to emotional excitement and is under the influence of a religious movement that brings into relief all of their personal conflicts and encourages the deflection of normal sexual and emotional behavior into abnormal channels and encourages outbursts of emotional excitement," the psychoses they diagnosed in Divine's followers proceeded along a course expected for any patient.[127]

Bender and Yarrell's study was published in the *Journal of Nervous and Mental Disease* in 1938, but reports of their work reached the media several years earlier when they delivered a research paper at the May 1935 meeting of the American Psychiatric Association.[128] The *New York Times* summarized the talk in an article on page 3 under the headline,

"16 of Divine's Cult Show Mental Ills," asserting that only two patients admitted to the hospital of the sample were found to be free of psychosis. In contrast to the conclusions in the published study that tempered attribution of psychoses in Divine's followers to racial traits, the newspaper account highlighted Bender and Yarrell's claim of development of "primitive behavior" in one patient and applied it to a larger group of Divine's followers. The article rendered the psychiatrists as finding among patients "a type of behavior characteristic of the primitive Negro with primitive dancing and chanting nonsense rhyme."[129] The Associated Press and other wire services provided stories about Bender and Yarrell's research that newspapers across the United States and Canada published in the days after their presentation, amplifying the sense that these new religious groups had created a major mental health crisis with a significant racial component.[130]

Newspaper reports of Bender and Yarrell's study followed attention the previous year to the mental health of Peace Mission members in Newark, New Jersey. Officials in the city's Social Service Bureau expressed concern about living conditions in the several Peace Mission heavens because of overcrowding and continuous religious services. As with Rebecca Isaac's case in Harlem, Newark officials focused on the disruption to families the group's theology produced. Marie Warrick, an African American social worker for the bureau, discussed the case in terms that echoed the assessments of Black psychiatrists and social scientists of the impact of urbanization and the rise of new religious movements on Black migrants.[131] In responding to reports that the state's Graystone Park Mental Hospital had seen the admission of large numbers of Peace Mission members who were said to have become mentally imbalanced soon after joining the group, Warrick told the press that members of these new groups "live in an imaginary world induced by their leaders. Their state of mind is like that produced by drugs. Later many, when forced to face life's realities, are mentally unbalanced by the sudden change from a dream life to real life."[132] That Warrick took this approach, which rejected racialized explanations in favor of analysis of social environment, including within religious groups, is not surprising, given that the Episcopalian and Philadelphian was the daughter of a physician and the niece by marriage to Solomon Carter Fuller, the first Black psychiatrist in the United States and mentor to several Tuskegee Veterans Hospital psychiatrists.[133] Warrick was also part of a "brain trust" of Black and white doctors, social workers, religious leaders, and journalists who worked with the Urban League's Ira De Augustine Reid to address the impact of the "increasing number of religious cults," with emphasis on the group's sense "that considerable insanity is accompanying this increase."[134]

Father Divine and Faithful Mary, a prominent Peace Mission leader, engaged with psychiatrists in New York City who treated members of the group. At Bender and Yarrell's invitation, Faithful Mary, accompanied by two of Divine's secretaries and fifteen members, visited Bellevue to explain Peace Mission beliefs and practices in relation to a recently admitted patient.[135] Divine met with a psychiatrist at Kings Park State Hospital on Long Island to discuss a patient and followed up with a letter defending the Peace Mission from racialized psychiatric analyses. Divine complained that "it has been said by a goodly number of the Physicians that MY Movement and its emotions are from the primitive ancestors of some special race or nationality."[136] He directed psychiatrists to study the history of all religions, especially the Shakers, which he insisted would show that the Peace Mission's utopian theology, idea of God in the flesh, and embrace of celibacy were not unusual or limited to the so-called colored race. In a sermon to his followers, Divine spoke about the press reports of Bender and Yarrell's study and expressed confusion that the psychiatrists described "the expression of the Holy Spirit in bodies" as mental illness. He asserted that, in seeking mental causes for spiritual expressions, they betrayed their ignorance of the history of religions. As with his response to the Kings Park psychiatrist, Divine likened his followers' religious experiences to those of the biblical figures of Jesus's disciples, Paul, Moses, and Abraham and wondered how modern psychiatrists would judge them. He went on to offer a lesson "not on mental hygiene especially, but on Spiritual Hygiene,—the mystery of GOD's presence in the consciousness of the people." Divine rejected the interpretation that his followers' behavior was abnormal and characterized it, instead, as a reflection of their efforts to connect to his consciousness and "reconceive GOD's Intelligence through the relaxation of [one's] conscious mentality."[137] He noted that history provided many accounts of religious groups cultivating the emotions and counseled psychiatrists to study this history. For Divine, the testimony of his many followers to the spiritual and emotional transformation wrought by their connection to him as God, in place of "all of their pleasures and all of their fancies," was proof enough of the benefits of the Peace Mission.

Neither Divine's response to the pathologizing of the Peace Mission's theology and worship nor the testimony of his majority Black female following about why they joined and remained changed public perception of the group as presenting a social problem. Indeed, this perception was grounded in ample evidence that did raise issues and present challenges for family members and public officials. Some observers, such as psychologists Hadley Cantril and Muzafer Sherif, argued that fear of Divine and his insistence that "cosmic forces are on his side and that he has the power of life and death" kept Peace Mission members from leaving the group.[138] In fact, accounts of some former members lent credence to such analysis, including from those who felt manipulated out of their money and labor and others who charged Divine with sexual abuse.[139] Moreover, the disruption of families that was a focus of Judge Jacob Panken's ire toward Divine had a real impact on those whose relatives entered Divine's kingdom. And while cases of women abandoning spouses or children received the most press coverage and attention from legal and medical authorities, men also embraced the celibate, sex-segregated life of the Peace Mission. In 1934, James Green moved into a Peace Mission residence in Harlem, not far from where he had lived with his wife, Mary, and young daughter. In keeping with Divine's theology, he would acknowledge Mary only as "sister" when passing her on the street and, according to Mary, "treats her and their daughter as dog." Seeking financial support from James, Mary Green told a judge that her case was not exceptional, and that the Peace Mission had caused much "domestic unhappiness."[140]

From the perspective of many African American religious and political leaders, the "problem of the cults" had serious implications for race relations because, in the words of an editorial in the Black press, they represented "an obstacle to our progress which must be effectively and diplomatically handled."[141] Black leaders who worried about what attracted people to these new movements in urban environments and questioned how traditional Black churches might be failing to meet the needs of migrants and young people in the modern era recognized the potential appeal of these groups. As Miles Mark Fisher, a Black Baptist minister who later earned a PhD in history from the University of Chicago, wrote in 1936, "The cults have anticipated many a denominational challenge of this social and economic order, diseased by greed, corruption, crime, poverty, immorality, intemperance and war. Unlike the Negro churches, the cults seek to cure the souls of bodies and men. They view social work differently from the Negro denominations that have no social technique while their community is needy, while their church buildings represent idle wealth, except periodically, and while their race has few social agencies."[142] For Fisher and other observers of the rise of "the cults," the new challenges of the urban environment combined with the failures of traditional churches to meet community needs accounted for the appeal of these groups, rather than racial propensities. With the turn away from what Horace Mann Bond described as "race, and race alone" to environment and understanding of individual lives, the notion of mental illness caused by the superstition, emotionalism, and credulity of "religious excitement" became less prominent in psychiatric theory. Increasingly, Black religious and political leaders and Black and white psychiatrists and social workers sought ways of attending to the individual experiencing mental distress in the context of their community, including their religious communities, rather than by committing them to state hospitals.

# 6

## Faith in Psychiatry

In 1935, James H. Robinson entered Union Theological Seminary, a prominent liberal Protestant seminary in New York City, as a graduate student. Robinson's path to Union to study with the theologian Eugene Lyman, New Testament scholar Mary Ely Lyman, and professor of practical theology and minister Harry Emerson Fosdick, among others, was unusual when compared with that of most of the student body. Born in Knoxville, Tennessee, to Henry, a laborer, and Willie Belle, a laundress, Robinson had a childhood marked by his mother's illness and death and his father's intense devotion to a Holiness church in Knoxville and, later, a Pentecostal church in Cleveland, Ohio.[1] In his 1950 autobiography, Robinson wrote of being emotionally wounded by the sermon the Pentecostal preacher delivered at his mother's funeral that "offered Mama no hope of eternal life because unlike my father, she was unsanctified" and described the religious doubts this perspective produced in him.[2] Living at different times with an aunt and uncle and grandparents during his childhood provided other church experiences for Robinson, including at a racially integrated Baptist church in Knoxville where he encountered racism from white children and adult members.[3] After his father married a fellow church member, whom Robinson found excessively deferential to white people and who tried to prevent him and his siblings from continuing their educations, Robinson left home.[4]

The support and guidance of African American religious leaders in Cleveland, especially Ernest Escoe, the head of a neighborhood Young Men's Christian Association, who welcomed Robinson into his family and the AME Church he attended, motivated Robinson to continue his education.[5] During those years he organized youth work in a local Congregational church where he met Charles Lee Jefferson, the pastor of St. Mark's Presbyterian Church. Jefferson encouraged him to consider the ministry and noted that the denomination would fund his education if he joined. Robinson wrote that this was an easy decision, since he considered himself already "part Baptist, Methodist, Sanctified, Christian, and Congregational. There was no appreciable difference so far as I knew or cared."[6] Robinson attended the historically Black Lincoln University in Pennsylvania, where he became consumed with fury about the injustices and terror African Americans were experiencing and described himself as growing neurotic: "It always seemed as if I could do nothing to control my emotions when along would come a white person to rub in once again the merciless stigmatization of race."[7] His growing anger was fueled by experiences during his summers working in a church in Beardon, Tennessee, facing threats from white residents, seeing local Black clergy's fears about political agitation, and enduring a mob attack on the church.[8] Robinson remembered his experience at Lincoln as helping him feel "the tremendous strength of my potentialities" and resist "succumbing to an emotional self-defeat."[9] He graduated in 1935 at the top of his class and was recognized by his fellow graduates as the student who had done the most for the graduating class.[10]

Arriving at Union Theological Seminary the fall after his graduation from Lincoln and following his father's death, Robinson expected that "color wouldn't matter here," but he "was blindly, painfully mistaken." Racial discrimination was compounded by his feelings of self-doubt around fellow students who had attended elite schools. Even with the support of several faculty members and an enriching fieldwork experience at the Union Neighborhood Center and a Brooklyn Congregational church led by fellow Lincoln and Union graduate Shelby Rooks, Robinson struggled to find his footing.[11] Although Robinson was determined to leave school, Professor Mary Ely Lyman convinced him to stay, but he continued to struggle and overwork himself on too little sleep. Becoming ill with stomach pains and indigestion, he was sent to Presbyterian Hospital. In his memoir, Robinson described a specialist examining him in a lecture room in front of twenty doctors, nurses, and interns. The white doctor prefaced his exam with remarks about race and disease immunity, spouting stereotypes about biological racial differences. Then, turning to what had brought Robinson to the hospital, he declared Robinson's pain imaginary and offered the fact that "the boy is a Negro" to support this conclusion. In Robinson's account, the doctor continued, declaring, "This boy (I winced at his condescension) is ambitious beyond his capacity. Only a few generations removed from the jungles of

Africa and slavery, he is unable to compete intellectually with men of the advanced white race. You'll find many similar cases."[12]

After offering a medical opinion in line with the long history of psychiatric framings of African Americans as savage, fit only for slavery, and unable to achieve civilization, this doctor counseled Robinson to leave the seminary, telling him, "Our minds have great power over our bodies and otherwise you will face a breakdown surely." He continued, "There is no future for you in competing with men of the best cultural and mental heritage. Go down South and get yourself a little church among your people." The doctor advised, "They need you and you can be somebody. None of you can hope to get beyond that level you yourself have attained." Robinson countered by pointing to "Negroes who have achieved great fame," which prompted the doctor to name Walter White of the NAACP, John Hope of Morehouse College, and Mordecai Johnson of Howard University, all light-skinned African Americans, smirkingly arguing that their achievements could be attributed to the amount of "white superiority which they have absorbed." Robinson shouted back that Frederick Douglass, Howard Thurman, Harriet Tubman, Sojourner Truth, and other important figures were "as black as I am," but was summarily dismissed without another glance.[13] He determined to prove the doctor wrong and, returning to his studies, was elected president of his class and performed well in academics and preaching. Upon his graduating in 1938, Union's president Henry Sloane Coffin encouraged him to take up work with Black Presbyterians in Harlem. Robinson took the opportunity to become the founding pastor of the Church of the Master, reinvigorating the formerly white Morningside Presbyterian Church, whose membership had merged with another white church rather than admit Black congregants.[14] His new wife, Helen, a North Carolinian, graduate of Johnson C. Smith University, and the daughter of a formerly enslaved Presbyterian minister and educator, joined him in this work.[15]

In his approach to pastoring this new church, Robinson viewed responding to the social and economic challenges Black residents of Harlem and Morningside Heights faced as fully within the congregation's purview. Robinson served on several committees concerned with local issues, national civil rights campaigns, and religious matters.[16] In seeking to make the church "a source of help as well as inspiration," Robinson, Helen, and several congregants embarked on a community survey to better understand the needs of the members of the church and the neighborhood. He wrote in his memoir that the door-to-door survey "revealed more problems than all the combined religious forces of the Harlem ghetto could relieve let alone solve," including profound poverty and exploitation by white doctors, druggists, and businesspeople. Added to this, he believed that the presence of "religious charlatans" in storefront churches, "who feed like leeches upon the ignorance and superstitions of the people," exacerbated the neighborhood's problems.[17] In this context in which most churches, in Robinson's estimation, made themselves available to the people only on Sundays when their doors were open, he understood some of the draw of figures like Father Divine "and a host of lesser imitators." Father Divine, he concluded, "at least, gave his followers inexpensive meals, clean living quarters and the ego-satisfying status of angels, but the ethics of the other gentlemen were highly questionable."[18] Robinson and his staff achieved success in demonstrating the broad services and support a committed local church could provide, and within two years the church's membership had reached four hundred, with Robinson reporting weekly attendance of six hundred.[19]

As he worked with young people in Harlem, Robinson became convinced that many would benefit from counseling or psychiatric care. In his assessment, "the tensions and repressions under which they lived could not help but breed terrific emotional and mental problems," but there were no options for care or treatment in the neighborhood. Realizing the depth of need, Robinson wrote that he "dreamed of a minister and a psychiatrist working together in an experiment in spiritual psychiatry. It would be no trick at all if two such persons of equal stature and mutual confidence and respect for one another's respective fields could be found who would deal with people both as moral and physical beings."[20] Visiting a congregant who had been admitted to Bellevue Hospital's psychiatric ward underscored for Robinson the need for access to preventative counseling. He wrote in his memoir that mentioning the idea of bringing psychiatry to Harlem to a clerical colleague was met with the suggestion that perhaps he, himself, needed psychiatric care. This colleague was not alone in thinking the idea radical, but Robinson insisted that it was "practical and certain that if given a fair trial it would prove a success."[21]

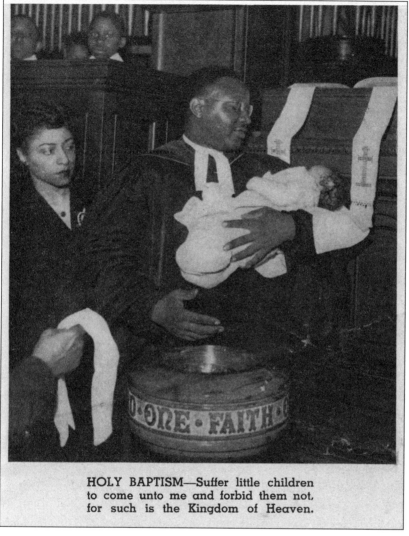

HOLY BAPTISM—Suffer little children
to come unto me and forbid them not,
for such is the Kingdom of Heaven.

Figure 6.1. Rev. James H. Robinson performing a baptism at the Church of the Master,
New York, ca. 1940s.

Robinson did not elaborate on what he meant by "spiritual psychiatry," but his desire to see Black Harlemites have access to mental hygiene and psychiatric services without discrimination, especially given his own experience while in seminary, placed him in the context of a broader movement for community-based mental health care in the years following the end of World War II. As Harlem had served as a laboratory for white and Black psychiatrists and social scientists of the 1930s interested in the psychological, social, and religious effects of African American migration and urbanization, so it did for postwar religious, political, and medical leaders concerned about lack of access to preventative care. Advocates of expanded mental hygiene resources for African Americans did not necessarily identify religion as a source of psychological destabilization, nor did they advocate explicitly religious counseling. They did, however, see the mission of Black churches as entailing recognizing psychological challenges in modern life and understanding that what may appear to be moral failing—as in the case of some of the young gang members with whom Robinson worked—was a response to how "the pernicious problem of race complicated the lives of Negroes."[22] Robinson and other local Black clergy, including Baptist Adam Clayton Powell Jr., Methodist Frederick Asbury Cullen, and Episcopalian Shelton Hale Bishop, realized that the resources of the pastor's study were not sufficient in many cases, but they suspected that treatment within a hospital was not always warranted. Elizabeth Bishop Davis, whose father, Shelton Hale Bishop, cofounded a mental health clinic in Harlem in 1946 and who herself became a psychiatrist at Harlem Hospital, recalled that these clergy "recognized, they had to, as part of their pastoral work, they were constantly confronted with people whose psychiatric, emotional needs they could not meet because they were not professionals and they had nowhere to send them."[23] Other African American community activists, social workers, and medical professionals, many whose work was animated by religious commitments, contributed to these developments, including the physician Arthur C. Logan, who was married to the sociologist and Young Women's Christian Association (YWCA) secretary Wenonah Bond Logan.[24]

Robinson's goal of providing community-based counseling resources aligned with broader changes in psychiatry in the postwar United States as psychodynamic psychiatry became more widespread. As the historian Martin Summers writes, "The ideas that everyone fell on a spectrum with mental illness and mental health at opposite poles, and that mental illness was essentially an individual's failure to adapt to his or her environment and the people within it, gained even more currency in the wake of the nation's war experience."[25] During the war, the government used psychiatric screening to identify potential difficulties soldiers might experience in adjusting to the military. These assessments reflected and mobilized racial bias that led to a higher rate of rejection of Black draft registrants, but they also helped to deepen attention to the impact not only of traumas like combat experience but of long-term stress on individual psyches throughout American society.[26] Greater attention to mental health in the postwar period led to the passage of the National Mental Health Act in 1946, which provided funding for the establishment of the National Institutes of Mental Health and the founding of the Group for the Advancement of Psychiatry in 1947, under William C. Menninger's leadership, to coordinate research in mental health.[27] The post–World War II "social psychiatry" movement, which the historian Matthew Smith describes as "an interdisciplinary approach to understanding mental health and illness that combined insights of the social sciences with those of psychiatry," with the aim of "prevention of mental illness," also contributed to the changing mental health care landscape.[28]

In addition to new frameworks for understanding the sources of mental illness, new approaches to treatment beyond the traditional model of confinement and labor in institutions and somatic therapies such as lobotomy and shock therapy came to the fore in this period.[29] Some African American psychiatrists in the postwar period, including Tuskegee Veterans Hospital's Alan P. Smith, promoted psychoanalysis as an important tool for treating the large group of Americans "suffering from some form of mental disease or personality disorder." Smith, who was a founding member of the National Guild of Catholic Psychiatrists in the 1950s, addressed Black doctors at the annual meeting of the National Medical Association in 1947 on "the role of psychoanalytic psychiatry in the practice of medicine." "Psychoanalysis," he argued, "has enriched [psychiatry] with a deeper understanding of the experientially determined development of an individual's motivations, interpersonal defenses and social adaptations."[30] Providing an overview of the stages of personality development and experiences of anxiety, drawing in part on Sigmund Freud's work, Smith framed personality through a universal human lens and indicated that the source of anxiety could be within the individual's personality or "fear that arises from the external situation," which allowed for accounting for racism and discrimination. He discussed several case studies from among the World War II veterans he had treated and described how psychotherapy had been successful in alleviating their anxiety and, in some cases, the physical manifestations of anxiety. Smith told his audience and readers of the published version in the *Journal of the National Medical Association* that "in therapy, we attempt to find the repressed material and bring the conflict situations out into the open, so that the patient can learn to handle them on a conscious level."[31] As a result of therapy, he argued, patients have a better sense of self through a process unlike other areas of "medical treatment in which the patient plays a passive role."[32] In this period, then, both African American patients and psychiatrists, as well as some white psychiatrists, turned to resources in psychotherapy and treatment grounded in ideas about universal "normal" human personality development and general responses to stress and trauma but also remained attentive to the specific sources of stress and trauma in African American life.

## Mental Hygiene for All

Prior to World War II, African American mental hygiene activists called for expanded access to counseling and preventative mental health treatment. The mental hygiene movement developed in the early twentieth century from the perspective of former patients and with the goal of inhibiting the development of mental illness. In the broader mental hygiene movement, the goal of prevention of mental illness aligned for some with calls for immigration restriction, eugenics, and compulsory sterilization, the latter of which was carried out programmatically within institutions in some states. The movement also promoted greater collaboration between psychiatrists, social workers, judges, and teachers to support the mentally ill outside of institutions.[33] The historian Gabriel Mendes describes the mental hygiene movement as "both a medical and political project" that "brought psychiatrists out of asylums and into the broader community, particularly into urban America."[34] Yet, even by the early 1940s, the white-run National Committee for Mental Hygiene, founded in the early twentieth century, did not engage the question of mental hygiene among African Americans and reportedly had no Black participants.[35] Thus, the kind of community work to prevent mental illness promoted by the National Committee for Mental Hygiene and related state organizations did not extend to Black communities. Nevertheless, African Americans chose to engage the mental hygiene movement to provide resources for care outside of state institutions, sometimes doing so in religious contexts.

Rosa A. Kittrell's work advocating for mental hygiene highlights the significance of religious commitment and institutions to the movement for some African Americans. Kittrell was born in 1902 in Henderson, North Carolina, the granddaughter of people who had been enslaved in that area, and the daughter of a farmer and a laundress who valued education for their eight children. Kittrell graduated from the Hampton Institute in Virginia in 1927 and, while in school there, was involved with the YWCA.[36] After graduating, she taught in the primary schools in Henderson before enrolling in the Bishop Tuttle Training School, an Episcopal social work school for African American women connected to Saint Augustine's College in Raleigh that opened in 1925. The Episcopal Church characterized the school as "a national center for the training of young women for Christian leadership in church and community."[37] The two-year curriculum consisted of three broad components: religious education (including the study of biblical literature, church history and organization, missions, sociology, education, and "the psychology of character"), social work (including casework, social research, community organization, and mental hygiene), and home management (home economics and practical nursing, among other topics).[38] One observer of the school wrote, comparing the curriculum of "this wonderful enterprise for the race" to those at white southern social service schools, that, "while the others train in cold, hard, Social Service, the Bishop Tuttle School mixes the religion of the Lord Jesus Christ, and that makes all the difference in the world."[39] After graduating from Bishop Tuttle in 1932, Kittrell took charge of a community center the school sponsored in Raleigh.[40]

While Kittrell had studied mental hygiene as part of Bishop Tuttle's social work curriculum, it was personal experience that turned her into an advocate for expanded access to mental health care in Black communities. She recounted some years later that, following a surgical procedure, she began to feel mental confusion and a disconnection between her mind and body and then experienced "violent spells of vomiting." She tried to return to work at the community center, fearing "the public would think I was crazy," but found herself unable to continue. Finding no physical problem, her doctor had her sent to a hospital in her hometown of Henderson, where she attempted to injure herself and was sedated. Throughout this terrifying six-week experience, Kittrell emphasized, no one talked with her about what she was experiencing, and she was allowed no family visitors. "I felt alone in a world where there were many strange people," she recalled.[41] After her release and relocation for another job to White Plains, New York, just north of New York City, Kittrell entered a cycle of hospitalizations and release. She received treatment that included hydrotherapy and sedation. She reported continued suicidal impulses, which resulted in twenty-one admissions between her hospitalizations in North Carolina and periods of several months at a time in institutions in New York State.[42] Kittrell punctuated her account of her mental health struggles and experiences of hospitalization with the repeated observation that "her people" had not established mechanisms of support for the mentally ill and that the only treatment option was commitment to state hospitals.[43]

Kittrell wrote that her condition improved with treatment for what she described as a glandular disturbance, but she resolved to work to reduce the stigma of mental illness for African Americans, to help create infrastructure to train Black psychiatrists and open options for short-term patient care.[44] "I had a burning desire to do something which would eliminate such trying experiences for others of my race," she wrote. Her interest in advocating from the patient's perspective led her to reread Clifford Beers's autobiography, *A Mind That Found Itself*, in which he described mistreatment in mental hospitals and his work to reform care for the mentally ill, which resulted in the formation of the National Committee for Mental Hygiene. Kittrell wrote to Beers to affirm the continued need for such work. She recalled that, in her letter and subsequent conversations with him, she noted that African Americans had specific mental hygiene needs because, she told him, the Black patient battled in "an alien white world where no opportunity is given for members of his own race to help him."[45] In 1938, with the help of Thomas P. Brennan, a white doctor at the Grasslands Hospital in Valhalla, New York, where she had been treated, she founded the White Plains Mental Hygiene Group. Although she was hesitant at first to trust a white doctor, her experience

ROSA KITTRELL

Figure 6.2. Rosa Kittrell, founder of the
Committee for Mental Hygiene for Negroes,
*Club Dial* (December 1943). Courtesy of the
Woman's Club of White Plains.

with Brennan persuaded her that he had "a real love of all races and a sincere desire to help the mentally ill," and that he was a dedicated advocate for the cause of mental hygiene in Black communities.[46]

The White Plains Mental Hygiene Group became the building block of the National Committee for Mental Hygiene for Negroes, in which physicians from several hospitals staffed by Black doctors participated, including from the psychiatric division of the Tuskegee Veterans Hospital, West Virginia's Lakin State Hospital, Howard University Medical School, and Meharry Medical College.[47] Kittrell served as executive secretary and Brennan as chairman. Over the next several years, Kittrell and Brennan's organization held national meetings and sponsored presentations on topics such as the training of Black psychiatrists, mental health care in the South, and child development.[48] The committee established two primary goals: the creation of a psychopathic hospital connected to a Black medical school to provide opportunities for training in psychiatry for Black doctors, nurses, and social workers, and the development of "regional lay mental hygiene groups."[49] The committee made progress on the latter goal when, in 1940, George C. Branche, a graduate of Boston University Medical School and psychiatrist at the Tuskegee Veterans Hospital, established the Mental Hygiene Society in Tuskegee on the model of the one Kittrell founded in White Plains.[50] In articulating his sense of the need for such groups, Barbadian immigrant Prince P. Barker, a Howard University Medical School graduate and a psychiatrist at the Tuskegee Veterans Hospital, emphasized the large numbers of people "affected with mild mental or nervous disorders" who, if given access to care, could be kept out of institutions. Mental hygiene resources, he argued, would reduce "the fearful social stigma" that led many to hide their needs and exacerbated their mental stress.[51]

Kittrell did not advocate for Christianity as a component of mental hygiene services, but she did see religious groups as important partners for the work of the Committee for Mental Hygiene for Negroes, and the group's work reflects the religious commitments and networks of participants. Frances Harriet Williams, an African American leader in the national YWCA, endorsed the project from its early days in White Plains and expressed hope that improved mental hygiene education would lead to "better relations between white and colored groups."[52] The committee's 1943 meeting, held at the Harlem Young Men's Christian Association, began with the singing of "God Bless America" and an invocation by Rev. Benjamin Richardson of the Abyssinian Baptist Church.[53] Later meetings of the national committee included clergy and hospital chaplains among participants, and Rev. Adam Clayton Powell Jr., Abyssinian's pastor, joined the Advisory Council from the start.[54] Churches and religious groups served as helpful partners for publicizing the mental hygiene movement among African Americans. The White Plains Mental Hygiene group had a theater unit and performed its 1941 production, *The Family Comes Thru*, at several local churches.[55] Brennan appeared on the Wings Over Jordan choir's radio show in 1942 to promote mental hygiene, which resulted in an inquiry from Leah T. Malone, an African American student at Smith College's School for Social Work, about the committee and a request for advice about a placement as a psychiatric social worker.[56]

Two years after the founding of the national committee, Kittrell began to look for financial resources to sustain and expand the work and turned to Black religious leaders for help. Powell suggested that she convene an interracial group of supporters whose endorsement he could use to approach a philanthropic foundation for funding. This plan seems not to have moved beyond the initial stages, however, and Viola W. Bernard, a professor of psychiatry at Columbia University whom Kittrell invited to be part of that group of supporters, evaluated the idea as premature and unrealistic, even as she endorsed the committee's goals.[57] Kittrell also approached George Edmund Haynes, an African American economist and religious leader and the executive secretary of the Department of Race Relations of the Federal Council of Churches, for assistance. Haynes was sympathetic to the project but, given his work on race relations, wondered why Kittrell was organizing a separate committee for African Americans and not working with the National Committee for Mental Hygiene. Viola W. Bernard replied to a query from Haynes that, while a representative of the National Committee for Mental Hygiene had addressed the annual meeting of Kittrell's group in 1943, it had shown no interest in engaging issues related to African Americans.[58] Thus, while Bernard found the plan to solicit financial support from a foundation to be premature, she recognized the need for Kittrell's work. World War II interrupted the work of Kittrell's committee, and following the war, she turned her attention to her local context as the founder and head of a community center. The partnership with African American religious institutions to support the mental health services she envisioned would be developed in Harlem's Lafargue Clinic after the war. Although the Lafargue Clinic was not the result of patient advocacy, as had been the case with the Committee for Mental Hygiene for Negroes, it would bring a national spotlight to community-based mental health care for African Americans.

## "An Experiment in Spiritual Psychiatry"

"One must descend to the basement and move along a confusing maze-like hall to reach it. Twice the passage seems to lead against a blank wall; then at last one enters the brightly lit auditorium. And here, finally, are the social workers at the reception desks; and there, waiting upon the benches rowed beneath the pipes carrying warmth and water to the floors above, are the patients. One sees white-jacketed psychiatrists carrying charts appear and vanish behind screens that form the improvised interviewing cubicles. All is an atmosphere of hurried efficiency; and the concerned faces of the patients are brightened by the friendly smiles and low-pitched voices of the expert workers. One has entered the Lafargue Psychiatric Clinic."[59] This is how the African American novelist and essayist Ralph Ellison described the Lafargue Clinic, promoted by its staff as "a mental hygiene clinic in and for the community of Harlem," which opened in March 1946 in the basement of the parish house of St. Philip's Episcopal Church on 133rd Street.[60] The clinic was the product of a collaboration between unlikely partners, all of whom had faith in the possibility that psychiatry, extended to the masses, could address a range of personal and social issues before they became acute and who viewed Harlem as a neighborhood that could benefit from this work.

Fredric Wertham, a German Jewish immigrant psychiatrist, provided medical expertise and brought professional experience that convinced him that psychiatry could be a social good if access to it were expanded. Wertham had interned at Emil Kraepelin's psychiatric institute in Munich in the 1920s, the period in which Kraepelin's system of classifying mental illness under the rubrics of dementia praecox and manic-depressive psychosis was gaining traction in European and American psychiatry.[61] The historian Gabriel Mendes conjectures that the alignment of Kraepelin's research with social Darwinism, eugenics, and reactionary politics in Germany after World War I influenced Wertham's search, in contrast, for "a place where psychiatry and progressive politics met, where the science of mental health was integrated into a broad effort at social betterment."[62] In the United States, his work at the Phipps Clinic at Johns Hopkins University in Baltimore, as well as at Bellevue Hospital and in other psychiatric services in New York City hospitals, amplified his desire to make psychotherapy accessible to those lacking financial resources and psychiatric institutions in their local communities. His time in Baltimore, where he said he was the only psychiatrist in the city who saw Black patients for private psychotherapy, had impressed upon him how difficult it was for African Americans to obtain psychiatric care.[63] The prohibitive cost of private psychotherapy for poor people also concerned Wertham and, in the African American novelist Richard Wright, he found a partner in making social psychiatry a reality for Black Harlemites in a context open to all regardless of race or wealth.[64] The two had become friends after Wright sent an admiring letter to Wertham following the 1941 publication of Wertham's book *Dark Legend: A Study in Murder*, which Wright found a fascinating psychological study.[65]

Wright brought to the Lafargue Clinic project a deep interest in the psychological effects of racism on African Americans. Born into a sharecropping family in Mississippi, Wright spent time as a child in a Methodist orphanage and with his Seventh-day Adventist relatives, but he never embraced Christianity, either emotionally or intellectually.[66] In 1927, he moved to Chicago, where he began to write, became involved in leftist politics, and joined the Communist Party, which he left in the early 1940s. In 1937, Wright relocated to New York, where he became part of the cultural, political, and social milieu of the Harlem Renaissance. His works in this period were varied, including writing for the Federal Writers Project, magazines, and short stories. His novel *Native Son* (1940), about a young Black man who commits murder, earned critical acclaim for its attention to the psychological damage of racism, fear, and social and economic marginalization in urban contexts.

His interest in broadening access to psychotherapy for African Americans struggling against the harms of racism and oppression may also have stemmed from his being disqualified for military service in 1944. Wright responded to his draft notice with a letter objecting to racial segregation in the military, arguing that "to serve in our armed forces is to fight in defense of such a system and to give my approval to it."[67] He noted that, should he be drafted, he would serve "passively," following orders but hoping that any efforts in support of continued segregation in which he was compelled to participate would fail.[68] The military classified Wright as 4F and not qualified for service, characterizing him as suffering from "psychoneurosis, severe, psychiatric rejection" and calling for additional "psychiatric and social investigation" at the local draft board where he had registered. An FBI agent investigating Wright's Communist Party affiliation summarized the military's decision as grounded in the local draft board's perception "that his interest in the problem of the Negro has become almost an obsession and it was said that he apparently overlooks the fact that his own rise to success refutes many of his own statements regarding the impossibility of the Negro's improving his personal position."[69] Wright's engagement of broad social factors shaping and limiting African Americans' opportunities countered the military's argument that his individual achievements meant that "the problem of the Negro" was no longer urgent. Moreover, the draft board's idea that Wright's concern about racial discrimination constituted a psychological problem highlights the kind of historical damage the field of psychiatry had done to African Americans that he and others sought to rectify.

Like Black psychiatrists and social scientists of the period, Wright was interested in the urban environment as a complex social and psychological factor in modern Black life, and he engaged it in both his fiction and his nonfiction writing, including in his *Twelve Million Black Voices* (1941), with images from the Farm Security Administration's photographic project.[70] *Twelve Million Black Voices* drew on works by Black social scientists, including E. Franklin Frazier, Ira De Augustine Reid, and Wright's friend Horace Cayton, who would go on to coauthor, with St. Clair Drake, the influential *Black Metropolis: A Study of Negro Life in a Northern City.* In a chapter titled "Death on the City Pavements," Wright discussed the psychological toll taken on the millions "who had had our personalities blasted with two hundred years of slavery" and the challenges of the transition from the rural South to the urban North, with its crowded, expensive, and dilapidated apartments, limited employment opportunities, and crime and disease.[71] In turning to the culture and joy that sustained urban Black communities, Wright included churches as "centers of social and community life" and contended that "it is only when we are within the walls of our churches that we are wholly ourselves, that we keep alive a sense of our personalities in relation to the total world in which we live, that we maintain a quiet and constant communion with all that is deepest within us."[72] He noted the prominent role of churches in the lives of Black women, arguing that "because their orbit of life is narrow—from the kitchenette to the white folk's kitchen and back home again—they love the church more than do our men, who find a large measure of the expression of their lives in the mills and factories."[73] In his view, many of these women were drawn to the intimate worlds of small storefront churches as a means to "retain the ardent religious emotionalism of which they are so fond."[74] As the religious studies scholar Josef Sorett argues, despite Wright's Marxist orientation and the fact that he was not himself religious, he "acknowledged the primary role of institutional Afro-Protestantism not only in addressing the spiritual appetites of black Harlem but in tending to its corporeal needs as well."[75]

Wright's recognition of the spiritual and social significance of Black churches in general, and in Harlem in particular, contextualizes how he and Wertham came to locate their free psychiatric clinic in the parish house basement of an Episcopal church in Harlem. And, indeed, Shelton Hale Bishop, the rector of St. Philip's Episcopal, welcomed the project when Wright approached him. A graduate of Columbia University and General Theological Seminary of the Episcopal Church, Bishop was a New Yorker and the son of Hutchens Chew Bishop, the first Black graduate of General Theological Seminary and a member of the National Association for the Advancement of Colored People's Board of Directors. Shelton Hale succeeded his father as rector of St. Philip's in 1933 and, in his ministry, expressed special concern for Harlem's young people and the desire to make the church a place that could shield them from crime and violence. The parish provided recreation in the Community Center, and Bishop himself negotiated a truce between neighborhood gangs to make the streets safer.[76] The opportunity for St. Philip's to support the Lafargue Clinic came in the wake of the 1943 police shooting of a Black soldier in a conflict over a woman's arrest and subsequent violence and property destruction in Harlem. Neighborhood clergy like Adam Clayton Powell Jr. of Abyssinian Baptist Church argued that the response of some Black Harlemites to the wounding of the soldier was grounded in "the blind, smoldering and unorganized . . . resentment against jim crow treatment of Negro men in the Armed Forces and the unusual high rents and cost of living forced upon Negroes in Harlem."[77] In the aftermath of the violence, the City-Wide Citizens' Committee on Harlem, an interracial, interfaith civic action group, included access to psychological services, particularly for young people, as one element of a broad response to improve social and economic conditions in Harlem.[78] Bishop's interest in preventing juvenile delinquency and supporting the neighborhood's youth made the prospect of offering counseling and social work services for adults and children appealing in this context.

Bishop's commitment to making psychiatry accessible beyond the space of psychiatric hospitals may also have had roots in two family crises. In the late 1920s and early 1930s, Bishop and his wife, Eloise Carey

Bishop, went through a fractious and public separation and child custody battle. Eloise, a teacher who had graduated from Northwestern University and the Chicago Normal School, was the daughter of Archibald J. Carey, a bishop in the AME Church in Chicago. The Black press had touted the couple's 1919 marriage as a high-society match. Shelton was then pastoring a church in Pittsburgh, and Eloise reportedly did not wish to move to New York when Shelton joined his father in ministry at St. Philip's, but did so reluctantly.[79] In 1929, Eloise took a leave from her teaching position and went to family in Chicago with the couple's three children, a move that prompted considerable speculation in the Black press about the state of the couple's marriage.[80] The *Pittsburgh Courier* reported that, according to family friends, "it is said that Mrs. Bishop is suffering from a nervous disorder, and that she had consulted different specialists in psychiatry, who have advised that she take treatments which might be necessary for a period of two years for her to become completely cured." These family friends characterized Shelton as hoping his wife would seek treatment, to no avail, but Eloise's perspective did not receive similar press attention.[81] Although they remained married, the Bishops separated, and the ensuing court battle for custody of the couple's children was acrimonious, with charges of cruelty levied by both parties.[82] Where Bishop's wife refused psychiatric treatment, he became familiar with institutional care when his younger sister, Estelle "Gussie" Booth, was hospitalized at Creedmoor State Hospital in Queens and died there in 1942.[83] It is possible that Bishop's belief that his wife had refused needed psychiatric care because the only available treatment options were so extreme, like those his sister experienced years later, motivated his collaboration with Wright and Wertham to host the Lafargue Clinic in the St. Philip's parish house.

## Human Happiness and Social Progress

In the winter of 1946, the newsletter of St. Philip's Episcopal Church carried an item announcing the birth of "a fine new child" in the form a mental clinic that would help to address the lack of resources for psychiatric treatment in the community and that represented "one more attempt on the part of this Parish to meet community needs in a very specific way." The newsletter informed parishioners that the clinic had been established at the church through a request by the famous novelist Richard Wright for Bishop's support; that the eminent Dr. Fredric Wertham headed it; and that Dr. Hilde Lachmann-Mosse, Wertham's colleague at Queens General Hospital, would supervise staff and work at the clinic. Mosse was from a prominent German Jewish family and had begun her medical education in Germany before the rise of the Nazis forced her family to flee to Switzerland, where she completed her degree. She arrived in New York in 1938 and became an important figure in child psychiatry in the city, working with Viola W. Bernard and Kenneth and Mamie Clark, the African American psychologists whose Northside Center for Child Development was a key site for research supporting the plaintiffs in the *Brown v. Board of Education* school desegregation case.[84] A brochure for the clinic informed prospective clients that it had been named after Paul Lafargue, a Cuban-born "physician, philosopher, and social reformer . . . of Negro parentage, on his father's side," and that "more than any other scientific writer on social subjects, he gave social progress meaning in terms of human happiness."[85] The clinic's board consisted of Wertham, Wright, and Bishop, the three main organizers, as well as two Black Harlem professionals, Earl Brown, a journalist and New York City council member, and Marion Pettiford Hernandez, a registered nurse and graduate of New York's Lincoln School for Nurses. Hernandez studied public health nursing at Columbia's Teachers College and had been the first African American nursing supervisor at the Henry Street Settlement. When she joined Lafargue's board, she worked at Planned Parenthood's Hannah Stone Center in Harlem. Brown was the son of a Baptist minister, and Hernandez was a member of St. Philip's, so both brought to the project a sense of religious and social mission.[86]

The clinic was open to the community for two hours on Tuesday and Friday evenings and free of charge, but clients who could afford to do so were asked to pay twenty-five cents or fifty cents if a staff member needed to visit court on the patient's behalf.[87] Monetary donations also supported the clinic, and both individuals and groups gave, as in the case of a contribution from Mary Jane Ward, the author of *The Snake Pit*, a bestselling novel about mental hospitals, and donations from Columbia University's Rho Chapter of the historically Black Delta Sigma Theta sorority.[88] Lafargue did not maintain data about patients' race or religion, but the limited data reported from the first three years indicate that the majority of patients were Black, and generally more men than women signed on as new patients each month. This was the case, in part, because the clinic sought and received authorization by the Veterans Administration to offer treatment to military veterans.[89] Lafargue's leaders announced special interest in "the behavior problems of children" because of the founders' concerns about juvenile delinquency, and although adults outnumbered them, children were always represented among the patients.[90] The clinic's space in the basement of the parish house consisted at first of two rooms but expanded to take up the entire basement, and counselors met with patients behind screens that afforded some privacy from other patients in counseling and those waiting to be seen.[91] The journalist Robert Bendiner, who wrote a profile of the clinic in 1948, described an informal and welcoming atmosphere in the basement, with children playing, adults in casual conversation, and a spirit of comradery and encouragement among the patients.[92] This environment was the leaders' ideal as put forth in an organizational document informing volunteers that "the atmosphere of the clinic should always be a positive psychotherapeutic one, with complete absence of hurry, crowding, tension, and unprofessional activities such as reading newspapers or loud discussion standing up or rushing around. There should ways be an open space for new persons coming in or new things happening."[93]

Doctors, nurses, medical and psychology students, psychiatric social workers, teachers, and office workers volunteered their time to staff the clinic, which was organized by groups with a psychiatrist or psychotherapist leading each team.[94] For many of the African American volunteers, participation in the clinic's work connected with efforts in which they had been engaged in other arenas of life and provided new or additional professional opportunities. June Jackson Christmas, who received her MD degree in psychiatry from Boston University in 1949, volunteered at Lafargue on Tuesday evenings during her internship at Queens General Hospital in 1949 and 1950, doing psychiatric interviewing, intake work, and some counseling. Christmas, one of the first three Black graduates of Vassar College, was motivated to apply to that college because of work Rev. James H. Robinson, then pastor of the Church of the Master in Harlem, had been doing to get Vassar to admit Black women. Christmas heard about his efforts through her Sunday school teacher at Christ Church in Cambridge, Massachusetts, where she and her family were members. Volunteering at a psychiatric clinic hosted by an Episcopal Church in an underserved African American neighborhood brought together Christmas's commitments to civil rights, psychiatry, and religion.[95] Another African American volunteer, a public schoolteacher in Brooklyn with a bachelor of arts degree in psychology from Hunter College, worked one or two nights a week in the clinic while she finished a master of arts degree at the City College of New York. She had learned of the clinic from members of her Delta Sigma Theta sorority who were also members of St. Philip's and had organized a fundraising campaign for Lafargue. Hilde Mosse wrote letters of recommendation for several of her applications for internships, and the volunteer contributed to one of Wertham's studies of the impact of racial integration on schoolchildren in Delaware.[96] White volunteers contributed as secretaries, teachers, and social workers, in addition to accounting for most of the psychiatric volunteers. Many, like Wertham and Mosse, were immigrants or children of immigrants.[97] The clinic's leadership was attentive to racial attitudes among white volunteers, ready to dismiss anyone who believed that Black staff "got all the breaks" because of racial preference rather than advancing at the clinic because of their experience and abilities. An unattributed note on this topic held up as an example of deserved achievement the Black psychiatrist André Tweed, born in New York City to immigrants from St. Croix, a graduate of Howard University medical school, and a member of the staff at Queens General Hospital.[98]

Work at Lafargue was focused on extending access to psychotherapy to Black patients who were limited in finding therapists because white practitioners did not take them as clients and because of the small number of Black therapists. Clinic leadership underscored this commitment to the volunteers and emphasized that the provision of psychotherapeutic care would not be limited to psychiatrists. "The clinic is entirely oriented to psychotherapy, to all the different forms of psychotherapy," an organizational document asserted. "Every staff member with the exception of the clerical workers should get instruction in psychotherapy on all different levels, even on the lowest such as counseling."[99] Religion was not an overt component of the therapeutic care offered at Lafargue, despite the clinic's location in St. Philip's Parish House basement, the religious commitments of many of the volunteers, and the fact that Bishop referred parishioners to the clinic. The case form used for patients asked the counseling staff to report on the results of a physical examination and mental tests, including several kinds of intelligence tests; memory, reading, and mental alertness tests; and Rorschach "projective technique" tests. In addition, the staff took a case history, soliciting information about the patient's medical, family, marital, educational, and employment history and assessing the patient's mood, all aimed at a diagnosis and recommendation for treatment.[100]

There were no questions about religion in the basic outline of topics for case histories at Lafargue, but staff could tailor the outline, and it seems likely that if religion arose as a factor in discussion with a patient, it would be pursued.[101] Even if religion did become a topic in the patient's case history, staff would have been encouraged to evaluate its influence quite differently from how earlier generations of psychiatrists had attended to the role of religion in Black mental health. Lafargue's approach was grounded in valuing what the historian Dennis Doyle characterizes as the clinic's "universal mind assumption," or the "premise that race had no intrinsic impact on the development of the human personality" and that "each individual psyche developed and operated along the same universally human set of psychodynamic principles, no matter the color of the body in which that psyche formed."[102] At the same time, Wertham was interested in mental disturbances "induced by the special problems of a segregated minority."[103] In this regard, the therapeutic emphasis was on helping the patient understand that they bore no responsibility for the discrimination they experienced, with some therapists reportedly framing racial discrimination as grounded primarily in economic exploitation. Others, notably André Tweed, presented to his patients models of African Americans who succeeded "in spite of the blocks put in their path by a hostile society."[104] In one case noted by the journalist Robert Bendiner, a woman attempted suicide after being forced by cramped living space to send her three children to live elsewhere. Bendiner described her as "a schizophrenic, she hears voices, particularly those of neighbors plotting to use voodoo on her and poison her water."[105] Earlier white psychiatrists like South Carolina State Hospital superintendent J. W. Babcock or the St. Elizabeths Hospital psychiatrist Arrah Evarts might have attributed her paranoia and mention of "voodoo" to an innate racial superstition. At Lafargue, the staff viewed her illness as resulting from having been "stimulated beyond the bounds of safety by the pressures of the community," namely, economic exploitation and discrimination.[106]

Because the late nineteenth-century and early twentieth-century psychiatric claim that African American religious beliefs or practices served as precipitating factors in the development of mental illness was no longer prominent in the field's theoretical and diagnostic landscape, the appearance in post–World War II literature of analysis of Black religion as pathological brought a critical backlash from Black psychiatrists and psychotherapists. As the historian Dennis Doyle shows, the publication of Columbia University psychiatrists Abram Kardiner and Lionel Ovesey's *The Mark of Oppression: A Psychosocial Study of the American Negro* (1951), based on twenty-five cases of Black residents of Harlem, became a flash point for many psychiatrists who subscribed to a universalist understanding of the human psyche.[107] Where universalists rejected biological arguments about racial psychology and insisted on a common human personality, Kardiner and Ovesey theorized the existence of a "basic Negro personality," not biologically based but shaped in the American context as a result of social discrimination.[108] While this understanding shares with the universalists' approach a recognition of the impact of racism on Black mental health, Kardiner and Ovesey grounded their view of "Negro personality" in racialized cultural arguments. As Doyle explains, in earlier work Kardiner "argued that each culture produced a specific type of human psyche . . . created to best fit that culture." Ethnopsychiatrists like Kardiner "held that the same basic human set of intrapsychic forces could produce a distinct psychic type when contained within a non-white, non-western body."[109]

When Kardiner turned his attention to "the effects of caste and class on [Negro] personality," he, along with his collaborator Ovesey, thought that the findings could "be used to explain other aspects of Negro social life, such as social cohesion, religion, marriage, crime, etc."[110] Negro personality, according to Kardiner and Ovesey, was formed from slavery by requiring forcible accommodation "to the conditions the white man imposes on him" and marked by the "degradation of self-esteem."[111] They held up "the American white man" as the standard for evaluation of Negro personality, contending that "both he and the Negro live under similar cultural conditions with the exception of a few easily identifiable variables existing for the Negro only," with the oppression of the American racial caste system being one.[112] Enumerating core "American" values of success, liberty, and "fair play," the authors did note white Americans' rationalizations as they touted these values yet had enslaved, and now segregated and oppressed, Black Americans. Nevertheless, Kardiner and Ovesey positioned white community life as the standard for evaluating "Negro adaptation," without naming the many social and economic advantages that supported white American families.[113]

Discussion of religion in African American life appears in some of the case histories across Kardiner and Ovesey's categories of lower-, middle-, and upper-class subjects. The authors describe the religious backgrounds and childhoods of many subjects and the comfort religion provided for some in adulthood amid hardship. This was so in the case of a "lower class" woman who became Catholic after being sent to a Catholic institution for "wayward girls" and who struggled with same-sex desire. She reportedly asserted faith that "some day God will make it all right" and had confidence that her sins would be forgiven.[114] Although none of the subjects presented in the study were members of Father Divine's Peace Mission, the authors devoted most of the section on religion in the chapter on "the expressions of Negro personality" to the group. Kardiner and Ovesey claim to have conducted extensive interviews with two female members with "schizoid personalities," and the authors express some admiration for how the regulated life within the movement and these women's sense of pride in belonging helped "keep their pathological symptoms under control."[115] In their view, the role of Peace Mission membership in increasing low self-esteem—"the Negro's most vulnerable psychological handicap"— and communal living's ability to relieve economic anxiety accounted for Divine's appeal.[116] But they considered the group, which for them stood out from among the broader group of "lower-class religious cults" because of its success and relative longevity, to offer only "illusory" gain.[117] On the role of religion in African American life in general, they concluded, "Religion does not answer their needs, hence they are constant prey to new religious adventurers. We have seen little evidence of genuine religiosity among Negroes. They have invented no religion of their own. The one that comes closest to it, that of Father Divine, encourages a grotesque flight into unreality by the crude device of denying the real world and creating an artificial one."[118]

Black psychiatrists' critiques of *The Mark of Oppression* focused primarily on the small sample size of twenty-five Black New Yorkers, the use of white middle-class men as the control group, and the assertion of the existence of a "basic Negro personality." On the latter point, Prince P. Barker, the chief of the neuropsychiatric service at Tuskegee Veterans Hospital and a member of Rosa Kittrell's National Committee for Mental Hygiene for Negroes, contributed to a roundtable on the book that was published in the *Journal of the National Medical Association*. Barker wrote that "racial personality, basic or otherwise, is probably as erroneous an assumption as racial vulnerability or immunity to disease. This has been disproved for the Negro."[119] Perhaps most critical was Charles W. Collins, a psychotherapist who had charge of a clinical team at Lafargue.[120] It was Collins's review of Kardiner and Ovesey's work in the *Journal of the National Medical Association* that had occasioned the roundtable discussion, and his analysis focused on the core criticisms regarding sample size, control group, and conclusions. He also called attention to confusing analysis regarding religion and race in Kardiner and Ovesey's study. In their discussion of S.A., a fifteen-year-old boy struggling in school and registering an attitude of hopelessness, the researchers insisted, despite S.A.'s denial, that "his self-esteem is further deflated by his race and his color."[121] When asked to name "the big negro names today," the fact that he struggled and finally listed sports figures as positive role models and Father Divine as a negative one, led Kardiner and Ovesey to conclude that S.A. suffered from "unconscious rejection of Negro-identification.[122] That S.A. denigrated Divine as a "cult leader" pretending to be God, just as the authors themselves did in writing about the religious leader, did not strike the researchers as evidence of the boy's independent evaluation of religious groups but as "the incorporation of the white man as ideal."[123] For his part, Collins emphasized that, more than anything, the inability of a Black boy to name Black heroes served as an indictment of "the school system which deliberately avoids any reference to negro heroes."[124]

African American critics of *The Mark of Oppression* did not generally highlight the presence of religion as part of Kardiner and Ovesey's discussion of expressions of "Negro personality." For them, its appearance in the widely read and controversial study represented something of a return to older ways of viewing African American religion as a pathological expression of a damaged culture. But Collins and other staff at Lafargue had moved away from this model, emphasizing a universal understanding of personality development and investing in social psychiatry as a key tool for facilitating social change. James H. Robinson, Rosa Kittrell, Richard Wright, Fredric Wertham, and other Lafargue staff agreed with Kardiner and Ovesey's insistence that the conditions of oppression that white people set in American society needed to be changed for the benefit of Black mental health. They were likely to have disagreed with the book's stark conclusion that "Negro self-esteem cannot be retrieved, nor Negro self-hatred destroyed, as long as the status is quo," however, because of its denial of any sources of individual or groups self-esteem not connected to white Americans.[125] Indeed, while at the Columbia Psychoanalytic Center as the first Black trainee after graduating from the College of Physicians and Surgeons, the psychiatrist and psychoanalyst Margaret Morgan Lawrence declined an offer from Kardiner to serve as a research assistant for *The Mark of Oppression.* Kardiner had wanted Lawrence, who had grown up in Vicksburg, Mississippi, the daughter of an Episcopal priest, to interview African Americans in the South. Sara Lawrence Lightfoot, Lawrence's daughter and biographer, wrote that her mother was "suspicious of his perspective and his methods, and worried that in his research Negroes might be portrayed as powerless and inarticulate" and saw the request as seeking legitimation from having a Black research assistant.[126] African American clergy, psychiatrists, and social workers advocating for new approaches to mental health care in this period would likely have rejected the absolute character of Kardiner and Ovesey's idea of "Negro self-hatred," knowing well the many resources, including religious ones, within Black communities that had long supported Black self-esteem beyond the ken of white researchers.

These activists fought for greater access to psychotherapy not out of a view of a profoundly damaged "Negro personality" but because they, in Ralph Ellison's words, had faith in the benefits of providing a Black patient with an "insight into the relation between his problems and his environment, and out of this understanding the will to endure in a hostile world."[127] Shelton Hale Bishop, whose support enabled Lafargue's opening in St. Philip's space in the heart of Harlem, saw the endeavor as connected to the church's religious mission, commenting that "the clinic is an invaluable source to my ministry in the parish. It is of great value to the entire community."[128] The Lafargue clinic closed in 1958 with Bishop's retirement, the inability of the leadership to secure state funding to continue the work, and Bishop's successor's broadening of the scope of health services supported at the parish.[129] Despite the clinic's relatively short life span, it offered services that derived, in part, from religious commitments but refused the long-standing white psychiatric view of African American religion as contributing to mental disorders. Similarly, Rosa Kittrell's campaign for mental hygiene services within Black communities and expanding access to psychiatric training for Black doctors drew on the resources and support of religious institutions. As these activists and professionals asserted and acted on their confidence that new approaches to psychiatry could help African Americans respond to challenging social conditions, many the unique result of American racism, they sought to undo the damage wrought by the long history of pathologizing African American religious expressions.

# Conclusion

George W. Bennett was eager to settle into life in Harlem after having served twenty-three years of a thirty-five-year sentence in New York State prisons.[1] Bennett's sentence for burglary was longer than what was customary for this crime because of a prior conviction in Pennsylvania for assault. Born in Edenton, North Carolina, in 1898, Bennett went to school in Edenton and Elizabeth City; served in the army in South Carolina during World War I; lived in Philadelphia, where he made his living gambling; and arrived in Harlem in 1931. His time in the neighborhood was short, however, as he was arrested and sent to Sing Sing prison in 1932. By his return to Harlem in 1955, he had spent time in Dannemora State Hospital, Clinton State Prison (known as "Little Siberia"), and Attica, in addition to Sing Sing. During his long incarceration, Bennett had become alienated from his family but reconnected with his youngest daughter upon release and moved into her Harlem apartment. It was not really the neighborhood or city life that drew him, or even the chance to be with family again. Bennett was focused singularly on the opportunity freedom provided to complete the book he had been writing, excited that he could distribute his work without the censorship that had characterized his life in prison. His aim was to spread the message God had commissioned him to deliver. He announced in one of his treatises: "I George, as known by the knowledge of men, but I by the wisdom of God, of the revelation of Jesus Christ has been called and ordained of God by the audible state of the Holy Ghost as His Apostle King of Truth, of all the present world of man. As King of Truth, God has given me the wisdom and the task to write, preach and teach the perfect road to the full reality of his being in the only truth in the life which is eternal within the Spirit of His being."[2]

Bennett was raised in a Christian family and a household in which "the Bible and other religious literature were the only reading material." "These people talked Bible and lived Bible from morning 'til night," he recalled. "My father was a great Bible man, and he believed everything within it was true from God and Jesus Christ."[3] He followed his father into the Methodist Church and at age twelve went to the mourner's bench at a revival to confess his sins, experienced conversion, and was baptized into the Baptist church. He reported that "these religious experiences only strengthened my conscience of wrong doing but did not stop me from doing wrong," particularly gambling, which would consume his attention for many years.[4] It was not only the lure of gambling that complicated his relationship to Christianity in his youth. Learning about slavery from the people around him who had lived through it, and his own experiences of white people's racism, raised profound questions for him. He refused to use his middle name of Washington when he learned that the president after whom he was named had enslaved people. Bennett wrote, "For I grew up to think that the institution of slavery was the greatest evil on earth, and a disgrace to God and man, especially in a so-called Christian society."[5] He imagined that Africans, the creators of civilization, had become "weak in their thinking over a long period of time," and that this had allowed white people "to make us slaves, and take our wealth and heritage away from us."[6] But his father had taught him pride in Blackness because this was how God had created them, and he dreamed of Africa and Black self-rule, his thinking enlivened by Marcus Garvey's program of race unity instead of what Bennett characterized as "begging to be accepted" and relying on "the goodwill of religious people" to solve racial problems.[7]

For Bennett, the failure of both white and Black clergy to preach forcefully against segregation constituted the most profound sign of the absence of true religion in American Christianity. If the God of this Christianity allowed the evil of segregation on earth, he mused, then the same fate would await him in heaven. "I had thought that the doctrine of a true God, that His members would reflect that truth in the earth with all mankind, without respect to persons," he wrote.[8] Although he had "got religion," was baptized, and joined the church, Bennett found American Christianity in theology and practice wanting. He concluded that "the teaching and the practice of religion is only useful to keep order in the society of men. But it does not make man any better morally or justly."[9] When he was admitted to Sing Sing, he saw the prison chaplain as part of the intake process and was offended when the chaplain gave him a New Testament. "It was not that I did not believe in God and Christ and everything in the Scriptures," he wrote, "but it was the resentment that I had for the cruel people who had treated me so unjustly. They professed to be good Christians but did not obey the Bible themselves."[10] Given his rejection of religion, Bennett's coming to understand himself as "God's Apostle King of Truth" was an unlikely outcome of his time in prison, but such spiritual transformations have been known to happen. Perhaps more unexpected was that this spiritual transformation would lead him to develop a theological and racial critique of psychiatry.

In his autobiography, Bennett writes of a process of dramatic awakening in 1936 that began with the Bible. An avid reader of classics, philosophy, and history—particularly the popular Black history of J. A. Rogers—he said that had not read the Bible once since his incarceration, but he recounted how, one day, "a mind led me to read the Master's sermon on the Mount." He became focused on divine forgiveness and on the command to love one's neighbor, undertaking prayer and contemplation to discern "the truth of God."[11] Bennett wrote that, one morning, "within my consciousness there was established a brightness which loomed larger than the entire elements of the universe." He felt surrounded by Eternity and reported that he was gifted with the ability to "see this Eternal state of being within everything that existed, but no man knew anything about it."[12] Sometime later he heard the voice of the Holy Spirit and had a vision of the day of judgment, after which the voice of God told him, "I have called you to be my King of truth, and the wise interpreter of all being by the knowledge of life and death: The knowledge of all truth from the knowledge of all err. And you shall write in a book every word of which you shall receive of me."[13] Bennett embraced this commission and reported it to the warden, hoping he would receive support to write the book, as God had commanded him. Bennett did not receive support, and his communication with the warden resulted in an examination by a psychiatrist and transfer to the Dannemora State Hospital for the Criminal Insane.[14] During his nine years in the hospital, he labored to fulfill his mission.

Bennett described the hospital as a brutal place, surpassing "the lowest depths of human misery and degradation" he had ever seen, but he also found it more conducive to writing his book because of the absence of the kind of censorship he had experienced at Sing Sing. Moreover, he found "that in this place no one payed [sic] any attention to what a man writes, because it is already assumed that he is only writing some sort of delusions which brought him here."[15] It is possible that he was diagnosed with dementia praecox or schizophrenia, as he wrote about both in his notes and treatise.[16] Bennett refused the diagnosis, writing that "anyone who is born of God, he nor she can never go mad, as in the cases where so-called Christians of the world go mad. But when a person is born of God, in reality of truth, he cannot go mad because he is born by the immortal Mind in God which is the only sane and perfect Mind in all of being."[17] He understood his divine mandate to be "to lead all mankind into the wisdom of God" and, through his book, to help people "come into the Eternal and perfect state of Mind and God."[18] Psychiatrists offered no true wisdom or insight into human being or the wisdom or mentality of God, Bennett insisted. In the perfect state, he taught, there would be no classification of insanity according to diagnoses of dementia praecox and schizophrenia or "predicting how each type will behave."[19] Moreover, he asked, what could "the psychological illusions of science" offer when it deemed sane the very people who oppressed, segregated, and lynched and "professes to determine the general characteristics of a person by one's physical characteristics?"[20] In his view, the damage wrought on Black people by race scientists damned scientific claims to knowledge. Indeed, he argued, "this opinion of racial superior [sic] is madness, but I have never heard an American psychologist, psychiatrist, preacher or anyone else confirm this truth. This is because the world has no psychologist, preachers or of any professions by the wisdom of God, by the revelation of Jesus Christ who was the greatest psychologist and of all being that the world will ever know."[21]

Bennett's early life in North Carolina and his migration to New York City, period of commitment to Dannemora State Hospital, and return to Harlem to spread his religious teachings span the arc of the history this book has traced. He grew up around people, including his grandparents, who had survived "the evils of slavery" and was deeply affected by knowledge of what the formerly enslaved had endured to create lives, families, and communities after slavery.[22] This was also the period in which southern white psychiatrists produced theories asserting Black people's psychological unfitness for the challenges of freedom and promoting racialized ideas about religious excitement as a precipitating factor for insanity. The religious world of Bennett's youth in North Carolina included two central components of white psychiatrists' conceptions of racialized religious excitement: "superstition" and "emotionalism." Bennett wrote of his only religious disagreement with his father over his father's claim to be able to see "spooks in all shapes and forms" who would "emerge as shadows" at night and who others could not see.[23] Bennett was initially afraid of the spooks but eventually reasoned that they could not be real. Nevertheless, his sense that most people in his community were attentive to the presence of specters of ancestors, spirits, or witches shows the influence of the Black supernaturalism white psychiatrists would frame as indicative of the superstitious disposition of the race with the potential to precipitate mental illness. He experienced the emotion of revivals, describing the minister's dramatic preaching of the classic "hell-bound train" sermon, which had the church "rocking with people shouting and weeping" and that motivated his own conversion.[24] This type of religious enthusiasm white psychiatrists also racialized and incorporated into theories of the role of religion in mental illness among African Americans in the late nineteenth and early twentieth centuries.

Bennett's migration to Harlem in the 1930s coincided with social and religious changes in Black life, including the emergence of new religious movements like Father Divine's Peace Mission, that responded to the conditions of Black urban life during the Depression. Psychiatrists and social scientists examining the appeal of these religious movements charted new approaches to interpreting the relationship of religion to mental illness. Black social scientists and psychiatrists invested in dismantling racial explanations for mental illness emphasized consideration of the kind of financial and social struggles Bennett and many other Black migrants faced in this period. His visionary religious experience and spiritual transformation that led to his transfer from prison to the state hospital for the criminally insane was like those of many African Americans committed to state hospitals for the insane across the country and whose doctors connected Black religion to their diagnoses of dementia praecox. When he returned to Harlem in 1955, the Lafargue Clinic was operating just a few blocks from where he would attempt to establish the King's Church of God. On a leaflet with a list of vital questions for which his church would provide answers, Bennett included the question "Are Psychiatry, Psychology and Psychoanalyze Sciences?"[25] Given his refusal of a psychiatric diagnosis and his religious critique of the medical specialty, the faith Lafargue's staff and patients had placed in a reformed and universal psychiatry would not have satisfied Bennett. He had a different mission from their goal of expanding access to psychiatric care.

Bennett's autobiography and religious writings offer uncommon insight into the perspective of someone diagnosed with a mental illness psychiatrists attributed to religious causes or saw manifested in religious forms. His critique of psychiatry was at once unverifiable beyond his own religious and visionary world—grounded in the claim that God had bestowed upon him the wisdom to understand that there is no insanity in the perfect state—and profoundly material in its highlighting of how psychiatry contributed to race science and the pathologizing of Black life and religious culture. The real madness, according to Bennett, came from the idea of white racial superiority and the practices of racism that stemmed from such an idea. In his life after commitment and prison, Bennett continued to hone his message, focusing more on establishing the King's Church of God than on critique of science and psychiatry. Nevertheless, he discussed psychiatry as a racial and spiritual problem in his autobiography and in his religious treatises. Within the Black communities of Norfolk, Virginia, where he relocated for a time to complete his books, and Harlem, Bennett was not entirely marginal to public life. There were notices in the Black press about the publication of his "interesting account of his life" and a recommendation to read his second book, "'The Meaning of Eternal Life,' which deals with God, faith, and religion in light of his own personal experience."[26] And when he inaugurated a radio broadcast in New York City, the *Amsterdam News* columnist Les Matthews noted it in his column.[27] In the 1960s and 1970s, Bennett placed ads in the *Amsterdam News* for his broadcast, one featuring a photograph of him in clerical attire, a collar, and a black biretta on his head.[28] It seems that for many around him, Bennett's excitement about conveying his religious message registered differently from the "religious excitement" late nineteenth-century white psychiatrists had racialized as Black and pathologized. He found an audience for his diagnosis of racism and psychiatry as the true madness and people who engaged his insistence on seeking different sources of knowledge than the white American Protestant scientific.[29]

This book has explored ideas about religion in late nineteenth-century and early twentieth-century psychiatric theory of the nature of the Black mind and the social, political, and medical impact of racialized conceptions of religious excitement and its legacies. Much has changed in American psychiatry since the 1950s, from expanded and more detailed diagnostic systems in the several editions of the *Diagnostic and Statistical Manual of Mental Disorders* to the emergence of pharmaceutical treatments. Since the 1970s, the closures of mental hospitals and the process of deinstitutionalization, coinciding with the rise of mass incarceration, have made America's jails and prisons the sites where significant numbers of mentally ill people are housed, generally without adequate treatment.[30] As the historian Jonathan Metzl has shown, these changes in theory and shifting sites and approaches to treatment have not necessarily diminished the role of racial thinking in psychiatry. He writes in his work about the racialization of schizophrenia as a Black disease, "To a remarkable extent, anxieties about racial difference shape diagnostic criteria, health-care politics, medical and popular attitudes about mentally ill persons, the structures of treatment facilities, and, ultimately, the conversations that take place there within."[31]

As we have seen, popular, political, and medical ideas about the nature of Black religious life—superstitious, emotional, excessive, irrational—have contributed powerfully to white Americans' understandings of racial difference across the decades after the end of slavery through the mid-twentieth century. Engaging this history reveals some of the material consequences of the psychiatric pathologizing of Black religion for African Americans in the Jim Crow era, including in institutionalization under the umbrella of "religious excitement." The work of scholars, journalists, and activists to uncover the histories of medical racism in the United States and seek avenues for repair has highlighted racial disparities in health outcomes and identified sources of suspicion among African Americans of American medicine. It is my hope that charting the shape of these psychiatric discourses and attending to how they contributed to the experiences of Black people in American courts, hospitals, and communities will offer tools for thinking about the afterlives of racialized religious excitement in American culture. Indeed, just as the structures that have perpetuated racial disparities in the care and treatment of Americans' bodies have persisted over time, albeit in ever-changing ways, so too have religiously inflected racialized conceptions of mental normalcy endured and shaped approaches to mind and body.

The rise of "excited delirium" in the 1980s as a cause of death listed in medical examiners' records and as a police justification for use of force resonates with the "excessive religious excitement" of the nineteenth century, and its deployment illuminates the power of entanglements of religion and race in American medical discourse and practice. Police and medical promoters of "excited delirium" describe it as an agitated, aggressive state of incoherence, often accompanied by extreme strength, and have claimed that it causes death in combination with drug use and restraint or the use of a taser. Police and medical examiners have mobilized it most commonly in connection with the deaths of Black men. The medical framework that designates excited delirium a neuropsychiatric syndrome obscures the role of racialized ideas about religion in its development and deployment. The anthropologist Aisha M. Beliso-De Jesús demonstrates that "excited delirium" as a cause of death emerged from the policing of the Afro-Cuban religion Santería in the United States, continuing the long history of pathologizing Africana religions as superstition and potentially promoting mental illness.[32] This diagnosis appeared in the case of the 2021 killing of Elijah McClain, whom Aurora, Colorado, police placed in a chokehold and injected with ketamine; the 2020 killing of Daniel Prude, whom Rochester, New York, police asphyxiated by placing a hood on him; and George Floyd, whom Minneapolis, Minnesota, police killed in 2020 by restraining him and kneeling on his neck. In each of these cases, and many more, authorities invoked excited delirium to explain both the agitation the victims exhibited in their encounters with police and their deaths.[33]

There is, of course, no straight line from the racialization of "religious excitement" at the end of the nineteenth century to the emergence of the diagnosis of "excited delirium" at the end of the twentieth century, and the pathologizing of African American religion has certainly followed yet other routes in recent years. Yet considering the broad history this book charts allows us to see to how such medical frames can be mobilized to render some religious beliefs and practices excessive or locate them outside the bounds of conceptions of proper religion. Attending to the afterlives of racialized religious excitement can be one step in attuning us to the potential consequences, often violent and deadly, of this pathologizing work and to seek different paths.

# ACKNOWLEDGMENTS

It is a delight to come to the end of this work and to have the opportunity to acknowledge the support I have received from so many colleagues, friends, and family. Andrew Walker-Cornetta's encouragement and feedback persuaded me to pursue the questions that led to this book, and Kathryn Lofton's unflagging enthusiasm for the project has meant so much. The members of the Black Religious Studies Working Group, especially Kim Akano, Vaughn Booker, Khytie Brown, Ras Michael Brown, Judith Casselberry, N. Fadeke Castor, Matthew Cressler, Jamil Drake, Ambre Dromgoole, Ahmad Greene-Hayes, Mélena Laudig, Laura McTighe, KB Dennis Meade, Eziaku Nwokocha, Alphonso Saville, Joseph Stuart, Nicole Myers Turner, and Alexis Wells-Oghoghomeh, have shown great care for me throughout the research process. Their generous engagement of the work has shaped my analysis and approach to writing the book. Thanks, as ever, to the DOPE crew—Annie Blazer, Jessica Delgado, Nicole Kirk, and Kathryn Gin Lum—for so much encouragement and fun over the years.

I'm grateful to have had the opportunity to discuss the work in progress provided by the many colleagues and friends who invited me to give lectures and participate in workshops and conferences. Thank you to all who offered helpful comments on early drafts, engaged me in conversation about the project, and supported my work in other ways, including George Aumoithe, Danielle Boaz, Constance Brown, Anthea Butler, Elizabeth Castelli, Heath Carter, Eden Consenstein, Gillian Frank, Ilyse Morgenstein Fuerst, Megan Goodwin, Kali Handelman, Paul Harvey, Sarah Imhoff, Alison Isenberg, Terence Keel, Sylvester Johnson, Lauren Kerby Langlois, Tanya Luhrmann, Adeana McNicholl, Samira Mehta, John Lardas Modern, Julia Robinson Moore, Katherine Moran, Elayne Oliphant, Anthony Petro, Dionne Powell, Sally Promey, Shari Rabin, Leslie Ribovich, Daniel Rivers, Barbara Savage, David Sehat, Tobin Miller Shearer, Kristy Slominski, Matthew Smith, Harvey Stark, William

Stell, Beth Stroud, Stephen Tuck, David Harrington Watt, Christopher White, and Michael Zogry. Ira Helderman, who has been a wonderful and supportive conversation partner as I entered the unfamiliar territory of the history of religion and psychiatry, offered detailed comments on the entire manuscript, for which I am enormously appreciative. Mélena Laudig provided vital research assistance, and Adele Logan Alexander, Mikael Awake, and Dennis Dickerson offered resources that enriched the book. Assistance from archivists and librarians at the California State Archives, the Columbia University Health Sciences Library, the Georgia Archives, the Library of Virginia, the National Archives and Records Administration, the South Carolina Department of Archives and History, the Schomburg Center for Research in Black Culture, Valdosta State University, and the White Plains Public Library was invaluable in the research process.

My thanks to graduate and undergraduate students in my courses who engaged the work with enthusiasm; to members of Princeton's Religion in the Americas Workshop; colleagues in the Department of Religion at Princeton, especially Leora Batnitzky, Wallace Best, Jenny Wiley Legath, AnneMarie Luijendijk, Elaine Pagels, and Seth Perry for their input and encouragement on the long road to this book; and to the department's wonderful staff, especially Mary Kay Bodnar and Kerry Smith, for being the department's anchors and for supporting me as department chair during a global pandemic.

I have been fortunate to have received research grants and fellowships in support of this work from the John Simon Guggenheim Memorial Foundation, the Schomburg Center for Research in Black Culture, and the National Endowment for the Humanities. Any views, findings, conclusions, or recommendations expressed in this book do not necessarily reflect those of the National Endowment for the Humanities. Jennifer Hammer at NYU Press has been wonderful to work with again, and her critical questions and careful engagement of the book have improved the work considerably. Thanks also to the NYU Press production team for their contributions to a smooth process.

I wrote much of this book during the first years of the pandemic and completed it in the long grieving wake of my mother's death from complications of COVID-19. Researching and analyzing racialized discourses of health, illness, social value, and disparate medical treatment in the American past amid a devastating global pandemic in our present in which so many have chosen individualism over solidarity and care for the vulnerable has been sobering. My mother's faith nourished her, and the night before she died, she read scripture in the monthly missal telling of the certainty of joy and fellowship, which motivates me to remain hopeful. I dedicate the book to my parents, grateful for all they endured to make and sustain a family in this country. Love to my family—Weisenfeld, Bailey, Fruhbauer, Széll, Hibbs, Collins—for sticking together through so many losses and joys in the past few years, and to Timea for sticking with me.

# ABBREVIATIONS

CSH/CP  Records of Central State Hospital, 1874–1961, Series II. Commitment Papers, 1874–1906. Accession 41741, State Government Records Collection, The Library of Virginia, Richmond, Virginia.

GWB  George W. Bennett Manuscript, Sc MG 240, Schomburg Center for Research in Black Culture, Manuscripts, Archives and Rare Books Division, The New York Public Library.

LCR  Lafargue Clinic Records, Sc MG 141, Schomburg Center for Research in Black Culture, Manuscripts, Archives and Rare Books Division, The New York Public Library.

SCSH/CF  South Carolina State Department of Mental Health, RG 190000, Series: SC State Hospital for the Insane, S190024 Commitment Files ca. 1840–1950, South Carolina Department of Archives and History.

SCSH/CH  South Carolina State Department of Mental Health, RG 190000, Series: SC State Hospital for the Insane, S190021 Case Histories, 1875–1915, South Carolina Department of Archives and History.

SEH/CFP  Records of St. Elizabeths Hospital, RG 418, Records of the Medical Records Branch, Case Files of Patients, 1855–1950, National Archives Building, Washington, DC.

SEH/CRB  Records of St. Elizabeths Hospital, RG 418, Records of the Medical Records Branch, Conference Record Books, National Archives Building, Washington, DC.

SEH/RC  Records of St. Elizabeths Hospital, RG 418, Records of the Medical Records Branch, Register of Cases, 1855–1941, National Archives Building, Washington, DC.

VWB  Viola W. Bernard Papers, Archives and Special Collections, Augustus C. Long Health Sciences Library, Columbia University.

# NOTES

INTRODUCTION

1  Judy B., Case Number 3985, Box 17, SEH/CFP.

2  See, for example, Sidlauskas, "Medical Portrait"; Rawling, "'She Sits All Day'"; Jordanova, "Portraits, Patients and Practitioners."

3  These photographs of Judy B. are not the only ones in the records of this hospital that feature someone's hands holding a patient's head in place.

4  Judy B., Conference report, June 10, 1906, Case Number 3985, Box 17, SEH/CFP.

5  For example, Judy B., conference reports January 5, 1910; May 17, 1911, Case Number 3985, Box 17, SEH/CFP.

6  Judy B., Conference report, June 8, 1915, Case Number 3985, Box 17, SEH/CFP.

7  Judy B., Conference report, May 17, 1911; December 1, 1910, Case Number 3985, Box 17, SEH/CFP.

8  Shepard, *Notes on Genealogy*, 88.

9  Judy B., Conference report, January 15, 1914; January 15, 1915, Case Number 3985, Box 17, SEH/CFP.

10  Evarts, "Ontogenetic." I am grateful for Martin Summers's work that connects this case to Evarts's article. Summers, *Madness*, 173.

11  Evarts, "Ontogenetic," 277 (emphasis added).

12  I use the term "Black religion" at times to signal the varied religious practices of people of African descent in the United States and at other times to point to how white psychiatrists crafted and deployed understandings of the religious expressions of Black people as the product of a uniform racial mind.

13  Summers, *Madness*, 3.

14  See Drake, *To Know the Soul of a People*; Savage, *Your Spirits Walk beside Us*; Evans, *Burden of Black Religion*.

15  Turner, *Soul Liberty*, 14; see also Harvey, *Freedom's Coming*.

16  Turner, "Politics of Interdependent Independence."

17  Wells-Oghoghomeh, *Souls of Womenfolk*, 196.

18  Chireau, *Black Magic*, 3, 4, 2.

19  Raboteau, *Slave Religion*, 66–74.

20  Hardy, "'No Mystery God'"; Weisenfeld, *New World A-Coming*.

21  Evans, *Burden of Black Religion*, 9.

22  See, for example, Prince, "'Driven Insane by Eddyism'"; Fluhman, *Peculiar People*; Curtis, "Sane Gospel"; Numbers and Numbers, "Millerism and Madness."

23 For a study of the destructive power of Western biomedical diagnoses to Native kinship medical systems in the institutionalization of Native Americans in the Canton Asylum for Insane Indians, see Burch, *Committed*.

24 Arthur K., Case Number 4002, Box 17, SEH/CFP.

25 Summers, *Madness*, 3.

26 The doctors questioned her regularly about whether she had been enslaved and recorded her as giving several names of enslavers, which may reflect her memory problems, or her status being held as the property of several people over the course of her life.

27 Gonaver, *Peculiar Institution*.

28 Lunbeck, *Psychiatric Persuasion*.

29 Gloege, *Guaranteed Pure*, 6. Rather than using the conventional theological divide of modernism and fundamentalism, Gloege characterizes late nineteenth-century and early twentieth-century American Protestantism along the lines of churchly Protestantism, that continued to vest religious authority in denominations, and corporate evangelicalism focused on evangelism and individual religious authority.

30 Harvey, *Freedom's Coming*, 63. On the Klan and religion, see Baker, *Gospel according to the Klan*.

31 Jemison, *Christian Citizens*, 103.

32 Gloege, *Guaranteed Pure*, 4–5.

33 Keel, *Divine Variations*, 150n32.

34 Walcott, *Long Emancipation*, 4.

35 Hogarth, *Medicalizing Blackness*.

36 Hucks, *Obeah, Orisa and Religious Identity*; Johnson, *Automatic Religion*; Sparkes, "Minds Overwrought by 'Religious Orgies'"; Boaz, "Obeah, Vagrancy"; Paton, *Cultural Politics of Obeah*; Smith, *Insanity, Race and Colonialism*; Moreira-Almeida, "History of 'Spiritist Madness.'"

37 Wheatley, "Colonial Governance"; Keller, *Colonial Madness*; Mahone, "Psychology of Rebellion"; Jackson, *Surfacing Up*; Sadowsky, *Imperial Bedlam*.

38 For example, Louis, "Black Women's Psychiatric Incarceration"; Segrest, *Administrations of Lunacy*; Summers, *Madness*; Nuriddin, "Psychiatric Jim Crow"; Willoughby, "Running Away from Drapetomania"; Gonaver, *Peculiar Institution*; Cooper Owens, *Medical Bondage*; Doyle, *Psychiatry and Racial Liberalism in Harlem*; Green, Mckiernan-González, and Summers, *Precarious Prescriptions*; Roberts, *Fatal Invention*; Metzl, *Protest Psychosis*; Rose, *Psychology and Selfhood*; Washington, *Medical Apartheid*; Scott, *Contempt and Pity*.

39 Cook and Powell, *Spirituality and Psychiatry*; Helderman, *Prescribing the Dharma*; Koenig, *Religion and Mental Health*; Vacek, *Madness*; Boyer, "Religion, 'Moral Insanity,' and Psychology"; Heinze, *Jews and the American Soul*; Rubin, *Religious Melancholy*.

40 Lum, *Heathen*.

41 Keel, *Divine Variations*, 139.

42 Modern, *Neuromatic*, 38.

43 On the status of many of the records of Virginia's Central State Hospital, which served Black patients, see the Central State Hospital Digital Library and Archives Project, https://coloredinsaneasylums.org/, founded by Dr. King Davis. Mab Segrest used patient case histories from the Georgia's Central State Hospital in Milledgeville for her 2020 study, *Administrations of Lunacy*, but I was informed in 2021 that the Georgia Archives had "been advised by legal counsel that Central State Hospital patient records are restricted by HIPAA and are not available for research." Author correspondence with Georgia Archives Reference, June 29, 2021.

44 Wells-Oghoghomeh, "'She Come Like a Nightmare.'"

45 Sadowsky, *Imperial Bedlam*, 5.

46 Helderman, *Prescribing the Dharma*, 245.

47 Lawrence, *Privacy and the Past*.

48 Thomas, "James H. Cone."

49 Hattie W. to C. H. Nichols, October 8, 1876; March 2, 1876; March 3, 1876, Case Number 3985, Box 17, SEH/CFP.

## CHAPTER 1. THE MAKING OF BLACK RELIGIOUS FANATICISM

1 1860 US Federal Census—Slave Schedule, 15th District, Liberty County, Georgia, p. 45; 1850 US Federal Census—Slave Schedule, Walthourville, Liberty County, Georgia, p. 17; *Thirteenth Report of the American Baptist Home Mission Society* (New York: John Gray, Printer, 1845), 24.

2 Raboteau, *Slave Religion*.

3 Exodus 13:18.

4 Brown, *African-Atlantic Cultures*, 201.

5 For example, Revelation 12:6; Fulop, "'The Future Golden Day of the Race.'"

6 "A Negro Fanatical Sect," *Wilmington Daily Republican*, July 30, 1889, 4.

7 "Georgia and Florida," *Savannah Morning News*, June 14, 1889, 6; "Liberty's Pseudo Christ," *Savannah Morning News*, June 23, 1889, 8; "A Georgia Jesus Christ," *Macon Weekly Telegraph*, July 3, 1889, 6; "A Sensational Drama," *Columbus Enquirer-Sun*, July 4, 1889, 1; "Thinks He Is Christ," *Fayetteville Weekly Democrat*, July 5, 1889, 1; Joseph, "Liberty," 4.

8 Following information in accounts of Bell's lunacy hearing in Savannah in 1888 under the name Belton Dupont and the work of the historian Thomas F. Armstrong, it is likely that Bell was born in Circleville, Ohio, in 1859 or 1860, the son of German immigrants William and Elisabeth Orth. William was a farmer and a United Brethren minister. Ephraim, the youngest of the family in 1860, matches Bell's account of his age and of having worked as a clerk in a store in Ohio prior to moving to Florida. 1860 US Federal Census, Circleville City, Pickaway County, Ohio, p. 42; 1880 US Federal Census, Wauseon, Fulton County, Ohio, Enumeration District 24, Family 4; "An Ohio Man Inspired," *Savannah Morning News*, April 15, 1888, 8; Armstrong, "Christ Craze of 1889," 239n10.

9   "Georgia and Florida," *Savannah Morning News*, June 14, 1889, 6. Overall, the Black population of Liberty County in 1890 (8,673) was more than double that of whites (4,207). *Bulletin of the Department of Labor, Volume VI.—1901* (Washington, DC: Government Printing Office, 1901), 735.

10   "Liberty's Pseudo Christ," 8.

11   "A False Messiah in Liberty County," *Savannah Morning News*, June 14, 1889, 6; "Liberty's Pseudo Christ," 8.

12   Brown, *African-Atlantic Cultures*, 212.

13   "Liberty's Pseudo Christ," 8.

14   "A Sensational Drama," *Columbus Enquirer-Sun*, July 4, 1889, 1; Dupont Bell lunacy proceedings, June 21, 1889, June 24, 1889, June 28, 1889, Georgia Probate Records, 1742–1990, Liberty, Miscellaneous probate records 1878–1891, vol. R, image 435–436; Court of Ordinary of Chambers, June 24, 1889; June 29, 1889, Georgia Probate Records, 1742–1990, Liberty, Miscellaneous probate records 1881–1934, vol. S, image 287, *FamilySearch*, May 20, 2014, https://FamilySearch.org.

15   "He Claims to Be Christ," *New York Times*, July 11, 1889, 3; "The Liberty County Messiah," *Atlanta Constitution*, July 14, 1889, 12; Armstrong, "Christ Craze of 1889," 240n17.

16   "A Sensational Drama," *Columbus Enquirer-Sun*, July 4, 1889, 1.

17   "A Corner in Wings: The Story of the New Messiah of Liberty," *Atlanta Constitution*, July 12, 1889, 3; "Selling Angels' Wings," *Louisville Courier-Journal*, July 12, 1889, 2. The article in the *Louisville Courier-Journal* was reprinted in several newspapers, including the Black-owned Minneapolis newspaper *The Appeal*, July 20, 1899, 1.

18   Turner, *Soul Liberty*, 4.

19   "Georgia, Augusta: The Negro Fanatics of Liberty County to Be Arrested and Punished," *New Orleans Times-Picayune*, July 27, 1889, 1.

20   "The False Christ," *Louisville Courier-Journal*, July 26, 1889, 6.

21   "Fanaticism and Crime," *New York Times*, July 24, 1889, 1. On deployments of the label "voodoo" in the United States, see Boaz, *Voodoo*.

22   "False Saviors," *Cincinnati Enquirer*, July 25, 1899, 1.

23   Eight men were indicted on November 20, 1889, for assault with intent to murder for the attack on Carter: Simon Walthour, John Douglas, L or Q (?) Roberts, Jack Pray, Ned Stevens, Dicky Maxwell, William Quarterman, and William Baty. Pray, Stevens, and Baty were found guilty on December 3, 1889, and sentenced to two years of hard labor in the penitentiary. Simon Walthour pled guilty on December 6, 1889, and was sentenced to two years of hard labor in the penitentiary. *Record of Minutes of Liberty County Superior Court* (November 1884–April 1890), 371, 377–79, 392–93, as cited in Rogers and Saunders, *Swamp Water and Wiregrass*, 200.

24   "False Christ," 6; "Claims to Be Christ," *Galveston Daily News*, July 30, 1889, 8.

25   "False Saviors," *Cincinnati Enquirer*, July 25, 1889, 1; "False Christ," 6. Newspaper accounts contain much conflicting detail about this crime and the identities of those involved. At first the press named the murderer as Laura Roberts and the

victim as her eight-year-old nephew, and later newspapers named her as Sarah Roberts and characterized her victim as a sixteen-month-old baby. Court records list her as Sarah Roberts. "For Butchering a Baby," *Columbus Enquirer-Sun*, November 19, 1889, 1; *State v. Sarah Roberts*, November 18, 1889, *Record of Minutes of Liberty County Superior Court* (November 1884–April 1890), 360, as cited in Rogers and Saunders, *Swamp Water and Wiregrass*, 199.

26  Rogers and Saunders, *Swamp Water and Wiregrass*, 198.

27  "Georgia, Augusta: The Negro Fanatics of Liberty County to Be Arrested and Punished," *New Orleans Times-Picayune*, July 27, 1889, 1; "Georgia Fanatics," *Wilkes-Barre News*, July 29, 1889, 1; "The New Messiah," *Athens Weekly Banner*, July 30, 1889, 1; Court of Ordinary, Lunacy Determination for Edward James, Georgia Probate Records, 1742–1990, Liberty, Miscellaneous probate records 1881–1934, vol. S, image 246, *FamilySearch*, May 20, 2014, https://FamilySearch.org.

28  "Georgia's Fanatics," *Harrisburg Telegraph*, July 31, 1889, 1.

29  "Put in a Safe Place," *Savannah Morning News*, August 3, 1889, 8.

30  Armstrong, "Christ Craze of 1889," 24n119.

31  "Liberty (Ga.) Sensation," *Baltimore Sun*, July 27, 1889, 5; "The Colored Messiah," *Daily Arkansas Gazette*, August 2, 1889, 7; "Georgia's Fanatics," *Harrisburg Telegraph*, July 31, 1889, 1.

32  "'King Solomon' Succeeds the Two Messiahs in Liberty County," *Atlanta Constitution*, July 29, 1889, 1.

33  "'King Solomon' Succeeds the Two Messiahs in Liberty County," 1.

34  "Georgia, Augusta: A Georgia Religious Lunatic Killed," *New Orleans Times-Picayune*, October 20, 1889; 3 "The Walthour Killing," *Savannah Morning News*, October 22, 1889, 8. "In Liberty's Courts," *Atlanta Constitution*, May 24, 1891, 18.

35  "King Soloman's [*sic*] Queen," *North Georgia Citizen*, August 8, 1889, 1. Most of the early accounts identified her as Laura Roberts, using the same name as the woman who had been arrested for murdering a child some weeks earlier.

36  "Colored Messiah," 7.

37  Rogers and Saunders, *Swamp Water and Wiregrass*, 201.

38  "The Fanatics Thinning Out," *Savannah Morning News*, August 7, 1889, 3.

39  "All Quiet in Liberty," *Savannah Morning News*, August 17, 1889, 8.

40  "Another of Bell's Victims," *Savannah Morning News*, August 18, 1889, 8.

41  "Georgia and Florida," *Savannah Morning News*, March 29, 1890, 6; "The Fire Signals Set Up for the Return of the False Christ," *Atlanta Constitution*, March 29, 1890, 2.

42  Armstrong, "Christ Craze of 1889," 223–45.

43  Armstrong, 233.

44  Raboteau, *Slave Religion*, 152–63.

45  Jones, "Religious Instruction of the Negroes," 7, 8, 25–27; Jones, *Religious Instruction of the Negroes*; Clarke, *Dwelling Place*, 97–179.

46  Clarke, *Dwelling Place*, 125–30, 133; Jones, *Catechism for Colored Persons*; Jones, *Suggestions on the Religious Instruction of the Negroes*.

47 Raboteau, *Slave Religion*, 162–65.

48 Jones, *Catechism for Colored Persons*, 92–95.

49 Jones, 95.

50 Jones, *Suggestions on the Religious Instruction of the Negroes*, 15–16 (emphasis in the original).

51 Clarke, *Dwelling Place*, 138.

52 Clarke, 50–51.

53 Clarke, 152–56. See also Manigault-Bryant, *Talking to the Dead*; Brown, *African-Atlantic Cultures*; Young, *Rituals of Resistance*.

54 This account relies primarily on Armstrong, "Building of a Black Church."

55 1880 US Federal Census, District 15, Liberty County, Georgia, Family 181; Edward James and Elizabeth Miller, September 5, 1883, Georgia, US, Marriage Records from Select Counties, 1828–1978.

56 Armstrong, "Building of a Black Church," 366; Hargis, "For the Love of Place," 843.

57 Letter from W. H. Styles, *Savannah Tribune*, September 15, 1888, 2; *Savannah Tribune*, October 6, 1888, 3.

58 "Georgia Baptists: The Missionary Association in Council," *Savannah Tribune*, June 2, 1888, 2.

59 Letter from W. H. Styles, *Savannah Tribune*, July 14, 1888, 2.

60 "Georgia Fanatics," *Wilkes-Barre News*, July 29, 1889, 1.

61 Joseph, "Liberty," 54–56.

62 "Atonement in Blood," *Washington Post*, August 8, 1888, 7.

63 "Atonement in Blood." For a similar account that emphasizes the "Puritan stock" of the white residents, see "Incredible Barbarism," *Woodson Democrat*, August 23, 1888, 2.

64 "Incredible Barbarism," 2.

65 "Incredible Barbarism," 2; "Fanatics in Georgia: Barbaric Worship of the Sable Children of the Wilderness," *San Francisco Examiner*, July 30, 1889, 1.

66 "Fanaticism and Crime," *New York Times*, July 24, 1889, 1; "Georgia Fanatics," *Wilkes-Barre News*, July 29, 1889, 1.

67 "Life in Liberty," *Athens Weekly Banner*, August 20, 1889, 8.

68 "Life in Liberty," *Athens Weekly Banner*, 8.

69 Grady, *New South*, 261. According to the *Savannah Morning News*, the African American man who lived on Hall's former property was Samuel A. McIver, elected in 1888 to the Georgia House of Representatives. "Life in Liberty," *Savannah Morning News*, August 15, 1889, 5.

70 "Life in Liberty," *Athens Weekly Banner*, 8.

71 "Negro Folly and Superstition," *Moulton Advertiser*, August 8, 1889, 2 (reprinted from the *Montgomery Advertiser*).

72 "Crazed and Mad," *Atlanta Constitution*, August 1, 1889, 4; "Atonement in Blood," *Washington Post*, August 8, 1889, 7; "Negro Orgies in Georgia," *Minneapolis Commercial*, August 21, 1889, 2.

73   "Crazed and Mad," 4; "Negro Orgies in Georgia," 2.

74   "He Claims to Be Christ," 3. See also "A Georgia Lunatic," *Austin American-Statesman*, July 30, 1889, 1; "All Crazy from Religion," *Leavenworth Standard*, August 1, 1889, 1.

75   "All Crazy from Religion," 1; "Life in Liberty," *Savannah Morning News*, 5; "King Solomon's Queen," *North Georgia Citizen*, August 8, 1889, 1.

76   "King George Schweinfurth's Denial," *Chicago Daily Tribune*, March 30, 1888, 2; "Thrown Out of the Church," *Chicago Daily Tribune*, March 28, 1889, 7; "A Pack of Howling Lunatics," *Atlanta Constitution*, April 23, 1888, 4; "I Am, That I Am," *Cincinnati Enquirer*, May 18, 1889, 14.

77   "Emotional Insanity," *Fayetteville Weekly Democrat*, August 9, 1889, 2.

78   "The Passing Show," *Summit County Beacon*, August 21, 1889, 6.

79   "The Beekmanite Impostor," *Chicago Daily Tribune*, May 16, 1889, 4.

80   "A Form of Insanity," *Anaconda Standard*, April 6, 1890, 2.

81   "Claims to Be Christ," 8; "Southern False Prophets," *Daily Inter Ocean*, July 30, 1899, 3; "The False Christ," *New Orleans Times-Democrat*, July 30, 1889, 1; Wright, *Who's Who in the General Conference*, 152.

82   *Catalogue of the Officers and Students of Atlanta University* (Atlanta: Constitution Printing, 1884), 11; "The False Christ in Jail," *Savannah Morning News*, July 29, 1889, 2. When Bell first arrived in Liberty County, Styles had succeeded in having him arrested on a vagrancy charge, but a judge released him. "A Georgia Jesus Christ," *Macon Weekly Telegraph*, July 3, 1889, 6; "A Sensational Drama," *Columbus Enquirer-Sun*, July 4, 1889, 1.

83   "The False Christ in Jail," 2.

84   Rev. G. B. Reid, "Our Church Contending for the Faith," *Christian Recorder*, September 28, 1889, 1. On the varied uses of the label "heathen" in American religious history, see Lum, *Heathen*.

85   "Life in Liberty," *Savannah Morning News*, 5.

86   "Incredible Barbarism," *Woodson Democrat*, August 23, 1889, 2.

87   "Crazed and Mad," *Atlanta Constitution*, August 1, 1889, 4.

88   "Southern False Prophets," *Daily Inter Ocean*, July 30, 1889, 3.

89   "Negro Folly and Superstition," 2. Ironically, Snelson himself would be sent to the Georgia State Hospital at Milledgeville in 1902, reportedly with delusions of grandeur and physical deterioration. He was released in 1904 but apparently still was not fully able to care for himself. He was struck and killed by a train while wandering on the tracks. "Snelson Insane," *Waycross Journal*, November 22, 1902, 3; "Floyd Snelson Killed Saturday," *Waycross Journal*, February 16, 1904.

90   "Town and Country News," *Eufalia Times and News*, August 8, 1889, 3.

91   "Judge Norwood's Address on Traits of Negro Race," *Atlanta Constitution*, January 6, 1908, 8.

92   "A Field for the Missionary," *Atlanta Constitution*, March 30, 1890, 18; Stacy, *History of the Presbyterian Church in Georgia*, 273, 274–75.

93 "A Strange Fanaticism in Georgia," *The Church at Home and Abroad* 7, no. 38 (February 1890): 149.

94 "Strange Fanaticism," 150.

95 "Strange Fanaticism," 151.

## CHAPTER 2. BLACK FREEDOM AND THE RACIALIZATION OF "RELIGIOUS EXCITEMENT"

1 Charles K., Synopsis of Record, December 10, 1896, Case Number 10110, Box 163, SEH/CFP.

2 Charles K., November 6, 1903, Hospital Cemetery, Washington, DC, US, Select Deaths and Burials Index, 1769 1960.

3 Charles K., Clinical Record, Ward Notes, January 4, 1901, January 19, 1901, February 28, 1901, January 14, 1903, Case Number 10110, Box 163, SEH/CFP.

4 Charles K., Ward Notes, December 23, 1900, Case Number 10110, Box 163, SEH/CFP; Otto, *St. Elizabeths Hospital*, 104–5.

5 Charles K., Ward Notes, September 14, 1901, September 21, 1901, November 2, 1901, December 7, 1901, February 7, 1902, March 22, 1902, April 5, 1902, April 12, 1902, November 22, 1902, Case Number 10110, Box 163, SEH/CFP.

6 Charles K., Ward Notes, January 1, 1902, February 3, 1902, May 19, 1903; Preliminary Report of Autopsy, November 5, 1903, Case Number 10110, Box 163, SEH/CFP.

7 1900 US Federal Census, Washington City, District of Columbia, Enumeration District 143, Sheet 18.

8 Gambino, "'Savage Heart.'"

9 The 1860 census separated out enslaved people classified as insane (a total of 405) and did not draw racial distinctions within the population of free people classified as insane (23,593). Kennedy, *Population of the United States in 1860*, lxxviii; Bainbridge, "Religious Insanity in America."

10 US Department of the Interior, *Eighth Census, U.S. Instructions &c.* (Washington, DC: George W. Bowman, Public Printer, 1860), 16–17.

11 Kennedy, *Population of the United States in 1860*, xc–xci. Bainbridge attributes this material to "the distinguished alienist and social scientist Pliny Earle." Bainbridge, "Religious Insanity in America," 224.

12 Bainbridge, "Religious Insanity in America," 227.

13 Bainbridge, 237 (emphasis in the original).

14 Gonaver, *Peculiar Institution* 1, 7.

15 Babcock, "Colored Insane." This is also published in Barrows, *Proceedings of the National Conference of Charities and Correction* (1895), 164–86.

16 Babcock, "Colored Insane," 424.

17 The state changed the name of the Georgia Lunatic Asylum to the Georgia State Sanitarium in 1897.

18 Perry, "Insanity and the Negro," 467. See also Powell, "Increase of Insanity"; Mays, "Increase of Insanity"; Hodges, "Effect of Freedom." For Perry's biography, see Connelly, *Standard History of Kansas and Kansans*, 2036–37.

19 Babcock, "Colored Insane," 426. At the 1873 annual meeting of the Association of Medical Superintendents, psychiatrists at state hospitals had also discussed an increase in admissions of Black patients, the causes, and the need for more room to accommodate them. "Proceedings of the Association of Medical Superintendents," *American Journal of Insanity* 30 (October 1873): 168–82.

20 "Freedom Fatal for the Negro," *Richmond Times*, May 24, 1900, 1, 6.

21 J. P. Hodges, 1860 US Federal Census, Slave Schedule, Harnett, North Carolina, p. 18; Hodges, "Effect of Freedom," 94.

22 Roberts, "Insanity in the Colored Race," 6; C. M. Rock, "A Tribute to Dr. Roberts by His Pastor," *Biblical Recorder*, July 7, 1908, 16. In 1860, Roberts's father, Gideon, is listed as holding twelve people in bondage, and his grandmother Anna, who lived with the family, enslaved eight people. Roberts's family on his father's side were enslavers in North Carolina as early as the late eighteenth century. In his will John Roberts (d. 1765) listed many items of farm equipment, household items, books (including one titled *The Progress of Religion*), and "Negroes": two men, two women, and two girls. 1860 US Federal Census Slave Schedule, Indian Springs District, Wayne County, North Carolina, pp. 37–38.

23 Babcock, "Colored Insane," 426.

24 "Many Minds Wrecked," *Washington Post*, July 7, 1901, 7. Eugene Rollin Corson, a white physician in Savannah, Gorgia, made a similar argument in an article on African Americans' prospects, claiming an increase in insanity, "mostly acute mania, of a religious type." Corson, "Vital Equation of the Colored Race," 158.

25 Turner, *Soul Liberty*; Harper, *End of Days*.

26 White physicians in the Caribbean and Latin America made similar arguments in this period about religious excitement as a driver of insanity among Black people. In his 1876 article "Notes on Lunacy in British Guiana," for example, Edinburgh-educated James S. Donald, resident surgeon in an asylum in British Guiana, wrote that mania was the most common diagnosis among Black patients and that "a large proportion of cases is complicated with delusions of a religious character. This may be accounted for from the fact that times of religious excitement are of frequent occurrence among the black population, and an increase in our inmates is no uncommon sequence to a so-called 'revival' of religion. A strong religious sentiment (to use the expression in its widest significance) exists in the mind of the negro, and it is not, therefore, a matter of surprise that when reason is unseated the previous prominent feelings should sway the wanderings of the 'mind diseased.'" James S. Donald, "Notes on Lunacy in British Guiana," *Journal of Mental Science* 22 (April 1876): 77.

27 Cartwright, "Diseases and Peculiarities," 331–33. Cartwright said he named the condition by combining the Greek for "a runaway slave" and "mad or crazy." On the influence of Cartwright's theories and the broader moral interpretations and medicalizing of resistance, see Myers, "'Drapetomania' Rebellion, Defiance and Free Black Insanity"; Gross, "Pandora's Box."

28 1850 US Federal Census, Slave Schedule, 1st Ward, Orleans Parish, Louisiana, p. 3.

29  In an earlier work Cartwright set out to persuade that Ham, Canaan's father, was "the parent or generator of the black race," through biblical interpretation, history, and physiological analysis. Cartwright, "Canaan Identified with the Ethiopian," 324. On the history of American interpretations of the story, see Keel, *Divine Variations*; Haynes, *Noah's Curse*; Johnson, *Myth of Ham*.

30  Cartwright, "Diseases and Peculiarities," 333.

31  Cartwright, 333.

32  Cartwright, 333.

33  Cartwright, 335.

34  For a discussion of how Cartwright's racial theories related to broader race science of the period, see Willoughby, "Running Away from Drapetomania."

35  Cartwright, "Diseases and Peculiarities," 336.

36  Green, "Psychoses among Negroes," 706. "Dr. E. M. Greene [*sic*] Will Leave Sanitarium," *Milledgeville Union-Recorder*, November 6, 1917, 1.

37  Evans, *Burden of Black Religion*, 108.

38  Curtis Evans makes a similar argument in his work on social scientists' assessments of Black religion at the end of the nineteenth century, writing, "Behind these seemingly clinical analyses of African American religion stood a massive moral argument against blacks, which was rooted in a normative liberal Protestant religious tradition." In exploring emerging psychiatric discourse, I find both greater representation of white southerners in the discussion than his emphasis on northern social scientists revealed and a strong influence of white southern conservative denominations. Evans, 106.

39  Joseph, "Liberty," 41–42; 1860 US Federal Census, Slave Schedule, Dalton, Whitfield County, Georgia, p. 5.

40  1860 US Federal Census Slave Schedule, Indian Springs District, Wayne County, North Carolina, pp. 37–38; "A Tribute to Dr. Roberts by His Pastor," *Biblical Recorder*, July 5, 1908; Norwood, *History of the First Baptist Church of Goldsboro, North Carolina*, 16–17.

41  On "churchly Protestantism" see Gloege, *Guaranteed Pure*, 6.

42  Roberts, "Insanity in the Colored Race," 6

43  Summers, *Madness*, 139.

44  Kiernan, "Race and Insanity" (April 1885), 174.

45  O'Malley, "Psychoses in the Colored Race," 310; Burton, "Mary O'Malley, M.D.," 11; "Mary O'Malley," in Downs, *Encyclopedia of American Biography*, 181–82.

46  Bevis, "Psychological Traits of the Southern Negro," 69; William Bevis, enlisted May 2, 1864, Florida 1st Infantry (Reserves), US, Confederate Soldiers Compiled Service Records, 1861–1865.

47  Wagner, "Comparative Study of Negro and White Admissions," 167.

48  Lind, "Phylogenetic Elements," 304.

49  Lum, "Historyless Heathen."

50  Beard, *American Nervousness*, 174. See also Buchanan, "Insanity in the Colored Race," 67.

51 Barrows, *Proceedings of the National Conference of Charities and Correction* (1899), 398.

52 Witmer, "Insanity in the Colored Race," 19; White, *National Cyclopaedia of American Biography*, 367–68.

53 Buchanan, "Insanity in the Colored Race," 67; 1860 US Federal Census—Slave Schedule, Mississippi, Chickasaw County, Division 1, pp. 59–60.

54 Babcock, "Colored Insane," 423.

55 In his controversial *Race Traits and Tendencies of the American Negro*, Frederick L. Hoffman, a German statistician for the Prudential Insurance Company, included a brief discussion of insanity, drawing on admission numbers to an asylum in Sierra Leone from 1843 to 1853. He concluded that the numbers "would clearly prove that insanity was not an uncommon disease among the natives of Africa at the time." Hoffman, who claimed that as a foreigner he was "free from the taint of prejudice or sentimentality," was also skeptical of claims of increasing rates of insanity among Blacks in the United States. Notably, Hoffman's wife, Ella, was from an enslaving family in Webster, Georgia. 1860 US Federal Census, Slave Schedule, Southern District, Webster, Georgia, p. 287; Hoffman, *Race Traits and Tendencies of the American Negro*, v, 126–34. Kelly Miller and W. E. B. Du Bois published lengthy, detailed, and scathing reviews of the work, rejecting Hoffman's overall conclusion that "race traits" accounted for poor health, declining material circumstances, and "moral degradation" of African Americans at the end of the century. Miller, "Review of Hoffman's Race Traits"; Du Bois, "Review of Frederick L. Hoffman's *Race Traits*."

56 Beard, *American Nervousness*, 188.

57 Roberts, "Insanity in the Colored Race," 9.

58 Barrows, *Proceedings of the National Conference of Charities and Correction* (1896), 459–60.

59 Miller, *Effects of Emancipation*, 5. For a similar argument, see J. P. Searcy's discussion of Alabama's Mt. Vernon Hospital for the Negro insane quoted in "The Negro Insane," *Charities* 10, no. 1 (January 3, 1903): 8; Ash, *Biographical History of North Carolina*, 377–78. North Carolina changed the name of the Eastern Insane Asylum to the Eastern Hospital in 1891.

60 Drewry, "Care and Condition of the Insane in Virginia," 312. Tyler, *Men of Mark in Virginia*, 108–11. Humphrey Drewry, William's great-great-grandfather, enslaved thirty-two Black people in 1830, and subsequent generations also did until the Civil War. Southampton County, Virginia, was the site of Nat Turner's 1830 rebellion, and the family certainly would have experienced the events in some way. 1830 US Federal Census, Southampton County, Virginia, p. 262.

61 Drewry, "Care and Condition of the Insane in Virginia," 312.

62 Drewry, 313.

63 Witmer, "Insanity in the Colored Race," 24–25.

64 Witmer, 25. There are many other examples of white physicians making similar arguments in this period. See, for example, Drewry, "Care and Condition of the Insane in Virginia," 312.

65 Beard, *American Nervousness*, 188.

66 Beard, 127.

67 For example, Nott, *Two Lectures*. For a discussion of Nott's scientific and religious sensibilities regarding racial hybridity and his theory of polygenism, see Keel, *Divine Variations*, chap. 2.

68 Hall, "Negro in Africa and America," 360.

69 O'Malley, "Psychoses in the Colored Race," 312–13.

70 "Proceedings of the American Medico-Psychological Association," *American Journal of Insanity* 50 (1893–94): 257; Hodges, "Effect of Freedom," 90.

71 Bevis, "Psychological Traits of the Southern Negro," 70.

72 Bevis, 70.

73 Bevis, 71.

74 N.Y. American, "Insanity of the Negro Race," *Botanico-Medical Recorder* 11, no. 24 (October 7, 1843): 379–80. See also "Distribution of Insanity in the United States," 1019.

75 Deutsch, "First U.S. Census of the Insane," 472.

76 John C. Calhoun to Richard Pakenham, April 18, 1844, in Crallé, *Works of John C. Calhoun*, 337.

77 Jarvis, "Insanity among the Coloured Population of the Free States"; Gross, "'Doctor Ripley's Church.'"

78 Smith, "Freedom and Slavery for Afric-Americans," 65; Townsend, *Faith in Their Own Color*.

79 In the 1840s, James M. Galt, superintendent of the Eastern Lunatic Asylum in Virginia, resisted claims that a disproportionate number of free Black people became insane because he did not think there were reliable statistics, but, as Wendy Gonaver has written, ultimately did endorse the idea "that the rate of insanity was directly proportionate to freedom and geography." Gonaver, *Peculiar Institution*, 31.

80 "Distribution of Insanity in the United States," 1019.

81 Buchanan, "Insanity in the Colored Race," 68; 1860 US Federal Census—Slave Schedule, Mississippi, Chickasaw County, Division I, pp. 59–60; *Biographical and Historical Memoirs of Mississippi* (Chicago: Goodspeed Publishing, 1891), 450. Buchanan was elected a deacon of First Presbyterian Church in Meridian, Mississippi, in 1914. *Presbyterian of the South* 88, no. 43 (October 1914), 13.

82 B. F. Lee, "How Rarely Colored Men Speak of the Virtues of Colored Men in Public," *Christian Recorder*, November 3, 1887, 4.

83 Du Bois, *Health and Physique of the Negro American*, 71.

84 R. F. Boyd, M.D., "Needs of the Negro—XI," *Southwestern Christian Advocate*, May 14, 1885, 1. On clergy on this topic, see "The Delusions of Legislators," *Southwestern Christian Advocate*, April 15, 1880, 2; Rev. J. L. P., "Dialogue between the Devil and the Rumseller," *Southwestern Christian Advocate*, January 15, 1885, 2; Rev. P. B. Peters, "The Temperance Question," *Christian Recorder*, February 19, 1885, 2.

85  J. T. Newman, M.D., "Alcohol the Cause of Insanity," *Southwestern Christian Advocate*, February 4, 1886, 6.

86  Rev. Daniel W. Shaw, "Why Total Abstinence Is Best," *Southwestern Christian Advocate*, June 5, 1902, 6. See also the anti-saloon article by the AME Church layman Reuben S. Lovinggood in which he argues that drinking "helps to fill the insane asylums." Lovinggood was the president of Samuel Huston College in Austin, Texas. R. S. Lovinggood, "Down with the Saloon," *Southwestern Christian Advocate*, May 30, 1907, 2.

87  *Afro-American Churchman*, March 5, 1887, 1.

88  William Hannibal Thomas, "Characteristics of Negro Christianity," *The Negro* 1, no. 1 (July 1886): 16, 17–18. On Thomas, see Smith, *Black Judas*.

89  "Our Symposium," *Southwestern Christian Advocate*, November 14, 1889, 6.

90  Stanford, *Tragedy of the Negro in America*, 196–98.

91  "The Religious Progress of the Negro," *A.M.E. Church Review* 9, no. 3 (January 1893): 306, responding to H. K. Carroll, "The Religious Progress of the Negro," *The Forum* 14 (September 1892): 75–85.

92  Maria J., Register Number 389, January 27, 1895, Box 1, Folder 10, CSH/CP.

93  Eliza K., Register Number 4842, February 18, 1903, Box 85, Folder 10, CSH/CP.

94  "Hanna Aids Ex-Slaves," *New York Times*, February 5, 1903, 3; Berry, *My Face Is Black Is True*.

95  Sallie W., Register Number 431, October 19, 1874, Box 2, Folder 5, CSH/CP; Dolly Ann D., Register Number 477, June 22, 1875, Box 2, Folder 12, CSH/CP; Nellie G., Patient Number 6615, January 7, 1898, Box 5, SCSH/CF, Vol. 13, SCSH/CH. See also Mary J., Register Number 1536, August 7, 1885, Box 1, Folder 10, CSH/CP.

96  Jacob F., Register Number 417, July 25, 1874, Box 1, Folder 7, CSH/CP.

97  Benjamin L., Patient Number 7006, April 11, 1894, Box 5, SCSH/CF; Vol. 14, SCSH/CH. The state would change the name of the South Carolina Lunatic Asylum to the South Carolina State Hospital in 1896.

98  1860 US Federal Census, Slave Schedule, Prince William Parish, Beaufort District, South Carolina, p. 33.

99  1900 US Federal Census, Georgetown City, Georgetown County, South Carolina, Enumeration District 48, Family 234; 1910 US Federal Census, Charleston City, Charleston County, South Carolina, Enumeration District 50, Family 81; Charleston, South Carolina Directory (1917), 611.

100  Ransom R., Patient Number 10051, August 9, 1902, Box 9, SCSH/CF; Vol. 17, SCSH/CH.

101  1900 US Federal Census, Township 6, Saluda County, South Carolina, Enumeration District 108, Family 35.

102  George W. Nickell, 1860 US Federal Census—Slave Schedule, Union Town, Monroe County, Virginia.

103  Frances F., Register Number 4054, June 1895, Box 48, Folder 4, CSH/CP; 1900 US Federal Census, Charlottesville, Albemarle County, Virginia, ED 91, Sheet, 5, Family 81.

104 Frances F., Register Number 4054, June 1895, Box 48, Folder 4, CSH/CP.

105 Barksdale's family moved residences four years before he was born, and his father put up the property, livestock, and "120 negroes, all born and raised on the plantation" for sale. Land, negroes, stock, &c. for sale . . . W. J. Barksdale, Haw-Branch, Amelia, Nov. 6, 1827, pdf, www.loc.gov. William Jones Barksdale, Will Books, 1734–1865; General Indexes to Wills, 1734–1974; Author: Virginia. County Court (Amelia County); Probate Place: Amelia, Virginia, July 7, 1851.

106 William F. Drewry, "Obituary: Dr. Randolph Barksdale," *American Journal of Psychiatry* 64, no. 4 (1908): 747.

107 "Proceedings of the Association of Medical Superintendents," *American Journal of Insanity* 32 (January 1876): 293.

108 "Proceedings of the Association of Medical Superintendents," 293.

109 *Annual Report of the Central State Hospital of the State of Virginia (Petersburg, VA) for the Fiscal Year Ending September 30, 1896* (Richmond: J. H. O'Bannon, Superintendent of Public Printing, 1896), 32; *Sixty-Ninth Annual Report of the Board of Directors and of the Superintendent of the Western State Hospital of Virginia for the Fiscal Year, 1895–'96* (Richmond: J. H. O'Bannon, Superintendent of Public Printing, 1896), 26; *One Hundred and Twenty-Third Annual Report of the Eastern State Hospital of Virginia for the Fiscal Year Ending September 30, 1896* (Richmond: J. H. O'Bannon, Superintendent of Public Printing, 1896), 19; *Annual Report of the Southwestern State Hospital at Marion Virginia to the General Assembly of Virginia for the Fiscal Year Ending September 30, 1896* (Richmond: J. H. O'Bannon, Superintendent of Public Printing, 1896), 18. In her survey of Central Asylum's commitment files from 1865 to 1881, Adia Awanata Brooks found religious causes listed for 33 percent of admitted patients. Brooks, "Politics of Race and Mental Illness," 85.

110 1900 US Federal Census, Charlottesville, Albemarle County, Virginia, ED 91, Sheet, 5, Family 81.

CHAPTER 3. PATHOLOGIZING BLACK SUPERNATURALISM

1 "Police Court," *Richmond Dispatch*, July 21, 1883, 1.

2 Ezekiel and Lichtenstein, *History of the Jews of Richmond*, 223.

3 "Dr. James Beale," *Richmond Dispatch*, July 2, 1890, 1.

4 Mumford, *Third Edition of the Code of Virginia*, 717–25.

5 Mary J., Register Number 1474, April 20, 1885, Box 17, Folder 12, CSH/CP.

6 Mary J., Register Number 1474, April 20, 1885, Box 17, Folder 12, CSH/CP.

7 Mumford, *Third Edition of the Code of Virginia*, 718–19.

8 *Report of the Central Lunatic Asylum for the Year 1885–6* (Richmond: A. R. Micou, Superintendent of Public Printing, 1886), 3.

9 Thompson, *Of Shattered Minds*, 18.

10 Chireau, *Black Magic*, 3.

11 Johnson, *African American Religions*, 58; see also Matory, *Fetish Revisited*.

12 "Voodooism, an Imported Relic of Barbarism Growing in Civilized Soil," *Louisville Courier-Journal*, September 29, 1873, 3.

13  Gonaver, *Peculiar Institution*, 106.

14  See, for example, Buckley, *Christian Science and Other Superstitions*.

15  Boaz, "Obeah, Vagrancy," 423; McCrary, "Superstitious Subjects," 56–70.

16  Chireau, *Black Magic*, 16–17; Brown, "Conjure/Doctors," 3–46. In his autobiography, William Wells Brown tells the story of Dinkie, "a full-blooded African" conjurer who used his spiritual authority and power to avoid being whipped by the overseer for refusing to work and gained the admiration of the enslaved around him, and Frederick Douglass tells of the protective claims of a conjurer's roots against punishment. In contrast, Henry Bibb writes of the failure of conjurers to deliver on his promise of protection from punishment and securing the attention of a woman. Brown, *My Southern Home*, 72–81; Bibb, *Narrative of the Life and Adventures of Henry Bibb*, 25–31; Douglass, *My Bondage and My Freedom*, 233–49.

17  Katherine D. Tillman, "Negro Superstition," *A.M.E. Church Review* 15, no. 3 (January 1889): 748–50; on Tillman's literary career, see Tate, *Domestic Allegories*.

18  Ferris, *African Abroad*, 253.

19  Ferris, 252, 236.

20  Ferris, 253.

21  Bruce, *Plantation Negro*, 111.

22  Bruce, vi.

23  Bruce, 245, 259–60.

24  "Vaudooism: African Fetish Worship among the Memphis Negroes," *Memphis Sunday Appeal*, October 25, 1868, 3.

25  "Certain Beliefs and Superstitions of the Negro," *Atlantic Monthly* 68, no. 406 (August 1, 1891): 286.

26  "Life in the Old Dominion," *New York Tribune*, February 14, 1881, 2.

27  Jones, *Negro Myths*, 169.

28  Jones, 176.

29  Bruce, *Plantation Negro*, 112.

30  "Alabama Negroes: Their Superstitions," *Chicago Daily Tribune*, November 28, 1874, 6.

31  Shepard, "Superstitions of the Negro," 49.

32  Shepard, 47; "Negro Superstition," *Cincinnati Enquirer*, September 22, 1882, 2; "Southern Superstitions," *Detroit Free Press*, February 24, 1884, 17.

33  "Negro Superstitions," *Harper's Bazaar*, September 1, 1888. On witchcraft belief in African American culture, see Chireau, *Black Magic*, 83–89; Wells-Oghoghomeh, *Souls of Womenfolk*, 173–93.

34  On the relationship of conjure and Christianity, see Chireau, *Black Magic*, 27–33.

35  "Voodooism," *Louisville Courier-Journal*, September 29, 1873, 3.

36  Chireau, *Black Magic*, 60.

37  "Negro Superstitions," *Harper's Bazaar* 21, no. 35 (September 1, 1888): 579.

38  Helm, *Upward Path*, 181; Bailey, "Race Ideology and the Missionary Quest of Lucinda and Mary Helm," 53–68.

39 "Globe Gleanings: Driven Insane by a Voodoo Spell," *San Francisco Chronicle*, September 1, 1884, 3.

40 "Voodouism in Macon," *Atlanta Constitution*, February 26, 1887, 2.

41 Bruce, *Plantation Negro*, 114.

42 Roberts, "Insanity in the Colored Race," 4.

43 Roberts, 4, 6.

44 Roberts, 7.

45 Buchanan, "Insanity in the Colored Race," 68.

46 Roberts, "Insanity in the Colored Race," 7.

47 Witmer, "Insanity in the Colored Race," 25.

48 He was influenced by Emmanuel Régis's assertion that "nothing is more communicable than ideas of religion and mysticism; for this reason the insanity they engender takes most frequently an epidemic type." Régis, *Practical Manual of Mental Medicine*, 37.

49 Babcock, "Communicated Insanity, 518–19.

50 Babcock, 521.

51 Lige C., Patient Number 6429, May 24, 1892, Box 5, SCSH/CF; Vol. 13, SCSH/CH.

52 1860 US Federal Census—Slave Schedule, Fairfield District, South Carolina, p. 150.

53 *Sixty-Ninth Annual Report of the South Carolina Lunatic Asylum for the Fiscal Year 1891–1892* (Columbia, SC: Charles A. Calvo, Jr., State Printer, 1892), 336; *Seventy-First Annual Report of the South Carolina Lunatic Asylum for the Fiscal Year 1893–1894* (Columbia, SC: Charles A. Calvo, Jr., State Printer, 1894), 10.

54 Thompson, *Of Shattered Minds*, 8.

55 1900 US Federal Census, Township 1, Fairfield County, South Carolina, Enumeration District 29, Family 399; 1910 US Federal Census, Township 1, Fairfield County, South Carolina, Enumeration District 47, Family 88.

56 Jennie J., Register Number 5047, Box 85, Folder 47, CSH/CP.

57 Rachel C., Patient Number 6183, August 18, 1891, Box 5, SCSH/CF; Vol. 13, SCSH/CH.

58 "John Wylie Quillian, M.D.," in Candler and Evans, *Cylcopedia of Georgia*, 141–42; 1860 US Federal Census, Slave Schedule, Abbeville, South Carolina, p. 235.

59 Rachel C., February 2, 1901, South Carolina State Hospital Cemetery Survey Index, Richland County Public Library, 2013, 49.

60 Mary F., Register Number 1506, May 27, 1885, Box 17, Folder 4, CSH/CP.

61 Malinda W., Patient Number 9353, June 6, 1900, SCSH/CF Box 8; SCSH/CH Vol. 19; 1900 US Federal Census, Florence City, Florence Township, South Carolina, Enumeration District 37, Family 179.

62 Thomas N., Register Number 3221, October 29, 1895, CSH/CP Box 49, Folder 10; "Arrested Last Night," *Norfolk Virginian*, October 22, 1895, 1.

63 *The Ordinances of the City of Norfolk* (Norfolk, VA: W. T. Barron and Co., 1894), 317; Richard H. Baker, 1850 US Federal Census, Slave Schedule, Norfolk City, Virginia, p. 17.

64 1900 US Federal Census, Namozine District, Dinwiddie County, Virginia, Enumeration District, p. 133A; *Two Hundredth Anniversary, Old St. Paul's Church*,

*Elizabeth River Parish, Norfolk, Virginia* (Norfolk, VA: Bicentennial Committee, 1939), 28, 31.

65 Lee R., Register Number 1770, July 10, 1887, Box 22, Folder 13, CSH/CP.

66 1900 US Federal Census, Verdier Township, Colleton County, South Carolina, Enumeration District 48, Family 151.

67 Robert N., Patient Number 7309, Box 6, SCSH/CF; Vol. 14, SCSH/CH.

68 1900 US Federal Census, Verdier Township, Colleton County, South Carolina, Enumeration District 48, Family 151.

69 "Revealed in a Vision," *Washington Post*, April 10, 1890, 2.

70 "Revealed in a Vision," *Washington Evening Star*, April 9, 1890, 2.

71 "Is Whisky a Life Elixir?" *Washington Daily Critic*, April 9, 1890, 4. Zora Neale Hurston describes Ruler's Root as effective in treasure hunts and, when hidden in a house "keep[s] things in your favor." Hurston, "Hoodoo in America," 413, 330.

72 Godding's obituary reported that he came from a devout Christian family and that he "was remarkable well-versed in Biblical history and could quote hundreds of passages from the Bible." *American Journal of Insanity* 56, no. 1 (July 1899): 185–97; *African Repository* 63, no. 2 (April 1887): 47–48; *Eighty-Third Annual Report of the American Colonization Society with the Minutes of the Annual Meeting and of the Board of Directors*, January 16, 1900 (Washington City: Judd and Detweiler Printers, 1900), 3.

73 Edward G. to William W. Godding, August 4, 1890. Edward G., Case Number 7775, Box 93, SEH/CFP.

74 Nelson T., Register Number 1431, October 11, 1884, Box 16, Folder 1, CSH/CP.

75 Henrietta M., Patient Number 9333, Box 8, SCSH/CF; Vol. 19, SCSH/CH.

76 Ed W., Patient Number 6216, Box 5, SCSH/CF; Vol. 13, SCSH/CH.

77 Alexis Wells-Oghoghomeh differentiates between witches and hags, "a designation applied exclusively to the female-imagined spirits believed to 'ride' their male and female victims during the night." Wells-Oghoghomeh, *Souls of Womenfolk*, 182.

78 Ed W., Patient Number 6216, Box 5, SCSH/CF; Vol. 13, SCSH/CH.

79 Martha B., Patient Number 8863, Box 7, SCSH/CF; Vol. 19, SCSH/CH. For other cases of African Americans describing snakes in their bodies because of conjure, see Chireau, *Black Magic*, 31, 106.

80 See, for example, *Seventy-Sixth Annual Report of the South Carolina State Hospital for the Insane for the Year 1900* (Columbia, SC: The State Company, State Printers, 1900), 25. This classification system derived from the work of the French physicians Philippe Pinel and his student Jean-Étienne Esquirol. Esquirol enumerated various moral and physical causes and explored the relationship between them in *Mental Maladies: A Treatise on Insanity*, published in 1838 and translated into English in 1845. See Porter, *Genetics in the Madhouse*, chap. 1.

81 Noll, *American Madness*, 66.

82 Noll, 73, 91. Noll writes that Kraepelin's first full description of dementia praecox, and manic-depressive psychosis as a separate disease, is found in the 1896 edition

of *Psychiatrie* and that the 1899 edition was particularly influential. Noll, 3; Kraepelin, *Psychiatrie*.

83 Kraepelin, *Dementia Praecox and Paraphrenia*, 3. On the increasing purchase of Kraepelin's categories in American psychiatry and opposition to his proposed disease categories, see also Lunbeck, *Psychiatric Persuasion*, chap. 5.

84 The language is from St. Elizabeths' Register of Cases, SEH/RC.

85 Charles D., Case Number 15241, March 29, 1905; Case Number 15617, October 21, 1905, Box 5, SEH/RC.

86 Quoted in Metzl, *Protest Psychosis*, 30. See also Summers, *Madness*, chap. 5.

87 Metzl, 30–31.

88 Engstrom and Crozier, "Race, Alcohol, and General Paralysis," 277n14. I am grateful to Ira Helderman for pointing me to this article.

89 Engstrom and Crozier, 274.

90 Strous, Opler, and Opler, "Reflections on 'Emil Kraepelin: Icon and Reality,'" 301.

91 Green, "Psychoses among Negroes," 707.

92 Green, 707.

93 O'Malley, "Psychoses in the Colored Race," 300. For an overview of St. Elizabeths' psychiatrists' ideas about race and dementia praecox, see Summers, *Madness*, 135–52.

94 O'Malley, "Psychoses in the Colored Race," 315.

95 *Woman's Medical Journal* 6, no. 7 (August 1897): 253; Burton, "Mary O'Malley, M.D.," 9–26.

96 O'Malley, "Psychoses in the Colored Race," 315.

97 O'Malley, 322.

98 O'Malley, 324.

99 Bevis, "Psychological Traits of the Southern Negro," 70–71.

100 Bevis, 72.

101 Bevis, 72, 73.

102 Bevis, 72–73.

103 Bevis, 74.

104 *Minneapolis Journal*, September 7, 1901; *Washington Evening Star*, February 15, 1915; Shepard, *Notes on Genealogy*, 88.

105 Evarts, "Dementia Praecox," 388.

106 Evarts, 391, 394.

107 Evarts, 391–92.

108 Evarts, 394.

109 Evarts, 400.

110 Evarts, 401–2.

111 Evarts, "Ontogenetic, 277–78. It is in this study that Judy B.'s case from this book's introduction appears.

112 Evarts, "Folk Lore of the Old Testament," 310. St. Elizabeths Hospital Superintendent William Alanson White also engaged Frazer in his work. See, for example,

W. A. White, "Psychoanalytic Parallels," *Psychoanalytic Review* 2 (January 1, 1915): 177–90.

113 Evarts, "Ontogenetic," 275–76. She cites J. G. Frazer, *The Golden Bough*, vols. 1 and 2, *The Magic Art and Evolution of Kings* (London: Macmillan, 1906, 1911).

114 Evarts, "Ontogenetic," 275.

115 Evarts, 276.

116 Evarts, 274, 276. She cites J. G. Frazer, *The Golden Bough*, vol. 9, *The Scapegoat* (London: Macmillan, 1914).

117 Evarts, "Ontogenetic," 287.

118 Evarts, 285.

119 See Conference Record Books, 1920–1922, 1929–1930, 1936 1938, SEH/CRB.

120 Lind, "Phylogenetic Elements," 309.

121 Lind, 319.

122 Lind, 323.

123 Lind, 324.

124 Scipio Y., Case Number 3188, Box 11, SEH/CFP; Conference reports, September 9, 1913; February 16, 1912, SEH/CRB.

125 Scipio Y., Case Number 3188, Box 11, SEH/CFP. He is listed as not literate in the census. 1910 US Federal Census, Washington, DC, Government Hospital for the Insane, Enumeration District 235, Sheet 1 B.

126 Lind, "Phylogenetic Elements," 330.

127 Charles T., Case Number 6740, Box 66, SEH/CFP.

128 His brother had him paroled against medical advice for a monthlong visit in 1905, during which time Charles had several "spells" that did not require immediate return to the hospital. Liza T. to St. Elizabeths Hospital, May 8, 1901; Ignatius T. to St. Elizabeths Hospital, August 1, 1905, Charles T., Case Number 6740, Box 66, SEH/CFP.

129 Lind, "Phylogenetic Elements," 324–25.

130 Charles T., Case Number 6740, March 14, 1916; February 25, 1917, Box 66, SEH/CFP.

131 Not all staff understood what he was doing. Notes from 1920 describe him as holding a cross in his hands and saying something to himself, while notes from 1921 identify him as praying the Rosary. Charles T., Case Number 6740, December 15, 1920, September 14, 1921, Box 66, SEH/CFP.

132 Charles's father was involved in a protracted legal dispute with the Visitation Sisters over the exact amount he would pay considering the death of one of his children and the birth of several children after the parties had entered into the agreement. Reidy, *Illusions of Emancipation*, 182.

133 Charles T., Case Number 6740, P. M. Lehman Memo, n.d. (ca. February 1940), Box 66, SEH/CFP.

134 See, for example, Pollock, "Mental Disease among Negroes."

135 Metzl, *Protest Psychosis*, 31.

CHAPTER 4. CONTAINING BLACK RELIGIOUS EMOTIONS

1 Daniel H., Case Number 15602, October 10, 1905, Box 275, SEH/CFP.

2 "Wanted Prophets [sic] Job," *Washington Evening Star*, October 9, 1905, 2; "Undoing of Weather Prophet," *Washington Post*, October 10, 1905, 10; "Spirits Turpentine," *Wilmington Morning Star*, October 11, 1905, 3.

3 "Undoing of Weather Prophet," 10; Daniel H., Case Number 15602, October 10, 1905, Box 275, SEH/CFP.

4 Daniel H., Case Number 15602, October 10, 1905, Box 275, SEH/CFP.

5 Davenport, *Primitive Traits*, 48. See also White, *Unsettled Minds*, 146–51.

6 For a discussion of ideas of emotionalism in late nineteenth-century and early twentieth-century social sciences, see Evans, *Burden of Black Religion*, in which he argues that "constructions of black emotionality were crucial to attempts to address and find a suitable explanation of the Negro problem in the United States" (125).

7 Stephens, *The Fire Spreads*, 8.

8 Butler, *Women in the Church of God in Christ*, 25–27.

9 Stephens, *The Fire Spreads*, 193–96.

10 Butler, *Women in the Church of God in Christ*, 28.

11 Yanni, *Architecture of Madness*.

12 Segrest, *Administrations of Lunacy*, 146.

13 "Death Takes Dr. T. O. Powell," *Atlanta Constitution*, August 20, 1907, 2; 1860 US Federal Census—Slave Schedules, Hancock, Georgia, p. 5.

14 *Reports of the Trustees, Superintendent and Resident Physician, and Other Officers of the Lunatic Asylum of the State of Georgia from October 1st, 1885–1st October, 1886* (Milledgeville, GA: Union and Recorder—Barnes and Moore Printers, 1886), 22.

15 Roberts, "Insanity in the Colored Race," 7.

16 On ideas about African Americans' "happy-go-lucky" nature, see Green, "Psychoses among Negroes," 703.

17 Buchanan, "Insanity in the Colored Race," 68.

18 Buchanan, 68.

19 C. H. Hughes, "Hospital Notes: Mississippi," *Alienist and Neurologist* 2, no. 3 (July 1, 1881): 443; "T. J. Mitchell," in *Biographical and Historical Memoirs of Mississippi*, vol. 2 (Chicago: Goodspeed Publishing Company, 1891), 449–50; 1830 US Federal Census, Limestone County, Alabama, p. 53.

20 Witmer, "Insanity in the Colored Race," 25.

21 Obituary, *American Practitioner and News* 23, no. 3 (February 6, 1897): 113–14; 1860 US Federal Census—Slave Schedule, Meade County, Kentucky, p. 20; Pusey, "Increase of Insanity," 350, 349.

22 Pusey, "Increase of Insanity," 349.

23 Pusey, 350.

24 Miller, *Effects of Emancipation*, 7.

25 Lydston, "Race Problem in America," 174–75. Lydston promoted eugenics beyond the medical world, as in the case of his play *The Blood of the Fathers* (1912).

26  Green, "Psychoses among Negroes," 708.

27  Green, 706.

28  O'Malley, "Psychoses in the Colored Race," 316.

29  Brigham, *Observations on the Influence of Religion*, v–vi.

30  Brigham, 234, 261, 296–97, 330–31.

31  Brigham, 331.

32  Imhoff, *Masculinity and the Making of American Judaism*, 41.

33  Brigham, *Observations on the Influence of Religion*, xii, xvi, 301.

34  "A Legal Inquiry," *St. Louis Post-Dispatch*, September 1, 1890; Theodore Diller, M.D., "Hypnotism in a Religious Meeting," *Medical News* 57 (July–December 1890): 304; Wright, "Theodore Diller," 584.

35  Curtis, *Faith in the Great Physician*, 130–38; Taves, *Fits, Trances, and Visions*, 241–47.

36  "Weak Souls Caught in Strange Toils," *St. Louis Post-Dispatch*, October 17, 1897, 10. The report also includes a phrenological analysis of Worley's head.

37  Corson, "Vital Equation of the Colored Race," 158; Corson, *Some Unpublished Letters of Helena Petrova Blavatsky*.

38  King, "Psychology of the Negro Revival," 459–60.

39  King, 459.

40  King, 460.

41  Payne, *Recollections of Seventy Years*, 253–54.

42  Brown, *My Southern Home*, 189.

43  Brown, 193.

44  Brown, 197.

45  Cooper, *Voice from the South*, 34.

46  White, *Too Heavy a Load*, 73.

47  Higginbotham, *Righteous Discontent*, 120–49.

48  Savage, *Your Spirits Walk beside Us*, 30.

49  Savage, 56–57.

50  See also Evans, *Burden of Black Religion*.

51  Washington, "Religious Life of the Negro," 22.

52  Ferris, *African Abroad*, 246.

53  Babcock, "Colored Insane," 424.

54  "Weird Babel of Tongues," *Los Angeles Times*, April 18, 1906, II1; see also "Rolling and Diving Fanatics 'Confess,'" *Los Angeles Times*, June 23, 1906, I7. On psychological language and tensions within evangelicalism in response to early Pentecostalism, see Curtis, "Sane Gospel."

55  "Women with Men Embrace: Whites and Black Mix in a Religious Frenzy," *Los Angeles Times*, September 3, 19–6, II1; "Holy Rollers Rave in Orgy," *Los Angeles Herald*, July 24, 1908, 1; "New Religious Sect Holds Weird Service," *San Diego Union and Daily Bee*, August 16, 1909, 12. The multiracial character of early Pentecostal meetings made them the target of white violence. In 1914 in Chico, California, for example, a group of twenty white boys attacked worshippers in a private home because they objected to "white men and women kissing the negro

minister and his wife after each sermon and upon leaving church." "Boys Lead Raid on Holy Roller Band," *Los Angeles Herald*, March 20, 1914, 5.

56  "Arrest Holy Roller," *Los Angeles Herald*, October 5, 1906, 7.

57  "Excitement on Benner St.," *Highland Park News-Herald and Journal*, April 20, 1907, 1.

58  1910 US Federal Census, Oakland City, Alameda County, California, Enumeration District 28, Family 233.

59  On Charles D. McGettigan, see "Dr. McGettigan, Leader in Coast Medicine, Dies," *San Francisco Call*, January 24, 1931; on Theodore Rethers, see *California and Western Medicine* 23, no. 1 (January 1925): 71–72, 78.

60  Arthur E., Patient Number 5119, July 30, 1915, Mendocino State Hospital Commitment Register, 330, California, US, State Hospital Records, 1856–1923.

61  Joseph E., WWII Draft Registration Card, Serial Number U2012, Local Board 61, Oakland, California, April 26, 1942, US, World War II Draft Registration Cards, 1942; "'Mother Jones,' 76, S.F. Negro Missionary," *San Francisco Examiner*, August 10, 1967, 47.

62  See, for example, the testimonies in *The Apostolic Faith* 1, no. 1 (September 1906): 1.

63  "Arrested for Jesus' Sake," *The Apostolic Faith* 1, no. 4 (December 1906): 3.

64  "Symptoms of Homicidal Mania," *Washington Post*, April 7, 1896, 3.

65  "The Courts" *Evening Star*, May 15, 1896, 15; Fannie S., Case Number 9883, Case Number 10101, Box 4, SEH/CFP; Registers of Cases, 1855–1941, December 31, 1890–December 16, 1900, 75, 84, SEH/RC; "She Wanted to Kill," *Washington Evening Times*, November 28, 1898, 1.

66  "Sent to the Asylum," *Washington Evening Star*, November 28, 1896, 3; "She Wanted to Kill," 1.

67  "A Madman in the Church," *Washington Morning Times*, July 10, 1897. There had been Black members of the parish since the mid-nineteenth century, and they participated in several segregated benevolent societies. *Historical Souvenir of the Consecration of Saint Dominic's Church, Washington, D.C., October 12, 1919* (Baltimore: St. Mary's Industrial School Electric Press, 1919), 59.

68  The ward notes in John T.'s file do not begin until 1901. See, for example, John T., Case Number 10348, Ward Notes, January 8, 1901; March 17, 1911, Box 171, SEH/CFP.

69  William T. to William A. White, Case Number 10348, October 8, 1911, Box 171, SEH/CFP.

70  Postmortem summary, n.d., John T., Case Number 10348, Box 171, SEH/CFP.

71  Hugh Hicklin, 1860 US Federal Census, Slave Schedules, Chester County, South Carolina, p. 75; 1900 US Federal Census, Lewisville Township, Chester County, South Carolina, Enumeration District 13, Family 302. Hicklin is buried in the Fishing Creek Presbyterian Cemetery in Chester, South Carolina.

72  Mariah H., Patient Number 8940, June 9, 1899, Box 7, SCSH/CF; Vol. 19, SCSH/CH.

73  A. B. Douglas, 1860 US Federal Census, Slave Schedules, Chester County, South Carolina, p. 44; Batson Jordan, 1840 US Federal Census, Darlington, South Caro-

lina, p. 22. Like Hicklin, Jordan was a Confederate veteran and is buried in the Fishing Creek Presbyterian Cemetery in Chester, South Carolina.

74 "Dug Treasure Hole," *Houston Post*, August 23, 1911, 10; 1910 US Federal Census, Houston City, Harris County, Texas, Enumeration District 71.

75 "Probate Court," *Houston Post*, September 27, 1911, 19.

76 "Negro Judged Insane," *Houston Post*, September 29, 1911, 11.

77 "What Is Religious Mania?" *Houston Post*, September 30, 1911, 7.

78 *Biennial Report of the Trustees and Superintendent of the State Lunatic Asylum to the Legislature of Mississippi for the Years 1886–1887* (Jackson, MS: R. H. Henry, State Printer, 1888), 8; *Biographical and Historical Memoirs of Mississippi*, vol. 2 (Chicago: Goodspeed Publishing, 1891), 449–50.

79 *Annual Report of the Central Kentucky Lunatic Asylum, Anchorage, Kentucky, for the Year Ending October 31, 1887* (Frankfort, KY: John D. Woods, Public Printer and Binder, 1887), 38.

80 Yanni, *Architecture of Madness*, 51, 79.

81 *Sixty-Ninth Annual Report of the South Carolina Lunatic Asylum for the Fiscal Year 1891–1892* (Columbia, SC: Charles A. Calvo, State Printer, 1892), 336; *Seventy-First Annual Report of the South Carolina Lunatic Asylum for the Fiscal Year 1893–1894* (Columbia, SC: Charles A. Calvo, State Printer, 1894), 10.

82 "Word from Florida," *Christian Recorder*, December 12, 1878, 1.

83 *Thirty-Fourth Annual Report of the Central State Hospital of Virginia for the Fiscal Year Ending 1904 and Historical Sketch of the Hospital* (Richmond: Public Printing, 1904), 12.

84 *Thirty-Fourth Annual Report of the Central State Hospital*, 37.

85 Segrest, *Administrations of Lunacy*, 205 209.

86 *Biennial Report of the Alabama Insane Hospital at Tuscaloosa for the Years Ending 30th September, 1891 and 1892* (Montgomery, AL: Smith Allred and Co. State Printers, 1892), 26.

87 *Digest of the Testimony Taken Before the Special Committee Appointed by the Speaker under a Resolution of the House of Representatives, Fifty-Ninth Congress, to Make a Full and Complete Investigation of the Management of the Government Hospital for the Insane* (Washington, DC: Government Printing Office, 1906), 201; 1860 US Federal Census, West Side Nottoway River, Southampton County, Virginia, pp. 5–6.

88 *Fortieth Annual Report of the Central State Hospital of Virginia for the Fiscal Year Ending September 30, 1910* (Richmond: Davis Bottom, Superintendent of Public Printing, 1910), 12.

89 "Excerpts from the Central State Hospital Annual Reports (1912–1923)," Western State Hospital Papers, Series I. Subseries H. General Files and Ledgers, 1828–1997, Box 89, Folder 6, Library of Virginia.

90 Michie, *Code of Virginia*, 209.

91 *Fifty-Ninth Annual Report of the Central State Hospital, of Virginia, 1928–1929* (Richmond: Division of Purchase and Printing, 1929), 16; "Rev. Hugh Henry," Richmond Times-Dispatch, February 16, 1912, 2.

92 This was out of a total of 2,454 inmates that year. *Fifty-Ninth Annual Report of the Central State Hospital, of Virginia, 1928–1929* (Richmond: Division of Purchase and Printing, 1929), 15.

93 *Sixty-First Annual Report of the Central State Hospital, Virginia* (Richmond: Division of Purchase and Printing, 1931), 10.

94 For an overview of eugenics and the politics of reproduction for African Americans, see Roberts, *Killing the Black Body*, chap. 2.

95 Thompson, *Of Shattered Minds*, 8.

96 *United States Congress House Special Committee on Investigation of the Government Hospital for the Insane*, 197.

97 *Sixth Biennial Report of the Board of Managers of the Crownsville State Hospital to His Excellency the Governor of Maryland, October 1, 1921 to September 30, 1923* (Baltimore: Department of Welfare, 1923), 28.

98 *Report of the Superintendent of the Florida State Hospital for the Period Beginning July 1, 1926, and ending June 30, 1928* (n.p.), 19.

99 Barrows, *Proceedings of the National Conference of Charities and Correction* (1896), 460.

100 *Superintendent's Report of the Eastern N.C. Insane Asylum, Also the Report of the Treasurer for the Year of 1887* (Wilmington, NC: Messenger Steam Power Presses, 1887), 4; *Superintendent's Report of the Eastern N.C. Insane Asylum, Also the Report of the Treasurer for the Year of 1889* (Wilmington, NC: Messenger Steam Power Presses, 1889), 19; *Sixty-Seventh Annual Report of the South Carolina Lunatic Asylum for the Fiscal Year 1889–90* (Columbia, SC: Charles A. Calvo State Printer, 1890), 218–19.

101 *Seventy-First Annual Report of the South Carolina Lunatic Asylum for the Fiscal Year 1893–94* (Columbia, SC: Charles A. Calvo State Printer, 1894), 15; *Sixty-Seventh Annual Report of the South Carolina Lunatic Asylum*, 216.

102 *Rules and Regulations for the Government of the Lunatic Asylum of South Carolina, Compiled by the Superintendent and Adopted by the Regents, October 8, 1891* (Columbia, SC: Presbyterian Publishing House, 1891), 18.

103 "A Funeral in the Asylum," *Christian Recorder*, June 30, 1898, 3.

104 Derieux, "Uncle Jaggers, 78–79, 121–22, 125–26; "Religion: Rev. Charles Jaggers," *Time*, September 1, 1924; Thompson, *Of Shattered Minds*, 57–60; *Souvenir and Official Program of the Mid-Winter Session of the Bishops' Council of the African Methodist Episcopal Church* (Columbia, SC: Allen University Print, 1923), 48.

105 "In the Colored Churches," *Richmond News Leader*, May 28, 1904, 7.

106 "In the Colored Churches," 7; "Religious Services There," *Richmond Planet*, January 12, 1901, 1; "Faithful Employee Dead," *Richmond Virginian*, June 22, 1911, 2.

107 "Baton Rouge District," *Southwestern Christian Advocate*, October 21, 1909, 10.

108 *Twenty-Seventh Annual Report of the Central State Hospital, of the State of Virginia for the Fiscal Year Ending September 30, 1897* (Richmond: J. H. O'Bannon, Superintendent of Public Printing, 1897), 8.

109 *Fortieth Annual Report of the Central State Hospital of Virginia for the Fiscal Year Ending September 30, 1910* (Richmond: Davis Bottom, Superintendent of Public Printing, 1910), 10, 13.

110 "Commencement of the Medical Department—Howard University," *Washington Evening Star*, March 8, 1882, 4. On the Readjuster Party and African American religion in Virginia, see Turner, *Soul Liberty*.

111 "Open New Hospital in West Virginia," *Baltimore Afro-American*, June 26, 1926, 4; Carter G. Woodson, "A Venture with Negro Management," n.d., Papers of Carter G. Woodson (microfilm) (Bethesda, MD: University Publications of America, 1999), Reel 5.

112 "Editorial: Opening of State Hospital for Colored Insane in West Virginia," *Journal of the National Medical Association* 18, no. 3 (July–September 1926): 136. See also "The Dawn of a Better Day," *Journal of the National Medical Association* 17, no. 4 (October–December 1925): 209–10.

113 "George I. Lythcott" in Caldwell, *History of the American Negro*, 616–18; "Dr. Lythcott Dies at Home in Oklahoma," *Chicago Defender*, May 14, 1938, 5.

114 Yenser, *Who's Who in Colored America* (1944), 246.

115 C. C. Barnett, "Lakin State Hospital," *The West Virginia Negro: Report of G. E. Ferguson, Director Bureau of Negro Welfare and Statistics of the State of West Virginia to Governor Wm. G. Conley* (Charleston, WV: Jarrett Printing Co., 1932), 38; F. G. Blackman, "Lakin Hospital Manned by Highly Trained Negro Staff," *Pittsburgh Courier*, April 25, 1936, A3.

116 "Negro Staffed Hospital Is Only One Approved in W. Va.," *New Journal and Guide*, July 30, 1932. 4.

117 Barnett, "Lakin State Hospital," 40.

118 *Annual Report of the Taft State Hospital for the Period November 1, 1939 to October 31, 1940*, Submitted by E. P. Henry, Medical Superintendent, to Governor Leon C. Phillips (Taft, OK: Taft State Hospital, 1940), 3.

119 C. C. Barnett, "Institution Report," *Tenth Biennial Report of the State Board of Control of West Virginia for the Period July 1, 1927, to July 30, 1930*, vol. 2 (Charleston, WV: Jarrett Publishing, 1930), 214.

120 Barnett, "Institution Report"; *Annual Report of the Taft State Hospital for the Period November 1, 1939 to October 31, 1940*, 3; E. L. Youngue, "Lakin State Hospital," *Biennial Report of Isaac M. Carter, Director, Bureau of Negro Welfare and Statistics of the State of West Virginia to Governor Homer A. Holt, 1937–1938* (Charleston, WV: Jarrett Printing, 1938), 59.

121 *Annual Report of the Taft State Hospital for the Period November 1, 1939 to October 31, 1940*, 3.

122 Barnett, "Lakin State Hospital," 40.

123 Barnett, 39.

124 Barnett, 40.

125 "Lakin Probe Asked by Mason County Delegate," *Hinton Daily News*, January 30, 1941, 8.

126 James D., Case Number 10960, October 3, 1895, Box 192, SEH/CFP.

127 "The School Trustees," *Washington Evening Star*, February 12, 1896, 12.

128 "Mistook Saul for Satan," *Washington Post*, October 2, 1895, 2.

129 1900 US Federal Census, District of Columbia, ED 44, Family 119.

130 Mrs. James D. to Dr. C. H. Latimer, December 8, 1897, Case Number 10960, Box 192, SEH/CFP.

131 In the hospital's annual report that year, Superintendent William Godding noted that the increasing numbers of "colored insane" had resulted in overcrowding, with portions of the West Lodge housing twice as many patients as it was designed to accommodate, and he called for an extension to be constructed. *Report of the Government Hospital for the Insane to the Secretary of the Interior* (Washington, DC: Government Printing Office, 1897), 19.

132 Mrs. James D. to Dr. W. W. Godding, November 17, 1898, Case Number 10960, Box 192, SEH/CFP.

133 James D. to Lizzie D., November 29, 1897, Case Number 10960, Box 192, SEH/CFP.

134 Mrs. James D. to Dr. C. H. Latimer, November 30, 1897, Case Number 10960, Box 192, SEH/CFP. Martin Summers writes that St. Elizabeths' superintendent William Godding, one of the doctors to whom Lizzie wrote, "unapologetically advocated for the inspection and, if necessary, censorship of patients' correspondence." Summers, *Madness*, 98.

135 "Deaths in the District," *Washington Evening Star*, April 14, 1906, 5.

136 "Trio of Insane People," *Washington Evening Star*, August 4, 1898; "Legal Record: District Courts," *Washington Post*, September 11, 1898.

137 Thomas G., Ward notes, April 1, 1901, Case Number 10815, Box 185, SEH/CFP. I have maintained the original spelling and grammar of the ward notes.

138 Thomas G., Ward notes, January 29, 1902, Case Number 10815, Box 185, SEH/CFP.

139 Mary C. to William W. Godding, September 5, 1898; December 11, 1898, Case Number 10815, Box 185, SEH/CFP.

140 Henry Y. to William W. Godding, August 30, 1898; November 28, 1898; March 5, 1899; September 7, 1899; April 24, 1901, Case Number 10815, Box 185, SEH/CFP.

141 Henry Y. to William W. Godding, November 28, 1898, Case Number 10815, Box 185, SEH/CFP.

142 "Many Minds Wrecked," *Washington Post*, July 7, 1901, 7.

143 Thomas G. to A. B. Richardson, February 22, 1901, Case Number 10815, Box 185, SEH/CFP.

144 *Report of the Special Committee on Investigation of the Government Hospital for the Insane.*

145 For another case of a patient who explicitly "resisted efforts at institutional control" and maintained that she was able to see and communicate with the dead, see Segrest, "Exalted on the Ward."

CHAPTER 5. THE SOCIAL ENVIRONMENT AND THE "NEGRO CULT"

1 1930 US Federal Census, New York City, New York County, New York State, Enumeration District 31-984, Family 121.

2 These events are covered in many works on Father Divine, including Watts, *God, Harlem U.S.A.*; "Leader of 'Heaven' Gets a Year in Jail," *New York Times*, June 5, 1932, 10; "Judge Who Sent Divine to Jail Dies Suddenly," *New York Amsterdam News*, June 9, 1932, 1; "Divine Hailed Here by 7,000 as He Quits Jail," *New York Amsterdam News*, June 29, 1932, 1.

3 Tevis, "'The People's Judge.'"

4 "White Woman, Seeking Writ, Scores Divine," *New York Amsterdam News*, September 15, 1934, 1; "Cult Leader is Hit in 'TIME': Pullman Porter Husband of Father Divine 'Angel' Tells of Practices—Wants 'GOD' Closed Up," *Atlanta Daily World*, January 13, 1934, 1; "Child Taken to 'Heaven'; Quiz Father Divine," *Chicago Defender*, March 9, 1935, 5; Fr. Divine Is Sued for $10,000 by N. Y. Husband, *Baltimore Afro-American*, March 23, 1935, 1.

5 "Panken Denounces Divine as a Menace," *New York Times*, February 11, 1940, 47; "Father Divine Scored by Judge," *New York Age*, May 11, 1935, 1.

6 "About Men and Things: A Judge Attempts a Definition of Religion," *Jewish Exponent*, February 23, 1940, 4. On Wiltwyck, see Ribovich, "Saving Black Boys."

7 "Divine in Court, Admits He Is Not 'Really' God," *Baltimore Afro-American*, March 9, 1935, 1. See also "Child Taken to 'Heaven'; Quiz Father Divine," 5.

8 "Divine in Court," 1.

9 "Not Really 'God,' Divine Concedes," *New York Times*, March 2, 1935, 17.

10 Bender and Yarrell, "Psychoses among Followers of Father Divine."

11 1950 US Federal Census, New York City, New York County, New York, Enumeration District 31-1133, Dwelling 100; 1940 US Federal Census, New York City, New York County, New York, Enumeration District 31-1940, Household 93.

12 On the concept of religio-racial identity and Black new religious movements, see Weisenfeld, *New World A-Coming*.

13 Reid, "Let Us Prey!," 276; "Ira De Augustine Reid," in Boris, *Who's Who in Colored America, 1928–1929*, 304.

14 For an influential early study by a Black anthropologist, see Fauset, *Black Gods of the Metropolis*.

15 Bond, "Insanity among Negroes," 304. He is referencing Bevis, "Psychological Traits of the Southern Negro."

16 Bond, "Insanity among Negroes," 304.

17 1930 US Federal Census, Central State Hospital for the Insane, Jefferson County, Kentucky, p. 4. In an unpublished autobiography written many years later, Bond rejected the idea that James's illness was "genetically induced" and described his brother's mind "as a battleground of individual and social tensions." Horace Mann Bond, "Books: Autobiography, unpublished draft, 1970," Horace Mann Bond Papers. I am grateful to Kimberly Akano for alerting me to Bond's autobiography.

18  Bond, "Insanity among Negroes," 304, 306.

19  Bond, 306.

20  Moore, "Introduction to a Study of Neuropsychiatric Problems" (1926), 1042.

21  On Black and white social scientists in this period on questions of religion, race, and environment, see, for example, Drake, *To Know the Soul of a People*; Savage, *Your Spirits Walk beside Us*; Evans, *Burden of Black Religion*.

22  Smith, "Mental Hygiene," 2.

23  Smith, 5.

24  Frazier, "Psychological Factors," 489.

25  Moore, "Introduction to a Study of Neuropsychiatric Problems" (1927), 887.

26  Moore, 896.

27  Mather, *Who's Who of the Colored Race*, 196.

28  Smith, McDaniel, and, Hardin, *Kentucky African American Encyclopedia*, 55.

29  Smith was one of few African American doctors who were elected members of the American Psychiatric Association, and he later became a member of the National Guild of Catholic Psychiatrists. "Dr. Alan P. Smith Elected to Membership in the American Psychiatric Association," *Journal of the National Medical Association* 22, no. 4 (October–December 1930), 205; "With High Commendation Dr. Smith Made Colonel," *Tuskegee Herald*, June 29, 1955, 1. On the short-lived Guild of Catholic Psychiatrists, see Nussbaum, "Profession and Faith."

30  Roberts, "Insanity in the Colored Race," 6.

31  Moore, "Introduction to a Study of Neuropsychiatric Problems" (1927), 892–93. Smith draws on Moore to make the same argument. Smith, "Mental Hygiene," 2.

32  Moore, "Introduction to a Study of Neuropsychiatric Problems" (1927), 892. See also Moore, "Introduction to a Study of Neuropsychiatric Problems" (1926), 1044.

33  Moore, Introduction to a Study of Neuropsychiatric Problems" (1927), 893, 895.

34  Moore, 893, 891.

35  Moore, Introduction to a Study of Neuropsychiatric Problems" (1926), 1043–44.

36  Moore, Introduction to a Study of Neuropsychiatric Problems" (1927), 889.

37  Frazier, "Psychological Factors," 489–90.

38  Smith, "Mental Hygiene," 5–6. On this shift from arguments about race to culture, see also Evans, *Burden of Black Religion*, 224.

39  "Dr. Richard A. Billings' Funeral Rites Today," *Atlanta Daily World*, February 9, 1968, 6; Joel W. Smith, "Dr. Billings Lived a Dedicated Life Bishop H. I. Bearden Says," *Atlanta Daily World*, February 10, 1968, 1, 6. Billings served on the AME's General Board and Education Board at different times.

40  Billings, "The Negro and His Church," 426.

41  Billings, 438.

42  Billings, 436.

43  Billings, 426.

44  He may have had in mind a church like Charles Manuel "Sweet Daddy" Grace's United House of Prayer for All People that flourished in the 1930s, combining a

charismatic leader's claim to divine power and enthusiastic Pentecostal worship. Dallam, *Daddy Grace.*

45 Billings, "The Negro and His Church," 430.

46 Billings, 428–29.

47 Billings, 432.

48 Billings, 440.

49 Fauset, *Black Gods of the Metropolis*, and Jones, *Comparative Study of Religious Cult Behavior among Negroes*, are important examples. For an extensive discussion of the social scientific literature, see Evans, *Burden of Black Religion*, chap. 7.

50 See, for example, "Insanity of the Negro Race," *Botanico-Medical Recorder* 11, no. 24 (October 7, 1843): 379–80.

51 "Distribution of Insanity in the United States," 1019. White, whose family lived in Massachusetts for several generations after coming to the United States from England and was raised in New York City, may have been a Unitarian. Rev. Ulysses B. Pierce of All Souls Unitarian Church in Washington, DC, presided at his wedding and preached at his funeral. "Funeral Rites Set for Dr. W. A. White," *Washington Evening Star*, March 9, 1937, A-10.

52 Horatio M. Pollock, a statistician for the New York State Hospital Commission, published an analysis in 1924 of data from hospital admissions and found higher rates of first admission for African Americans than whites, especially in the North. Pollock, "Mental Disease among Negroes." On the growing influence of statistics in psychiatric research in this period, see Horowitz and Grob, "Checkered History of American Psychiatric Epidemiology."

53 Malzberg, "Migration and Mental Disease," 112. For more on Malzberg and the context for his work in the 1930s, see Doyle, *Psychiatry and Racial Liberalism in Harlem*, chap. 1.

54 Malzberg, "Mental Disease among American Negroes," 399, 396.

55 Malzberg, 373, 395. S. P. Rosenthal, a New York City schoolteacher who became a psychologist, also questioned the statistical findings of earlier studies and named Babcock, Bevis, Green, and O'Malley, as presenting unreliable statistics. Rosenthal, "Racial Differences in the Mental Diseases," 317.

56 Malzberg, "Mental Disease among Negroes in New York State," 510, 512.

57 Wagner, "Comparative Study of Negro and White Admissions," 179–80.

58 Wagner, 181.

59 Frazier, "Psychological Factors," 489.

60 Smith, "Mental Hygiene," 6. Also see Moore, "Introduction to a Study of Neuropsychiatric Problems among Negroes" (1927), 896.

61 On religious change in Black Chicago in this period, see Best, *Passionately Human.*

62 Frazier, *Negro Family in Chicago*, 78.

63 Rosenthal cites Frazier, "Psychological Factors," and Wagner cites Locke, *New Negro.*

64 Dwyer, "Psychiatry and Race during World War II," 122.

65 Jenkins, *Mystics and Messiahs*, 48.

66 See, for example, Prince, "'Driven Insane by Eddyism'"; Fluhman, *Peculiar People*; Jenkins, *Mystics and Messiahs*, 46–69.

67 For an early application of the "Voodoo cult" label, see the 1912 case of Clementine Barnabet in Louisiana, in which she was convicted of murders that supposedly involved conjure and a "Church of Sacrifice" and was sentenced to a term of life in Louisiana's Angola Penitentiary. A lunacy commission was convened to evaluate Barnabet's fitness to stand trial; its report characterized her as "morally depraved, unusually ignorant and of a low grade of mentality" but not insane. "Lunacy Commission Named," *New Orleans Daily Picayune*, October 18, 1912, 16; Barnabet Girl Found to Be Sane," *New Orleans Daily Picayune*, October 22, 1912, 16; E. M. Hummel, John Tolson, R. D. Voorhies, Lunacy Commission Report, October 21, 1912, Federal Writers Project Collection, Folder 45, Northwestern State University of Louisiana, Cammie G. Henry Research Center. For a longer discussion of discourses around the Barnabet case, see Greene-Hayes, "'A Very Queer Case.'"

68 Boaz, "Voodoo Cult of Detroit," 19. See also Ramsey, *Spirits and the Law*.

69 Boaz, "Voodoo Cult of Detroit," 19–20.

70 "Hideous Blot of Voudoo Murders Stains the West Indies Still," *New York Tribune*, December 14, 1913, D4.

71 Fard's origins and history are unclear, but he was probably an immigrant from New Zealand or Afghanistan, who had spent time in Oregon and California before his arrival in Detroit. See, for example, Clegg, *Original Man*.

72 Weisenfeld, *New World A-Coming*, 56–73.

73 Elijah and Clara are listed in the 1931 Detroit city directory under the surname Poole and in the 1932 directory under the surname Karriem. *Polk's Detroit City Directory*, vol. 69 (R. L. Polk and Co., Publishers, 1931), 1350; *Polk's Detroit City Directory*, vol. 70 (R. L. Polk and Co., Publishers, 1932), 820.

74 "Leader of Cult Admits Slaying at Home Altar," *Detroit Free Press*, November 21, 1932, 1; 2; "Voodoo Slayer Admits Plotting Death of Judges," *Detroit Free Press*, November 22, 1932, 1.

75 "Leader of Cult Admits Slaying at Home Altar," 2.

76 "See, for example, "Raided Temple Bares Grip of Voodoo in City," *Detroit Free Press*, November 23, 1932, 1, 3; "Suburbs Also in Voodoo Net," *Detroit Free Press*, November 29, 1932, 9; "Voodoo's Reign Here Is Broken," *Detroit Free Press*, December 7, 1932, 7.

77 Boaz, "Voodoo Cult of Detroit," 18.

78 W. D. Fard, "No Connection between Islam and Robert Harris, Alleged Voodoo Killer of Detroit," *Baltimore Afro-American*, December 31, 1932, 6.

79 "Probe Weird Rites of Detroit Voodoo Cult," *Chicago Defender*, December 3, 1932, 4.

80 Lost Found Moslem Lesson no. 1, question 10, Fard FBI File, Part 1, 116.

81 "Intended Voodoo Victims' Number Still Mounting," *Detroit Free Press*, November 27, 1932, 1.

82 "Voodoo Chief Held Unsound," *Detroit Free Press*, November 30, 1932, 3.

83 "Voodoo's Reign Here Is Broken," 7.

84 Russel J. Cowans, "Probe Weird Rites of Detroit Voodoo Cult," *Chicago Defender*, December 3, 1932, 1

85 Fard, "No Connection between Islam and Robert Harris, Alleged Voodoo Killer of Detroit," 6.

86 "Voodoo's Reign Here Is Broken," "Declare Voodoo King Insane," *Chicago Defender*, December 17, 1932, 1.

87 Robert Harris, Certificate of Death, Michigan Department of Health, Division of Vital Statistics, June 19, 1935, State Office Number 434 256, *Michigan, U.S., Death Records, 1867–1952*.

88 "Raided Temple Bares Grip of Voodoo in City," 1.

89 Weisenfeld, *New World A-Coming*, 42–55.

90 "Voodoo Slayer Admits Plotting Death of Judges," 1, 3.

91 "New Human Sacrifice with a Boy as Victim Is Averted by Inquiry," *Detroit Free Press*, November 26, 1932, 2; "Pastors Decry Growth of Cult Practices Here," *Detroit Free Press*, November 28, 1932, 2.

92 "Raided Temple Bares Grip of Voodoo in City," 3.

93 "Negro Claims to Be God," *Valdosta Daily Times*, February 5, 1914.

94 "Negro Preacher Arrested," *Valdosta Daily Times*, February 6, 1914; "Black 'Messiah' at Valdosta in Prison," *Atlanta Georgian and News*, February 10, 1914, 2; *Valdosta Daily Times*, February 21, 1914, quoted in Pearson and Tomberlin, "John Doe, Alias God," 45. The lunacy hearing was overseen by Ordinary Judge James Oglethorpe Vardenoe, a Presbyterian elder and Confederate veteran from Liberty County, Georgia, where the Children of the Wilderness had come to public attention in 1889. *History and Catalogue of the Sigma Alpha Epsilon Fraternity* (Harrisburg, PA: Myers Printing House, 1893), 108; 1860 US Federal Census—Slave Schedules, District 15, Liberty County, Georgia, p. 21; Stacy, *History of the Midway Congregational Church*, 106–7.

95 "Is Everybody Crazy?" *Valdosta Daily Times*, March 2, 1914.

96 "Messenger Was Adjudged Unsound Mind," *Valdosta Daily Times*, February 27, 1914.

97 Moseley, *Manifest Victory*, 106–9. Mosely described meeting the Messenger in Valdosta and requesting that his friend Copeland represent him. He encountered him again in Americus, Georgia, and in Brooklyn, New York, realizing that this acquaintance "was becoming famous as Father Divine." Moseley, 107.

98 "Moorish American Chief Facing Court," *Trenton Evening Times*, January 14, 1933, 2.

99 *The Municipal Court of Philadelphia: Address by Charles L. Brown, President Judge of the Municipal Court of Philadelphia at the Lutheran Church of the Redeemer, 35th and Midvale Avenue, Philadelphia, Monday evening, March 14, 1921* (n.p., 1921), 6, 21.

100 "Herbert Hoover Dodges Grand Sheik of the Moors," *Baltimore Afro-American*, February 4, 1933, 14. Way Bey's reference to "Asiatics of the Northwest" refers to Moorish Science Temple geography in which the Moroccan empire, from which

they claim to descend, is called Northwest Amexem. *Koran Questions for Moorish Americans* (Chicago, n.d.), 2.

101 "Moorish Sheik Held in Philly," *Baltimore Afro-American*, February 11, 1933, 13.

102 "Elijah Poole," SAC Chicago, January 27, 1958, CG 100-6989, p. 6, Elijah Muhammad FBI File, Part 2, 62.

103 "Elijah Poole," SAC Chicago, January 27, 1958, CG 100-6989, p. 6, Elijah Muhammad FBI File, Part 2, 62.

104 Lauretta Bender, "Autobiographical Sketch," 1965, Box 18, Folder 4, The Papers of Lauretta Bender, Brooklyn College Archives and Special Collections, Brooklyn College Library.

105 "Patton Adds Psychiatrist," *San Bernardino County Sun*, October 31, 1956, 15.

106 Bender and Yarrell, "Psychoses among Followers of Father Divine," 423.

107 "Dr. James A. Brussel, Criminologist, Is Dead," *New York Times*, October 23, 1982, 10.

108 Brussel, "Father Divine," 215.

109 Brussel, 219.

110 On Black clergy's and journalists' responses to the Peace Mission, see Weisenfeld, *New World A-Coming*, chap. 7.

111 Brussel, "Father Divine," 219; McKay, "'There Goes God!'"

112 Brussel, "Father Divine," 219.

113 Bender and Yarrell, "Psychoses among Followers of Father Divine," 422; Du Bois, *Souls of Black Folk*, 190.

114 H. Snyder, "A Plantation Revival Service," *Yale Review*, October 1920, 172, quoted in Bender and Yarrell, "Psychoses among Followers of Father Divine," 422.

115 Bender and Yarrell, "Psychoses among Followers of Father Divine," 422.

116 Brussel, "Father Divine," 219.

117 Brussel, 222.

118 Brussel, 222–23.

119 On Bender and racial analysis, see Doyle, "'Racial Differences Have to Be Considered.'"

120 Bender and Yarrell, "Psychoses among Followers of Father Divine," 430, 436.

121 Bender and Yarrell, 425.

122 Bender and Yarrell, 425.

123 Bender and Yarrell, 431–32.

124 Bender and Yarrell, 434.

125 Bender and Yarrell, 448.

126 Bender and Yarrell, 425.

127 Bender and Yarrell, 448–49.

128 *American Journal of Insanity* 92, no. 2 (September 1935): 451.

129 "16 of Divine's Cult Show Mental Ills," *New York Times*, May 17, 1935, 3.

130 For example, "'Messiah' Accused of Creating Such Religious Fervor Some Become Insane," *Evansville Courier*, May 17, 1935, 2; Gardner Bridge, "Negro 'Messiah' Declared Menace," *Montreal Gazette*, May 17, 1935, 11; "Mind Diseases Strike Cult," *Cincinnati Post*, May 16, 1935, 2.

131 "30 Social Workers Hear Ira Reid," *Baltimore Afro-American*, November 18, 1933, 10.

132 "Jerseyites Crazy from Religious Cult Practices," *Baltimore Afro-American*, December 22, 1934, 10.

133 1930 US Federal Census, Philadelphia City, Philadelphia County, Pennsylvania, Enumeration District 51–636, Family 274; 1880 US Federal Census, Philadelphia City, Philadelphia County, Pennsylvania, Enumeration District 147, Family 152; Kaplan, *Solomon Carter Fuller*, 64–65.

134 "Drinking, Insanity, Cults Increase, N.J. Women Learn," *Baltimore Afro-American*, July 28, 1934, 20.

135 Bender and Yarrell, "Psychoses among Followers of Father Divine," 420.

136 Father Divine to Dr. Parker, May 17, 1935," *California Eagle*, May 31, 1935, 10.

137 "Father Divine's Message at the Banquet Table, 20 W. 115th Street, New York City, Thursday, May 16, 1935, Midnight," *California Eagle*, May 31, 1935, 10.

138 Cantril and Sherif, "Kingdom of Father Divine," 159.

139 Former members Verinda and Thomas Brown sued Divine to reclaim money and personal belongings they brought with them to the movement. *Verinda Brown v. Father Divine*, Supreme Court of the State of New York, Appellate Division, Record on Appeal (New York: Ackerman Press, Inc., 1938), 44–45. Several former members charged that Divine promoted sexual contact with him as part of their spiritual development. Faithful Mary, *'God,' He's Just a Natural Man* (New York: Universal Light Publishing Co., 1937); "Divine Is Accused by Widow," *Baltimore Afro American*, April 17, 1937; Ruth Boaz, "My Thirty Years with Father Divine," *Ebony*, May 1965, 88–98; Carol Sweet Hunt, "I Was One of Father Divine's Angels," *Confidential* 4, no. 2 (May 1956): 34–36, 64.

140 "Crowd Battles Police to Free Father Divine," *New Journal and Guide*, March 16, 1935, 1.

141 "The Problem of the Cults," *Cleveland Plain Dealer*, March 22, 1935, 7, reprinted from the *Chicago Bee*.

142 Miles Mark Fisher, "Negroes Gets Religion," *Opportunity: Journal of Negro Life* 14, no. 1 (January 1936): 150; Yenser, *Who's Who in Colored America* (1937), 185.

CHAPTER 6. FAITH IN PSYCHIATRY

1 Robinson, *Road without Turning*, 31, 90–91.

2 Robinson, 96.

3 Robinson, 85.

4 Robinson, 117, 124, 127.

5 Robinson, 131–32.

6 Robinson, 138.

7 Robinson, 142.

8 Robinson, 176–85.

9 Robinson, 171.

10 *The Lion: A Record of Achievements* (Lincoln University, PA: Lincoln University, 1935), 28.

11  Robinson, *Road without Turning*, 205.

12  Robinson, 210–12.

13  Robinson, 212.

14  Robinson, 220, 227; "Presbyterians Will Attend Opening of New Ritzy Harlem Church," *New York Amsterdam News*, April 30, 1938, 10.

15  Nancy Griffith, "Furman L. Brodie: Pastor and Educator," *News of Davidson*, December 19, 2019, https://newsofdavidson.org.

16  Robinson, *Road without Turning*, 229.

17  Robinson, 230–31.

18  Robinson, 231.

19  "400 Members in Two Years Record of New York Church," *Pittsburgh Courier*, October 5, 1940, 2.

20  Robinson, *Road without Turning*, 253.

21  Robinson, 253.

22  Robinson, 252.

23  "Oral history interview with Dr. Elizabeth Bishop Davis," conducted by Jean Blackwell Hutson, Schomburg Center for Research in Black Culture, 1983.

24  "Oral history interview with Dr. Elizabeth Bishop Davis." On the Harlem YWCA, see Weisenfeld, *African American Women and Christian Activism*.

25  Summers, *Madness*, 249.

26  Dwyer, "Psychiatry and Race during World War II," 123–29; Smith, *First Resort*, 54–59.

27  Smith, *First Resort*, 58–59; Summers, *Madness*, 225. Menninger grew up in a Presbyterian family in Topeka, Kansas, and led a Boy Scout troop connected with the First Presbyterian Church. Allison et al., *With Christ in Kansas*, 89, 95, 106.

28  Smith, *First Resort*, 3. See also Mendes, *Under the Strain of Color*, 108; Scott, *Contempt and Pity*, 74; also Summers, *Madness*, 255–56.

29  Raz, *Lobotomy Letters*.

30  Smith, "Role of Psychoanalytic Psychiatry," 147.

31  Smith, 152.

32  Smith, 152.

33  For an overview of the origins of the movement, the National Committee for Mental Hygiene, its institutional arm, and connections to eugenics, see Grob, *Mental Illness and American Society*, chap. 6.

34  Mendes, *Under the Strain of Color*, 65.

35  C. P. Oberndorf to Viola W. Bernard, June 24, 1943; Viola W. Bernard to George Edmund Haynes, July 7, 1943, VWB, Box 388, Folder 4.

36  *Southern Workman* 52, no. 11 (November 1923): 553.

37  *Southern Workman* 57, no. 1 (January 1928): 45; *Le Cheval: Senior Class Yearbook*, vol. 1 (Raleigh, NC: Saint Augustine's College, 1934), 21; *Sixty Fourth Annual Catalogue of Saint Augustine's College* (Raleigh, NC, 1930–31), 13. The school was named after the recently deceased Bishop Daniel S. Tuttle.

38  *Saint Augustine's Record, Saint Augustine's College, Seventy-First Catalogue Number* (Raleigh, NC, 1937–38), 37.

39  Quoted in Grace Lindley, "A Satisfying Enterprise to All Concerned: The Bishop
    Tuttle Memorial House Reflects Spirit of Great Bishop," *Spirit of Missions* 92, no. 6
    (June 1927): 363.

40  *Southern Workman* 62, no. 2 (February 1933): 94.

41  Rosa Kittrell, "No Hiding Place," *Club Dial*, December 1943, 8.

42  Dorothy P. Scott, "White Plains, N.Y.," *New York Amsterdam News*, December 6,
    1933, 10; Kittrell, "No Hiding Place," 24–25.

43  Kittrell, "No Hiding Place," 25.

44  "5-Year Mental Fight Won, Woman Helps Sufferers," *Chicago Defender*, March 27,
    1943, 7; Kittrell, "No Hiding Place," 26.

45  Kittrell, "No Hiding Place," 25; Beers, *A Mind That Found Itself*.

46  Brennan was born in St. Louis and graduated from St. Louis University and the
    St. Louis University School of Medicine, which may indicate that he was Catholic.
    "Dr. Thomas P. Brennan," *New York Times*, December 20, 1965, 35.

47  Kittrell, "No Hiding Place," 25–26; "Psychopathic Care Is Planned at N.C. Meet,"
    *Baltimore Afro-American*, December 16, 1939, 5.

48  "Mental Hygiene Committee Holds Third Annual Meeting," *New Journal and
    Guide*, March 6, 1943, A20; "Report of the Third Annual Meeting: The Committee
    for Mental Hygiene for Negroes," *Journal of the National Medical Association* 35,
    no. 4 (July 1943): 146–47.

49  Thomas P. Brennan and Rosa Kittrell, "A Committee for Mental Hygiene for
    Negroes," September 1941, VWB, Box 388, Folder 4.

50  Thomas P. Brennan and Rosa Kittrell, "The Committee for Mental Hygiene for
    Negroes," January 10, 1943, VWB, Box 388, Folder 4; "George C. Branche," *Wash-
    ington Post and Times Herald*, September 14, 1956, 36.

51  Prince P. Barker, "Frontiers of Mental Hygiene," *Journal of the National Medical
    Association* 38, no. 1 (January 1946), 15; "Barker to Be Buried," *New York Amster-
    dam News*, February 13, 1971, 27.

52  "Mental Hygiene Group in White Plains Has Birthday Celebration for One Year
    of Work," *New York Age*, April 20, 1940, 10. On Williams's work with the YWCA
    on race relations, see Robertson, *Christian Sisterhood, Race Relations*, chaps. 6 and
    7.

53  "Program: The Committee for Mental Hygiene for Negroes," February 17, 1943;
    Report of the Third Annual Meeting: The Committee for Mental Hygiene for
    Negroes," February 17, 1943, VWB, Box 388, Folder 4.

54  "Mental Hygiene Group Observes 1st Anniversary," *Chicago Defender*, April 27,
    1940, 17; "Hygiene Group Holds All-College Day," *Baltimore Afro-American*,
    August 17, 1940, 23; Rosa Kittrell to Viola Bernard, September 19, 1941, VWB, Box
    388, Folder 4.

55  "Amateur Players' Production Proves Popular," *New York Amsterdam News*, Sep-
    tember 6, 1941, 10.

56  Kittrell, "No Hiding Place," 26; Leah T. Malone to Thomas P. Brennan, July 18,
    1943, VWB, Box 388, Folder 4.

57 Rosa Kittrell to Viola W. Bernard, June 5, 1942; Viola W. Bernard to Rosa Kittrell, June 11, 1942, VWB, Box 388, Folder 4.

58 George Edmund Haynes to Viola W. Bernard, June 18, 1943; Viola W. Bernard to George Edmund Haynes, July 7, 1943; Report of the Third Annual Meeting: The Committee for Mental Hygiene for Negroes," February 17, 1943, VWB, Box 388, Folder 4.

59 Ellison, "Harlem Is Nowhere," 294.

60 Lafargue Clinic brochure, n.d., Box 1, Folder 15, LCR.

61 Mendes, *Under the Strain of Color*, 59.

62 Mendes, 62.

63 Therese Pol, "Psychiatry in Harlem," *The Protestant*, July 1947, 28, Box 1, Folder 13, LCR.

64 Mendes, *Under the Strain of Color*, 55.

65 Mendes, 2–4.

66 For the outlines of Wright's early life and his childhood experiences in various churches, see Wright, *Black Boy*.

67 Quoted in Rowley, *Richard Wright*, 285.

68 Rowley, 286.

69 FBI File No. 100-41674, "Richard Nathaniel Wright," July 8, 1944, 2–3. https://vault.fbi.gov.

70 Wright, *Twelve Million Black Voices*. On religion and photography in *Twelve Million Black Voices*, see McDannell, *Picturing Faith*, chap. 8.

71 Wright, *Twelve Million Black Voices*, 97.

72 Wright, 130–31.

73 Wright, 131. In his contribution on Harlem to the Federal Writers' Project book *New York Panorama* (1938), Wright made a similar argument about the significance of churches which, he argued, played "the central role in the life of the Harlem Negro." Federal Writers' Project, *New York Panorama*, 140. On Wright's involvement with the project, see Sorett, *Spirit in the Dark*, 71.

74 Wright, *Twelve Million Black Voices*, 135.

75 Sorett, *Spirit in the Dark*, 72.

76 "A Conversation between Mrs. Elizabeth Simonoff and the Rev. Shelton Hale Bishop," March 22, 1949, Box 3, Folder 4, LCR; "Biggest Episcopal Church: Harlem's St. Philip's Tops U.S. in Membership," *Ebony* 8, no. 1 (November 1952): 66. On the Community Center, initially called the Fun Center, see Doyle, "Universal Mind Assumption," 319–22.

77 Quoted in Greenberg, *Or Does It Explode?*, 212.

78 "Findings and Recommendations of the City-Wide Citizens' Committee on Harlem, Monday, May 29, 1944," 2, Box. 388, Folder 2, VWB. On the committee's work prior to 1943, see Greenberg, *Or Does It Explode?*, 205–6.

79 Dickerson, *African American Preachers and Politics*, 62.

80 See, for example, "Church and Social Circles Get Jolts as Breach Appears," *New York Amsterdam News*, March 6, 1929, 1; "Bishop Denies Marital Rift," *Baltimore Afro-American*, March 9, 1929, 11.

81  "Bishops Separate, Report," *Pittsburgh Courier*, March 9, 1929, 1.

82  "Rev. Bishop Gets Children by Decision," *New York Amsterdam News*, October 26, 1932, 1.

83  1940 US Federal Census, Queens Village, Queens County, New York, Enumeration District 41-776, Sheet 15B; "Gussie Bishop Booth Dead," *New York Age*, May 2, 1942, 12.

84  "The Mosse Family," *The Mosse Art Restitution Project*, accessed August 5, 2023, https://mosseartproject.com/. On Northside, see Markowitz and Rosner, *Children, Race, and Power*.

85  Lafargue Clinic Brochure, n.d., Box 1, Folder 15, LCR.

86  "Earl Brown Is Dead; Former Councilman," *New York Times*, April 15, 1980, 43; "Promoted," *New York Amsterdam News*, March 16, 1927, 8; Thoms, *Pathfinders*, 109–10; Doyle, "Universal Mind Assumption," 313n16; Doyle, "'A Fine New Child,'" 187.

87  Many patients did pay the fee for services. In 1947, for example, of 1,483 visits to the clinic, 940 were paid and 543 unpaid, resulting in $234.80 in fees paid for the year. Lafargue Clinic Statistics (1948–1956), Box 1, Folder 9, LCR.

88  Leonard Lyons, "Lyons Den," *Louisville Courier-Journal*, December 27, 1948, 7; "Pyramid Club Contributions," *New York Amsterdam News*, January 10, 1948, 7.

89  Lafargue Clinic Statistics (1948–1956); "Lafargue Clinic Approved by VA," *Baltimore Afro-American*, March 8, 1947, 3.

90  Lafargue Clinic Statistics (1948–1956).

91  Sidney M. Katz, "Jim Crow Is Barred from Wertham's Clinic," reprint from *Magazine Digest*, September 1946, Box 3, Folder 2, LCR; Theresa Pol, "Psychiatry in Harlem," *The Protestant* (June–July 1947), 29, Box 3, Folder 5, LCR.

92  Robert Bendiner, "Psychiatry for the Needy," *Tomorrow*, April 1948, 23, Box 3, Folder 2, LCR.

93  Lafargue Clinic Organization, September 1, 1952, Box 3, Folder 17, LCR.

94  Lafargue Clinic Staff List, September 1953, Box 1, Folder 12, LCR.

95  "Oral History Interview with Dr. June Jackson Christmas," conducted by Jean Blackwell Hutson, Schomburg Center for Research in Black Culture, 1985. Christmas would go on to have a long career in private practice and in varied positions including in the Department of Psychiatry at Harlem Hospital, as New York City's "commissioner of mental health and mental retardation services," and as the founder of the Harlem Rehabilitation Center, a community-based mental health services program.

96  Box 2, Folder 2, LCR. The files of the clinic's staff are restricted, so I have not named volunteer staff whose materials appear in the restricted filed. I have named those who appear on the unrestricted Lafargue Clinic Staff List, September 1953, Box 1, Folder 12, LCR, and in other public materials.

97  See Lafargue Clinic Staff List, September 1953.

98  Lafargue Clinic Organization, September 1, 1952, Box 1, Folder 11, LCR; 1930 US Federal Census, Bronx, New York City, New York, Enumeration District 3-692,

Family 618; Bendiner, "Psychiatry for the Needy," 24. Tweed became the first African American psychiatrist to be board certified in California and, an avid collector of religious artifacts from Ethiopia, donated a large collection to Howard University. The university repatriated a Christian manuscript from the collection to Ethiopia in 2021. Kurian, "Combatting Empire's Blinkered History."

99 Lafargue Clinic Organization.

100 Lafargue Clinic Testing Material, 1947, Box 1, Folder 13; Blank Case History Form, LCR, Box 1, Folder 14, LCR.

101 Blank Case History Form; "Mrs. Zucker's suggestions for first examination," Box 1, Folder 12, LCR. In my reading of the patient files, I did not see discussion of religion as a context for mental stress or illness in the histories of adults or children, but the clinic's archival collection includes only twenty-seven patient files from the almost fifteen hundred patients seen during the clinic's existence from 1946 to 1958. The records focused on problems like costly housing, employment, poverty, substance abuse, sexual abuse, illness, and war trauma.

102 Doyle, "Universal Mind Assumption," 4–5; Doyle, "'A Fine New Child,'" 174.

103 Bendiner, "Psychiatry for the Needy," 23.

104 Bendiner, 24.

105 Bendiner, 24.

106 Bendiner, 24.

107 Kardiner and Ovesey, Mark of Oppression. The authors changed the subtitle in the revised edition to Explorations in the Personality of the American Negro.

108 Kardiner and Ovesey, 317.

109 Doyle, "Universal Mind Assumption," 59.

110 Kardiner and Ovesey, Mark of Oppression, 12.

111 Kardiner and Ovesey, 51, 47.

112 Kardiner and Ovesey, 11.

113 Kardiner and Ovesey, 36–37.

114 Kardiner and Ovesey, 132, 138.

115 Kardiner and Ovesey, 355.

116 Kardiner and Ovesey, 353, 355.

117 Kardiner and Ovesey, 353, 356.

118 Kardiner and Ovesey, 385.

119 Collins et al., "Discussion of Psychoanalysis of Groups," 456.

120 Lafargue Staff List.

121 Kardiner and Ovesey, Mark of Oppression, 267.

122 Kardiner and Ovesey, 268.

123 Kardiner and Ovesey, 271.

124 Collins, "Psychoanalysis of Groups," 168.

125 Kardiner and Ovesey, Mark of Oppression, 387.

126 Lightfoot, Balm in Gilead, 181.

127 Ellison, "Harlem Is Nowhere," 302.

128 Earl Brown, "Timely Topics," New York Amsterdam News, February 15, 1947, 10.

129 Doyle, *Psychiatry and Racial Liberalism in Harlem*, 121; Mendes, *Under the Strain of Color*, 160–61.

CONCLUSION

1 This account of his life draws on Bennett, *Life behind the Walls*.
2 George W. Bennett, "The Reality of God and the Interpretation of Being: Introduction," n.d., 1, Box 1, Folder 2, GWB.
3 Bennett, *Life behind the Walls*, 8.
4 Bennett, 24.
5 Bennett, 6.
6 Bennett, 32.
7 Bennett, 12, 36–37.
8 Bennett, 46.
9 Bennett, 33.
10 Bennett, 83.
11 Bennett, 88–89, 95, 97. By this time, the Jamaican immigrant Joel Augustus Rogers was publishing history columns in the Black press that Bennett may have read and had also published *From Superman to Man* (1917) and *100 Amazing Facts about the Negro* (1934).
12 Bennett, *Life behind the Walls*, 98–99.
13 Bennett, 107–8.
14 Bennett, 113–14.
15 Bennett, 120. 116.
16 George W. Bennett, "Miscellaneous Handwritten Notes," n.d., Box 3, Folder 38, GWB. On the decline of dementia praecox as a diagnosis in the United States, see Noll, *American Madness*.
17 George W. Bennett, "The Correction of the Criminal and the Insane, in the Perfect State," n.d., 36, Box 1, Folder 16, GWB.
18 Bennett, "Reality of God," 3.
19 George W. Bennett, "The Wisdom of Normal and Abnormal Psychology and Psychiatry," n.d., 41, Box 1, Folder 6, GWB.
20 Bennett, "Wisdom," 19, 21, 27, 29.
21 Bennett, 41.
22 Bennett, *Life behind the Walls*, 14–15. Bennett's father, Diamond, was born in 1871, and his mother, Rebecca in 1879. 1900 US Federal Census, Bethel Township, Perquimans County, North Carolina, Enumeration District 84, Family 53. Diamond's father, Arthur, was born in 1846 and his mother in 1851. 1900 US Federal Census, Bethel Township, Perquimans County, North Carolina, Enumeration District 84, Family 52.
23 Bennett, *Life behind the Walls*, 8–9.
24 Bennett, 34.
25 "The King's Church of God," Box 3, Folder 36; "The King's Baptist Church of God Questions, Box 3, Folder 36, GWB.

26 "Ordination Held for Rev. Bennett," *New Journal and Guide*, January 30, 1965, A15; "The Church World: From Philadelphia," *New York Amsterdam News*, November 26, 1966, 27. See also "Author Gets New Vision in Prison," *New Journal and Guide*, December 10, 1966, A11.

27 Les Matthews, "Mr. 1-2-5 Street," *New York Amsterdam News*, August 31, 1974, A10.

28 Rev. George W. Bennett, display ad, *New York Amsterdam News*, July 19, 1969, 29.

29 This resonates with Black Studies scholar La Marr Jurelle Bruce's "mad methodology" and the commitments of Black madness studies. Bruce, *How to Go Mad without Losing Your Mind*, 234.

30 See Parsons, *From Asylum to Prison*.

31 Metzl, *Protest Psychosis*, xi.

32 Beliso-De Jesús, *Excited Delirium*.

33 Bellware, "Police Had No Legal Reason to Place Elijah McLain in Chokehold"; Clossen and Shanahan, "Black Man Died of Suffocation"; Orr, "How Daniel Prude Suffocated as Rochester Police Restrained Him"; O'Hare, Budhu, and Saadi, "Police Keep Using 'Excited Delirium' to Justify Brutality"; Santo, "Officer Suggested George Floyd Had 'Excited Delirium'"; Sullivan, "Death by Excited Delirium." In 2023, California became the first state to ban the use of excited delirium as a cause of death. Ives, "California Bans 'Excited Delirium' as a Cause of Death."

# BIBLIOGRAPHY

MANUSCRIPT SOURCES

Brooklyn College Archives and Special Collections, Brooklyn College Library
   Papers of Lauretta Bender
California State Archives
   Department of Mental Hygiene, Records of Mendocino State Hospital
   Department of Mental Hygiene, Records of Stockton State Hospital
Columbia University Health Sciences Library, Archives and Special Collections
   Viola Wertheim Bernard Papers
Library of Virginia
   Auditor of Public Accounts (1776–1928), Central State Hospital records, 1864–1890,
      Accession APA 127, State Government Records Collection, The Library of Vir-
      ginia, Richmond, Virginia
   Records of Western State Hospital, 1825–2000, State Government Records Collec-
      tion, The Library of Virginia, Richmond, Virginia
National Archives and Records Administration
   Records of St. Elizabeths Hospital
Schomburg Center for Research in Black Culture, The New York Public Library, Astor,
   Lenox, and Tilden Foundations
   George W. Bennett Manuscript
   Meta Warrick Fuller Papers
   Lafargue Clinic Records
South Carolina Department of Archives and History
   State Department of Mental Health
University of Massachusetts Amherst Libraries, Special Collections and University
   Archives
   Horace Mann Bond Papers, 1830–1979 (MS 411)

ONLINE DATABASES

Ancestry.com Operations Inc., Provo, Utah
   California, US, State Hospital Records, 1856–1923, www.ancestry.com/search/
      collections/9206/
   District of Columbia, US, Select Deaths and Burials Index, 1769–1960, www.ances-
      try.com/search/collections/60260/
   Georgia, US, Marriage Records from Select Counties, 1828–1978, www.ancestry.
      com/search/collections/4766/

Lancaster, Pennsylvania, US, Mennonite Vital Records, 1750–2014, www.ancestry.com/search/collections/60592/

Michigan, US, Death Records, 1867–1952, www.ancestry.com/search/collections/60872/

US, Colored Troops Military Service Records, 1863–1865, www.ancestry.com/search/collections/1107/

US, Confederate Soldiers Compiled Service Records, 1861–1865, www.ancestry.com/search/collections/2322/

US, Federal Census Collection, www.ancestry.com/search/categories/usfedcen/

US, Freedman's Bureau Records, 1865–1878, www.ancestry.com/search/collections/62309/

US, World War II Draft Registration Cards, 1942, www.ancestry.com/search/collections/1002/

FamilySearch.org

Georgia Probate Records, 1742–1990, www.familysearch.org.

Federal Bureau of Investigation Records: The Vault

Father Divine, https://vault.fbi.gov/father-divine

W. D. Fard, https://vault.fbi.gov/Wallace%20Fard%20Muhammed

Elijah Muhammad, https://vault.fbi.gov/elijah-muhammad

Richard Nathaniel Wright, https://vault.fbi.gov/Richard%20Nathaniel%20Wright


STATE HOSPITAL ANNUAL REPORTS

Alabama Insane Hospital

Central Kentucky Lunatic Asylum

Central Lunatic Asylum, Virginia (Central State Hospital)

Crownsville State Hospital, Maryland

Eastern Insane Asylum, North Carolina (Eastern State Hospital)

Eastern State Hospital, Virginia

Florida Hospital for the Insane (Florida State Hospital)

Georgia Lunatic Asylum (Georgia State Hospital)

Government Hospital for the Insane (St. Elizabeths Hospital, District of Columbia)

Lakin State Hospital, State Board of Control of West Virginia

Mississippi State Lunatic Asylum

South Carolina Lunatic Asylum (South Carolina State Hospital)

Southwestern State Hospital, Virginia

Taft State Hospital, Oklahoma

Western State Hospital, Virginia


NEWSPAPERS AND JOURNALS

*African Repository*

*Afro-American Churchman*

*Alienist and Neurologist*

*A.M.E. Church Review*

*American Journal of Insanity*

American Journal of Psychiatry
American Practitioner and News
Anaconda Standard
The Appeal
The Apostolic Faith
Athens Weekly Banner
Atlanta Constitution
Atlanta Daily World
Atlanta Georgian and News
Atlantic Monthly
Austin American-Statesman
Baltimore Afro-American
Baltimore Sun
Biblical Recorder
Botanico-Medical Recorder
California and Western Medicine
California Eagle
Charities
Chicago Daily Tribune
Chicago Defender
Christian Recorder
The Church at Home and Abroad
Cincinnati Enquirer
Cincinnati Post
Cleveland Plain Dealer
Club Dial
Columbus Enquirer-Sun
Confidential
Daily Arkansas Gazette
Daily Inter Ocean
Detroit Free Press
Ebony
Eufalia Times and News
Evansville Courier
Fayetteville Weekly Democrat
The Forum
Galveston Daily News
Harper's Bazaar
Harrisburg Telegraph
Highland Park News-Herald and Journal
Hinton Daily News
Houston Post
Jewish Exponent

*Journal of Mental Science*
*Journal of the National Medical Association*
*Leavenworth Standard*
*Los Angeles Herald*
*Los Angeles Times*
*Louisville Courier-Journal*
*Macon Weekly Telegraph*
*Medical News*
*Memphis Sunday Appeal*
*Milledgeville Union-Recorder*
*Minneapolis Commercial*
*Minneapolis Journal*
*Montreal Gazette*
*Moulton Advertiser*
*The Negro*
*New Journal and Guide*
*New Orleans Daily Picayune*
*New Orleans Times-Democrat*
*New Orleans Times-Picayune*
*New York Age*
*New York Amsterdam News*
*New York Times*
*New York Tribune*
*Norfolk Virginian*
*North Georgia Citizen*
*Opportunity: Journal of Negro Life*
*Pittsburgh Courier*
*Presbyterian of the South*
*The Protestant*
*Psychoanalytic Review*
*Richmond Dispatch*
*Richmond News Leader*
*Richmond Planet*
*Richmond Times*
*Richmond Times-Dispatch*
*Richmond Virginian*
*San Bernardino County Sun*
*San Diego Union and Daily Bee*
*San Francisco Call*
*San Francisco Chronicle*
*San Francisco Examiner*
*Savannah Morning News*
*Savannah Tribune*

*Southern Workman*
*Southwestern Christian Advocate*
*Spirit of Missions*
*St. Louis Post-Dispatch*
*Summit County Beacon*
*Time*
*Tomorrow*
*Trenton Evening Times*
*Tuskegee Herald*
*Valdosta Daily Times*
*Washington Daily Critic*
*Washington Evening Star*
*Washington Evening Times*
*Washington Morning Times*
*Washington Post*
*Washington Post and Times Herald*
*Waycross Journal*
*West Virginia Negro*
*Wilkes-Barre News*
*Wilmington Daily Republican*
*Wilmington Morning Star*
*Woman's Medical Journal*
*Woodson Democrat*

## PRIMARY SOURCES

Babcock, J. W. (James Woods). "The Colored Insane: I. Insanity in the Negro Ii. State Provision for Colored Insane." *Alienist and Neurologist (1880–1920)* 16, no. 4 (October 1, 1895): 423–47.

———. "Communicated Insanity and Negro Witch-Craft." *American Journal of Psychiatry* 51, no. 4 (April 1, 1895): 518–23.

Barrows, Isabel C., ed. *Proceedings of the National Conference of Charities and Correction at the Twenty-Second Annual Session Held in New Haven, Connecticut, May 24–30, 1895.* Boston: Geo. Ellis, 1895.

———. *Proceedings of the National Conference of Charities and Correction at the Twenty-Third Annual Session Held in Grand Rapids, Mich., June 4–10, 1896.* Boston: Geo. Ellis, 1896.

———. *Proceedings of the National Conference of Charities and Correction at the Twenty-Sixth Annual Session Held in the City of Cincinnati, Ohio, May 17–23, 1899.* Boston: Geo. Ellis, 1899.

Beard, George M. *American Nervousness: Its Causes and Consequences.* New York: G. P. Putnam's Sons, 1881.

Beers, Clifford Whittingham. *A Mind That Found Itself: An Autobiography.* New York: Longmans, Green, 1908.

Bender, Lauretta. "Behavior Problems in Negro Children." *Psychiatry* 2, no. 2 (May 1, 1939): 213–28.

Bender, Lauretta, and M. A. Spaulding. "Behavior Problems in Children from the Homes of Followers of Father Divine." *Journal of Nervous and Mental Disease* 91, no. 4 (April 1940): 460–72.

Bender, Lauretta, and Zuleika Yarrell. "Psychoses among Followers of Father Divine." *Journal of Nervous and Mental Disease* 87, no. 4 (April 1938): 418–49.

Bennett, George W. *Life behind the Walls of My Self-Made Fate.* Self-published, 1964.

Bevis, W. M. "Psychological Traits of the Southern Negro with Observations as to Some of His Psychoses." *American Journal of Insanity* 78 (July 1921): 69–78.

Bibb, Henry. *Narrative of the Life and Adventures of Henry Bibb, an American Slave, Written by Himself.* New York: published by the author, 1849.

Billings, R. A. "The Negro and His Church: A Psychogenetic Study." *Psychoanalytic Review* 21 (1934): 425–41.

Bond, Horace Mann. "Insanity among Negroes: A Symptom of Social Disorganization." *Opportunity: Journal of Negro Life* 10, no. 10 (October 1932): 304–8, 324.

Brigham, Amariah. "Miscellaneous: Exemption of the Cherokee Indians and Africans from Insanity." *American Journal of Insanity* 1, no. 3 (January 1845): 287–88.

———. *Observations on the Influence of Religion upon the Health and Physical Welfare of Mankind.* Boston: Marsh, Capen and Lyon, 1835.

Brown, William Wells. *My Southern Home: or, The South and Its People.* Boston: A. G. Brown, 1880.

Bruce, Philip Alexander. *The Plantation Negro as a Freeman: Observations on His Character, Condition, and Prospects in Virginia.* New York: G. P. Putnam's Sons, 1889.

Brussel, James A. "Father Divine: Holy Precipitator of Psychosis." *American Journal of Psychiatry* 92, no. 1 (July 1, 1935): 215–23.

Buchanan, J. M. "Insanity in the Colored Race." *New York Medical Journal* 44 (July 17, 1886): 67–70.

Buckley, J. M. *Christian Science and Other Superstitions.* New York: The Century Co., 1899.

Cantril, Hadley, and Muzafer Sherif. "The Kingdom of Father Divine." *Journal of Abnormal and Social Psychology* 33, no. 2 (April 1938): 147–67.

Cartwright, Samuel. "Canaan Identified with the Ethiopian." *Southern Quarterly Review* 2, no. 4 (October 1842): 321–83.

———. "Diseases and Peculiarities of the Negro Race." *DeBow's Review of the Southern and Western States* 11, no. 3 (September 1851): 331–36.

Collins, Charles W. "Psychoanalysis of Groups: Critique of a Study of a Small Negro Sample." *Journal of the National Medical Association* 44, no. 3 (May 1952): 165–71.

Collins, Charles W., P. Barker, Ernest Y. Williams, Rutherford B. Stevens, and E. L. Youngue. "Discussion of Psychoanalysis of Groups: Critique of a Study of a Small Negro Sample." *Journal of the National Medical Association* 44, no. 6 (November 1952): 455–61.

Cooper, Anna Julia. *A Voice from the South: By a Black Woman of the South.* New York: Oxford University Press, 1988 [1892].

Corson, Eugene Rollin, ed. *Some Unpublished Letters of Helena Petrova Blavatsky*. London: Rider and Co. Paternostra House, 1929.

———. "The Vital Equation of the Colored Race and Its Future in the United States." In *The Wilder Quarter-Century Book: A Collection of Original Papers Dedicated to Professor Burt Green Wilder at the Close of His Twenty-Fifth Year of Service in Cornell University (1868-1893) by Some of Former Students*, 115–75. Ithaca, NY: Comstock Publishing, 1893.

Crallé, Richard K., ed. *Works of John C. Calhoun*. Vol. 5, *Reports and Public Letters of John C. Calhoun*. New York: D. Appleton and Co., 1859.

Davenport, Frederick. *Primitive Traits in Religious Revivals: A Study in Mental and Social Evolution*. New York: Macmillan, 1905.

"The Distribution of Insanity." *Medical Record* 64, no. 26 (December 26, 1903): 1019.

Douglass, Frederick. *My Bondage and My Freedom*. New York: Miller, Orton and Mulligan, 1855.

Drewry, William F. "Care and Condition of the Insane in Virginia." In *Proceedings of the National Conference of Charities and Correction at the Thirty-Fifth Annual Session Held in the City of Richmond, Virginia, May 6–13, 1908*, edited by Alexander Johnson, 307–15. Fort Wayne, IN: Fort Wayne Printing Co., 1908.

Du Bois, W. E. B. "Review of Frederick L. Hoffman's *Race Traits and Tendencies of the American Negro*." *Annals of the American Academy of Political and Social Sciences* 9 (1897): 127–33.

———. *The Souls of Black Folk*. Chicago: A. C. McClurg, 1903.

Du Bois, W. E. B., and Conference for the Study of the Negro Problems. *The Health and Physique of the Negro American*. Atlanta: Atlanta University Press, 1906.

Ellison, Ralph. "Harlem Is Nowhere." In *The Shadow and the Act*, 294–302. New York: Vintage Books, 1972.

Evarts, Arrah B. "Dementia Praecox in the Colored Race." *Psychoanalytic Review* 1 (1914): 388–403.

———. "Folk Lore of the Old Testament, by J. G. FRAZER (Book Review)." *Psychoanalytic Review* 7 (January 1, 1920): 310.

———. "The Ontogenetic against the Phylogenetic Elements in the Psychoses of the Colored Race." *Psychoanalytic Review* 3 (January 1, 1916): 272–87.

Fauset, Arthur Huff. *Black Gods of the Metropolis: Negro Religious Cults of the Urban North*. Philadelphia: University of Pennsylvania Press, 1944.

Federal Writers' Project. *New York Panorama*. New York: Random House, 1938.

Ferris, William Henry. *The African Abroad, or, His Evolution in Western Civilization, Tracing His Development under Caucasian Milieu*. New Haven, CT: The Tuttle, Morehouse and Taylor Press, 1913.

Frazier, E. Franklin. *The Negro Family in Chicago*. Chicago: University of Chicago Press, 1932.

———. "The Pathology of Race Prejudice." *The Forum* 77, no. 6 (June 1927): 856–61.

———. "Psychological Factors in Negro Health." *Journal of Social Forces* 3, no. 1 (January 1, 1924): 488–90.

Grady, Henry Woodfin. *The New South*. New York: R. Bonner's Sons, 1890.

Green, E. M. "Manic-Depressive Psychosis in the Negro." *American Journal of Insanity* 73, no. 4 (April 1, 1917): 619–26.

———. "Psychoses among Negroes—A Comparative Study." *Journal of Nervous and Mental Disease* 41 (1914): 697–708.

Hall, G. Stanley. "The Negro in Africa and America." *Pedagogical Seminary* 12, no. 3 (September 1, 1905): 350–68.

Helm, Mary. *The Upward Path: The Evolution of a Race*. New York: Young People's Missionary Movement of the United States and Canada, 1909.

Hodges, J. Allison. "The Effect of Freedom upon the Physical and Psychological Development of the Negro of the South." In *Proceedings of the American Medico-Psychological Association at the Fifty-Sixth Annual Meeting Held in Richmond, Virginia, 88–98*. Utica, NY: American Medico-Psychological Association, 1900.

Hoffman, Frederick L. *Race Traits and Tendencies of the American Negro*. New York: Macmillan, 1896.

Hurston, Zora. "Hoodoo in America." *Journal of American Folklore* 44, no. 174 (1931): 317–417.

Jarvis, Edward. "Insanity among the Coloured Population of the Free States." *American Journal of Medical Sciences*, January 1844, 71–84.

Jones, Charles C., Jr. *Negro Myths from the Georgia Coast, Told in the Vernacular*. Columbia, SC: State Company, 1925.

Jones, Charles Colcock. *A Catechism for Colored Persons*. Charleston, SC: Observer Office Press, 1834.

———. "The Religious Instruction of the Negroes, A Sermon Delivered before Associations of Planters in Liberty and M'Intosh Counties, Georgia." 4th ed. Princeton, NJ: D'Hart and Connolly, 1832.

———. *The Religious Instruction of the Negroes in the United States*. Savannah, GA: Thomas Purse, 1842.

———. *Suggestions on the Religious Instruction of the Negroes in the Southern States*. Philadelphia: Presbyterian Board of Publication, 1847.

Jones, Raymond Julius. *A Comparative Study of Religious Cult Behavior among Negroes with Special Reference to Emotional Group Conditioning Factors*. Washington, DC: Howard University, 1939.

Kardiner, Abram, and Lionel Ovesey. *The Mark of Oppression: A Psychosocial Study of the American Negro*. New York: Norton, 1951.

Kennedy, Joseph C. G. *Population of the United States in 1860, Compiled from the Original Returns of the Eighth Census under the Direction of the Secretary of the Interior*. Washington, DC: Government Printing Office, 1864.

Kiernan, Jas. G. "Race and Insanity: The Negro Race." *Journal of Nervous and Mental Disease* 12, no. 2 (April 1885): 174–75.

———. "Race and Insanity: The Negro Race." *Journal of Nervous and Mental Disease* 12, no. 3 (July 1885): 290–93.

———. "Race and Insanity: The Negro Race." *Journal of Nervous and Mental Disease* 13, no. 2 (February 1886): 74–76.

———. "Race and Insanity." *Journal of Nervous and Mental Disease* 13, no. 4 and 5 (May 1886): 229–44.

King, Howard D. "The Psychology of the Negro Revival." *Journal of the South Carolina Medical Association* 10, no. 1 (January 1914): 459–60.

Kraepelin, Emil. *Dementia Praecox and Paraphrenia.* Translated by R. Mary Barclay. Edited by George M. Robertson. Edinburgh: Livingstone, 1919.

———. *Psychiatrie: Ein Lehrbuch für Studirende und Aerzte.* Leipzig: Verlag von Johann Abrosius Barth, 1899.

Lind, John E. "The Color Complex in the Negro." *Psychoanalytic Review* 1 (January 1, 1913): 404–14.

———. "The Dream as a Simple Wish-Fulfilment in the Negro." *Psychoanalytic Review* 1 (1914): 295–300.

———. "Phylogenetic Elements in the Psychoses of the Negro." *Psychoanalytic Review* 4 (January 1, 1917): 303–32.

Locke, Alain. *The New Negro: An Interpretation.* New York: Albert and Charles Boni, 1925.

Lydston, G. Frank. *The Blood of the Fathers.* Chicago: Riverton Press, 1912.

———. "The Race Problem in America in Its Relation to Criminal Sociology." *American Journal of Clinical Medicine* 17, no. 2 (February 1910): 170–75.

Malzberg, Benjamin. "Mental Disease among American Negroes: A Statistical Analysis." In *Characteristics of the American Negro*, edited by Otto Kleinberg, 373–99. New York: Harper and Brothers, 1944.

———. "Mental Disease among Negroes in New York State." *Human Biology* 7, no. 4 (December 1935): 471–513.

———. "Migration and Mental Disease among Negroes in New York State." *American Journal of Physical Anthropology* 21, no. 1 (1936): 107–13.

Mays, Thomas J. "Increase of Insanity and Consumption among the Negro Population of the South since the War." *Boston Medical and Surgical Journal* 136, no. 22 (June 3, 1897): 537–40.

McKay, Claude. "'There Goes God!': The Story of Father Divine and His Angels," *The Nation* 140, no. 3631 (February 6, 1935): 151–53.

Michie, Thomas Johnson, ed. *The Code of Virginia as Amended to Adjournment of General Assembly 1924.* Charlottesville, VA: Michie Company, 1924.

Miller, J. F. *The Effects of Emancipation upon the Mental and Physical Health of the Negro of the South.* Wilmington, DE, 1896.

Miller, Kelly. "A Review of Hoffman's Race Traits and Tendencies of the American Negro." Occasional Papers, No. 1. Washington, DC: American Negro Academy, 1897.

Moore, George S. "Introduction to a Study of Neuropsychiatric Problems among Negroes." *U.S. Veterans' Bureau Medical Bulletin* 2, no. 1 (January 1926): 1042–45.

———. "Introduction to a Study of Neuropsychiatric Problems among Negroes." *U.S. Veterans' Bureau Medical Bulletin* 3, no. 9 (September 1927): 887–97.

Mumford, George W. *Third Edition of the Code of Virginia, Including Legislation to January 1, 1874*. Richmond: James E. Goode, 1873.

Nott, Josiah C. *Two Lectures on the Natural History of the Caucasian and Negro Races*. Mobile, AL: Dade and Thompson, 1844.

O'Malley, Mary. "Psychoses in the Colored Race." *American Journal of Psychiatry* 71, no. 2 (October 1914): 309–37.

Payne, Daniel A. *Recollections of Seventy Years*. Nashville, TN: Publishing House of the A.M.E. Sunday School Union, 1888.

Perry, M. L. "Insanity and the Negro." *Current Literature* 34, no. 4 (October 1902): 467.

Pollock, Horatio. "Mental Disease among Negroes in the United States." *State Hospital Quarterly* 11, no. 1 (November 1925): 47–66.

Powell, Theophilus O. "The Increase of Insanity and Tuberculosis in the Southern Negro since 1860, and Its Alliance, and Some of the Supposed Causes." *Journal of the American Medical Association* 27, no. 23 (December 5, 1896): 1185–88.

Prichard, James Cowles. *A Treatise on Insanity and Other Disorders Affecting the Mind*. London: Sherwood, Gilbert, and Piper, 1835.

Pusey, H. K. "The Increase of Insanity and Mental Defectiveness." *New York Medical Journal* 48 (September 29, 1888): 348–50.

Régis, Emmanuel. *A Practical Manual of Mental Medicine*. 2nd ed. Translated by H. M. Bannister. London: Baillere, Tindall and Cox, 1895.

Reid, Ira De A. "Let Us Prey." *Opportunity* 4, no. 45 (September 1926): 274–78.

*Report of the Special Committee on Investigation of the Government Hospital for the Insane in Two Volumes*. Washington, DC: Government Printing Office, 1907.

Roberts, J. D. "Insanity in the Colored Race." Goldsboro, NC: Argus Job Print, 1883.

Robinson, James H. *Road without Turning: The Story of Reverend James H. Robinson; An Autobiography*. New York: Farrar, Straus, 1950.

Rosenthal, S. P. "Racial Differences in the Mental Diseases." *Journal of Abnormal and Social Psychology* 28, no. 3 (October 1933): 301–18.

Shepard, Eli. "Superstitions of the Negro." *Cosmopolitan* 5, no. 1 (March 1888): 47–50.

Smith, Alan P. "Mental Hygiene and the American Negro." *Journal of the National Medical Association* 23, no. 1 (March 1931): 1–10.

———. "The Role of Psychoanalytic Psychiatry in the Practice of Medicine." *Journal of the National Medical Association* 40, no. 4 (July 1948): 147–53.

Smith, James McCune. "Freedom and Slavery for Afric-Americans" (1844). In *The Works of James McCune Smith: Black Intellectual and Abolitionist*, edited by John Stauffer, 61–74. New York: Oxford University Press, 2006.

Stanford, P. Thomas. *The Tragedy of the Negro in America: A Condensed History of the Enslavement, Suffering, Emancipation, Present Conditions and Progress of the Negro Race in the United States of America*. Boston, 1897.

Wagner, Philip Sigmund. "A Comparative Study of Negro and White Admissions to the Psychiatric Pavilion of the Cincinnati General Hospital." *American Journal of Psychiatry* 95, no. 1 (July 1, 1938): 167–83.

Washington, Booker. "The Religious Life of the Negro." *North American Review* 181, no. 584 (July 1, 1905): 20–23.

Witmer, A. H. "Insanity in the Colored Race in the United States." *Alienist and Neurologist* 12, no. 1 (January 1, 1891): 19–30.

Wright, Richard. *Black Boy*. New York: Harper and Brothers, 1945.

———. *Twelve Million Black Voices: A Folk History of the Negro in the United States*. With photo-direction by Edwin Rosskam. New York: Viking Press, 1941.

BOOKS, ARTICLES, THESES, DISSERTATIONS

Allison, George W., Mrs. John C. Water, Barton P. Phelps, and H. C. Sticher. *With Christ in Kansas: A History of the First Presbyterian Church of Topeka, Kansas, 1859–1934*. Topeka, KS: Committee on the Seventy-Fifth Anniversary, n.d.

Armstrong, Thomas F. "The Building of a Black Church: Community in Post–Civil War Liberty County, Georgia." *Georgia Historical Quarterly* 66, no. 3 (October 1, 1982): 346–67.

———. "The Christ Craze of 1889: A Millennial Response to Economic and Social Change." In *Toward a New South? Studies in Post–Civil War Southern Communities*, edited by Orville Vernon Burton and Robert C. McMath Jr., 223–45. Westport, CT: Greenwood Press, 1982.

Ash, Samuel A., editor in chief. *Biographical History of North Carolina from Colonial Times to the Present*. Vol. 1. Greensboro, NC: Charles L. Van Noppen, 1905.

Bailey, Fred A. "Race Ideology and the Missionary Quest of Lucinda and Mary Helm: What Kentucky Patricians Thought They Knew about the 'Negro Element.'" *Register of the Kentucky Historical Society* 99: 1 (2001): 53–68.

Bainbridge, William Sims. "Religious Insanity in America: The Official Nineteenth-Century Theory." *Sociological Analysis* 45, no. 3 (1984): 223–39.

Baker, Kelly J. *Gospel According to the Klan: The KKK's Appeal to Protestant America, 1915–1930*. Lawrence: University Press of Kansas, 2011.

Bartholomew, Robert E., and Julian David O'Dea. "Religious Devoutness Construed as Pathology: The Myth of 'Religious Mania.'" *International Journal for the Psychology of Religion* 8, no. 1 (1998): 1–16.

Beliso-De Jesús, Aisha. *Excited Delirium: Race, Police Violence, and the Invention of a Disease*. Durham, NC: Duke University Press, 2024.

Bellware, Kim. "Police Had No Legal Reason to Place Elijah McLain in Chokehold, Probe of Death Finds." *Washington Post*, February 23, 2021. www.washingtonpost.com.

Berry, Mary Frances. *My Face Is Black Is True: Callie House and the Struggle for Ex-Slave Reparations*. New York: Alfred A. Knopf, 2005.

Best, Wallace D. *Passionately Human, No Less Divine: Religion and Black Culture in Chicago, 1915–1952*. Princeton, NJ: Princeton University Press, 2005.

Boaz, Danielle N. *Banning Black Gods: Law and Religions of the African Diaspora*. University Park: Pennsylvania State University Press, 2021.

———. "Obeah, Vagrancy, and the Boundaries of Religious Freedom: Analyzing the Proscription of 'Pretending to Possess Supernatural Powers' in the Anglophone Caribbean." *Journal of Law and Religion* 32, no. 3 (2017): 423–48.

———. "The Voodoo Cult of Detroit: Race, Human Sacrifice, and the Nation of Islam from the 1930s to the 1970s." *Journal of Interreligious Studies* 23 (May 2018): 17–30.

———. *Voodoo: The History of a Racial Slur*. New York: Oxford University Press, 2023.

Boris, Joseph L., ed. *Who's Who in Colored America, 1928–1929*. New York: Who's Who in Colored America Corporation, 1929.

Boyer, Jodie. "Religion, 'Moral Insanity,' and Psychology in Nineteenth-Century America." *Religion and American Culture: A Journal of Interpretation* 24, no. 1 (January 1, 2014): 70–99.

Brooks, Adia Awanata. "The Politics of Race and Mental Illness in the Postemancipation US South: Central Lunatic Asylum for the Colored Insane in Historical Perspective." Master's thesis, University of Texas at Austin, 2014.

Brown, David H. "Conjure/Doctors: An Explanation of a Black Discourse in America, Antebellum to 1940." *Folklore Forum* 23, no. 1 (January 1, 1990): 3–46.

Brown, Ras Michael. *African-Atlantic Cultures and the South Carolina Lowcountry*. Cambridge: Cambridge University Press, 2012.

Bruce, La Marr Jurelle. *How to Go Mad without Losing Your Mind: Madness and Black Radical Creativity*. Durham, NC: Duke University Press, 2021.

Burch, Susan. *Committed: Remembering Native Kinship in and beyond Institutions*. Chapel Hill: University of North Carolina Press, 2021.

Burton, Katherine B. "Mary O'Malley, M.D." *Psychoanalytic Review* 85, no. 1 (February 1, 1998): 9–26.

Butler, Anthea D. *Women in the Church of God in Christ: Making a Sanctified World*. Chapel Hill: University of North Carolina Press, 2007.

Caldwell, A. B., ed. *History of the American Negro: South Carolina Edition*. Atlanta: A. B. Caldwell, 1919.

Candler, Allen D., and Clement A. Evans, eds. *Cylcopedia of Georgia*. Vol. 3. Atlanta: State Historical Association, 1906.

Chireau, Yvonne P. *Black Magic: Religion and the African American Conjuring Tradition*. Berkeley: University of California Press, 2006.

Clarke, Erskine. *Dwelling Place: A Plantation Epic*. New Haven, CT: Yale University Press, 2005.

Clegg, Claude Andrew. *An Original Man: The Life and Times of Elijah Muhammad*. New York: St. Martin's Press, 1997.

Clossen, Troy, and Ed Shanahan. "Black Man Died of Suffocation after Officers Put Hood on Him." *New York Times*, September 2, 2020. www.nytimes.com.

Connelly, William E. *A Standard History of Kansas and Kansans*. Vol. 4. Chicago: Lewis Publishing, 1918.

Cook, Chris, and Andrew Powell, eds. *Spirituality and Psychiatry*. 2nd ed. Cambridge: Cambridge University Press, 2022.

Cooper Owens, Deirdre. *Medical Bondage: Race, Gender, and the Origins of American Gynecology.* Athens: University of Georgia Press, 2017.

Curtis, Heather. *Faith in the Great Physician: Suffering and Divine Healing in American Culture, 1860–1900.* Baltimore: Johns Hopkins University Press, 2007.

———. "A Sane Gospel: Radical Evangelicals, Psychology, and Pentecostal Revival in the Early Twentieth Century." *Religion and American Culture: A Journal of Interpretation* 21, no. 2 (2011): 195–226.

Dallam, Marie W. *Daddy Grace: A Celebrity Preacher and His House of Prayer.* New York: New York University Press, 2007.

Derieux, James C. "Uncle Jaggers Who Preached Ten Thousand Sermons from Just One Text." *Good Housekeeping* 93, no. 6 (December 1931): 78–79, 121–22, 125–26.

Deutsch, Albert. "The First U.S. Census of the Insane (1840) and Its Use as Pro-slavery Propaganda." *Bulletin of the History of Medicine* 15, no. 5 (May 1, 1944), 469–82.

Dickerson, Dennis C. *African American Preachers and Politics: The Careys of Chicago.* Jackson: University Press of Mississippi, 2010.

Downs, Winfield Scott, ed. *Encyclopedia of American Biography,* n.s., vol. 2. New York: American Historical Society, 1934.

Doyle, Dennis A. "'A Fine New Child': The Lafargue Mental Hygiene Clinic and Harlem's African American Communities, 1946–1958." *Journal of the History of Medicine and Allied Sciences* 64, no. 2 (2009): 173–212.

———. *Psychiatry and Racial Liberalism in Harlem, 1936–1968.* Rochester, NY: University of Rochester Press, 2016.

———. "'Racial Differences Have to Be Considered': Lauretta Bender, Bellevue Hospital, and the African American Psyche, 1936–52." *History of Psychiatry* 21, no. 2 (June 1, 2010): 206–23.

———. "The Universal Mind Assumption: Harlem and the Development of a New Racial Formation in American Psychiatry, 1938—1968." PhD diss., State University of New York at Stony Brook, 2006.

———. "'Where the Need Is Greatest': Social Psychiatry and Race-Blind Universalism in Harlem's Lafargue Clinic, 1946–1958." *Bulletin of the History of Medicine* 83, no. 4 (2009): 746–74.

Drake, Jamil W. *To Know the Soul of a People: Religion, Race, and the Making of the Southern Folk.* New York: Oxford University Press, 2022.

Dwyer, Ellen. "Psychiatry and Race during World War II." *Journal of the History of Medicine and Allied Sciences* 61, no. 2 (2006): 117–43.

Engstrom, Eric J., and Ivan Crozier. "Race, Alcohol and General Paralysis: Emil Kraepelin's Comparative Psychiatry and His Trips to Java (1904) and North America (1925)." *History of Psychiatry* 29, no. 3 (September 1, 2018): 263–81.

Evans, Curtis J. *The Burden of Black Religion.* New York: Oxford University Press, 2008.

Ezekiel, Herbert T., and Gaston Lichtenstein. *The History of the Jews of Richmond from 1769 to 1917.* Richmond: Herbert T. Ezekiel, 1917.

Fluhman, J. Spencer. *A Peculiar People: Anti-Mormonism and the Making of Religion in Nineteenth-Century America.* Chapel Hill: University of North Carolina Press, 2012.

Fulop, Timothy E. "'The Future Golden Day of the Race': Millennialism and Black Americans in the Nadir, 1877–1901." *Harvard Theological Review* 84, no. 1 (1991): 75–99.

Gambino, Matthew. "'The Savage Heart beneath the Civilized Exterior': Race, Citizenship, and Mental Illness in Washington, D.C., 1900–1940." *Disability Studies Quarterly* 28, no. 3 (July 31, 2008). https://doi.org/10.18061/dsq.v28i3.114.

———. "'These Strangers within Our Gates': Race, Psychiatry and Mental Illness among Black Americans at St Elizabeths Hospital in Washington, DC, 1900–40." *History of Psychiatry* 19, no. 4 (December 1, 2008): 387–408.

Gilman, Sander L. *Difference and Pathology: Stereotypes of Sexuality, Race, and Madness*. Ithaca, NY: Cornell University Press, 1985.

Gloege, Timothy. *Guaranteed Pure: The Moody Bible Institute and the Making of Modern Evangelicalism*. Chapel Hill: University of North Carolina Press, 2015.

Gonaver, Wendy. *The Peculiar Institution and the Making of Modern Psychiatry, 1840–1880*. Chapel Hill: University of North Carolina Press, 2018.

Green, Laurie B., John Mckiernan-González, and Martin Summers. *Precarious Prescriptions: Contested Histories of Race and Health in North America*. Minneapolis: University of Minnesota Press, 2014.

Greenberg, Cheryl Lynn. *Or Does It Explode? Black Harlem in the Great Depression*. New York: Oxford University Press, 1997.

Greene-Hayes, Ahmad. "'A Very Queer Case': Clementine Barnabet and the Erotics of a Sensationalized Voodoo Religion." *Nova Religio* 26, no. 4 (May 2023): 58–84.

Grob, Gerald N. *From Asylum to Community: Mental Health Policy in Modern America*. Princeton, NJ: Princeton University Press, 1991.

———. *The Inner World of American Psychiatry, 1890–1940: Selected Correspondence*. New Brunswick, NJ: Rutgers University Press, 1985.

———. *Mental Illness and American Society, 1875–1940*. Princeton, NJ: Princeton University Press, 1983.

Gross, Ariella. "Pandora's Box: Slave Character on Trial in the Antebellum Deep South." *Yale Journal of Law and the Humanities* 7, no. 2 (1995): 267–316.

Gross, Robert A. "'Doctor Ripley's Church': Congregational Life in Concord, Massachusetts, 1778–1841." *Journal of Unitarian Universalist History* 33 (2009–10): 21–24.

Hardy, Clarence E., III. "'No Mystery God': Black Religions of the Flesh in Pre-war Urban America." *Church History* 77, no. 1 (March 1, 2008): 128–50.

Hargis, Peggy G. "For the Love of Place: Paternalism and Patronage in the Georgia Lowcountry, 1865–1898." *Journal of Southern History* 70, no. 4 (2004): 825–64.

Harper, Matthew. *The End of Days: African American Religion and Politics in the Age of Emancipation*. Chapel Hill: University of North Carolina Press, 2016.

Hartman, Saidiya. "Venus in Two Acts." *Small Axe: A Journal of Criticism* 12, no. 2 (2008): 1–14.

———. *Wayward Lives, Beautiful Experiments: Intimate Histories of Social Upheaval*. New York: W. W. Norton, 2019.

Harvey, Paul. *Freedom's Coming: Religious Culture and the Shaping of the South from the Civil War through the Civil Rights Era.* Chapel Hill: University of North Carolina Press, 2005.

Haynes, Stephen R. *Noah's Curse: The Biblical Justification of American Slavery.* New York: Oxford University Press, 2007.

Heinze, Andrew R. *Jews and the American Soul: Human Nature in the Twentieth Century.* Princeton, NJ: Princeton University Press, 2004.

Helderman, Ira. *Prescribing the Dharma: Psychotherapists, Buddhist Traditions, and Defining Religion.* Chapel Hill: University of North Carolina Press, 2019.

Higginbotham, Evelyn Brooks. *Righteous Discontent: The Woman's Movement in the Black Baptist Church, 1880–1920.* Cambridge, MA: Harvard University Press, 1993.

Hogarth, Rana A. *Medicalizing Blackness: Making Racial Difference in the Atlantic World, 1780–1840.* Chapel Hill: University of North Carolina Press, 2017.

Horowitz, Allan V., and Gerald N. Grob. "The Checkered History of American Psychiatric Epidemiology." *Milbank Quarterly* 89, no. 4 (December 2011): 628–57.

Hucks, Tracey E. *Obeah, Orisa and Religious Identity in Trinidad: Africans in the White Colonial Imagination.* Durham, NC: Duke University Press, 2022.

Imhoff, Sarah. *Masculinity and the Making of American Judaism.* Bloomington: Indiana University Press, 2017.

Ives, Mike. "California Bans 'Excited Delirium' as a Cause of Death." *New York Times,* October 11, 2023. www.nytimes.com.

Jackson, Lynette A. *Surfacing Up: Psychiatry and Social Order in Colonial Zimbabwe, 1908–1968.* Ithaca, NY: Cornell University Press, 2005.

Jemison, Elizabeth L. *Christian Citizens: Reading the Bible in Black and White in the Postemancipation South.* Chapel Hill: University of North Carolina Press, 2020.

Jenkins, Philip. *Mystics and Messiahs: Cults and New Religions in American History.* New York: Oxford University Press, 2000.

Johnson, Paul C. *Automatic Religion: Nearhuman Agents of Brazil and France.* Chicago: University of Chicago Press, 2021.

Johnson, Sylvester A. *African American Religions, 1500–2000: Colonialism, Democracy, and Freedom.* Cambridge: Cambridge University Press, 2015.

———. *The Myth of Ham in Nineteenth-Century American Christianity: Race, Heathens, and the People of God.* New York: Palgrave Macmillan, 2004.

Jordanova, Ludmilla. "Portraits, Patients and Practitioners." *Medical Humanities* 39, no. 1 (June 1, 2013): 2–3.

Joseph, J. Walter, III. "Liberty: An Archaeological Examination of Social Identity within the Plantation Culture of the Lowcountry of Georgia." PhD diss., University of Pennsylvania, 1993.

Kaplan, Mary. *Solomon Carter Fuller: Where My Caravan Has Rested.* Lanham, MD: University Press of America, 2005.

Keel, Terence. *Divine Variations: How Christian Thought Became Racial Science.* Stanford, CA: Stanford University Press, 2018.

Keller, Richard C. *Colonial Madness: Psychiatry in French North Africa*. Chicago: University of Chicago Press, 2007.

Koenig, Harold G. *Religion and Mental Health: Research and Clinical Applications*. London: Academic Press, 2018.

Kurian, Philip. "Combatting Empire's Blinkered History: The Landmark Repatriation of Tweed MS 150." *Los Angeles Review of Books*, August 21, 2021. https://lareviewofbooks.org/.

Lawrence, Susan C. *Privacy and the Past: Research, Law, Archives, Ethics*. New Brunswick, NJ: Rutgers University Press, 2016.

Lightfoot, Sara Lawrence. *Balm in Gilead: Journey of a Healer*. Reading, MA: Addison-Wesley, 1988.

Louis, Diana Martha. "Black Women's Psychiatric Incarceration at Georgia Lunatic Asylum in the Nineteenth Century." *Journal of Women's History* 34, no. 1 (2022): 26–48.

Lum, Kathryn Gin. *Heathen: Race and Religion in America*. Cambridge, MA: Harvard University Press, 2022.

———. "The Historyless Heathen and the Stagnating Pagan: History as Non-native Category?" *Religion and American Culture: A Journal of Interpretation* 28, no. 1 (2018): 52–91.

Lunbeck, Elizabeth. *The Psychiatric Persuasion: Knowledge, Gender, and Power in Modern America*. Princeton, NJ: Princeton University Press, 1994.

Mahone, Sloan. "The Psychology of Rebellion: Colonial Medical Responses to Dissent in British East Africa." *Journal of African History* 47, no. 2 (2006): 241–58.

Manigault-Bryant, LeRhonda S. *Talking to the Dead: Religion, Music, and Lived Memory among Gullah-Geechee Women*. Durham, NC: Duke University Press, 2014.

Markowitz, Gerald, and David Rosner. *Children, Race, and Power: Kenneth and Mamie Clark's Northside Center*. New York: Routledge, 2000.

Mather, Frank Lincoln, ed. *Who's Who of the Colored Race: A General Biographical Dictionary of Men and Women of African Descent*. Chicago: Frank Lincoln Mather, 1915.

Matory, J. Lorand. *The Fetish Revisited: Marx, Freud, and the Gods Black People Make*. Durham, NC: Duke University Press, 2018.

McCrary, Charles. "Superstitious Subjects: US Religion, Race, and Freedom." *Method and Theory in the Study of Religion* 30, no. 1 (January 2, 2018): 56–70.

McDannell, Colleen. *Picturing Faith: Photography and the Great Depression*. New Haven, CT: Yale University Press, 2004.

McKittrick, Katherine. "On Plantations, Prisons, and a Black Sense of Place." *Social and Cultural Geography* 12, no. 8 (2011): 947–63.

Mendes, Gabriel N. *Under the Strain of Color: Harlem's Lafargue Clinic and the Promise of an Antiracist Psychiatry*. Ithaca, NY: Cornell University Press, 2015.

Metzl, Jonathan. *The Protest Psychosis: How Schizophrenia Became a Black Disease*. Boston: Beacon Press, 2009.

Modern, John Lardas. *Neuromatic or, A Particular History of Religion and the Brain.* Chicago: University of Chicago Press, 2021.

Moreira-Almeida, A. "History of 'Spiritist Madness' in Brazil." *History of Psychiatry* 16, no. 1 (March 1, 2005): 5–25.

Moseley, J. R. *Manifest Victory: A Quest and a Testimony.* Rev. ed. New York: Harper and Brothers, 1947.

Myers, Bob Eberly. "'Drapetomania' Rebellion, Defiance and Free Black Insanity in the Antebellum United States." PhD diss., University of California, Los Angeles, 2014.

Noll, Richard. *American Madness: The Rise and Fall of Dementia Praecox.* Cambridge, MA: Harvard University Press, 2011.

Norwood, Charles S. *A History of the First Baptist Church of Goldsboro, North Carolina: Organized in 1843 in Old Waynesborough.* Goldsboro, NC: Hillburn Printing, 1988.

Numbers, Ronald L., and Janet S. Numbers. "Millerism and Madness: A Study of 'Religious Insanity' in Nineteenth-Century America." *Bulletin of the Menninger Clinic* 49, no. 4 (July 1, 1985): 289–320.

Nuriddin, Ayah. "Psychiatric Jim Crow: Desegregation at the Crownsville State Hospital, 1948–1970." *Journal of the History of Medicine and Allied Sciences* 74, no. 1 (2019): 85–106.

Nussbaum, Abraham. "Profession and Faith: The National Guild of Catholic Psychiatrists, 1950–1968." *Catholic Historical Review* 93, no. 4 (2007): 845–65.

Otto, Thomas. *St. Elizabeths Hospital: A History.* Washington, DC: United States General Services Administration, 2013.

Parsons, Anne E. *From Asylum to Prison: Deinstitutionalization and the Rise of Mass Incarceration after 1945.* Chapel Hill: University of North Carolina Press, 2018.

Paton, Diana. *The Cultural Politics of Obeah: Religion, Colonialism and Modernity in the Caribbean World.* New York: Cambridge University Press, 2015.

Pearson, Fred Lamar, Jr., and Joseph Aaron Tomberlin. "John Doe, Alias God: A Note on Father Divine's Georgia Career." *Georgia Historical Quarterly* 60, no. 1 (April 1, 1976): 43–48.

Porter, Theodore M. *Genetics in the Madhouse: The Unknown History of Human Heredity.* Princeton, NJ: Princeton University Press, 2018.

Prince, Alexandra. "'Driven Insane by Eddyism': Christian Science, Popular Psychopathology, and a Turn-of-the-Century Contest over Faith and Madness." *Religion and American Culture* 31, no. 3 (2021): 379–418.

O'Hare, Méabh, Joshua Budhu, and Altaf Saadi. "Police Keep Using 'Excited Delirium' to Justify Brutality. It's Junk Science." *Washington Post*, July 17, 2020. www.washingtonpost.com.

Orr, Steve. "How Daniel Prude Suffocated as Rochester Police Restrained Him." *Rochester Democrat and Chronicle*, September 2, 2020. www.democratandchronicle.com.

Raboteau, Albert J. *Slave Religion: The "Invisible Institution" in the Antebellum South.* New York: Oxford University Press, 1978.

Ramsey, Kate. *The Spirits and the Law: Vodou and Power in Haiti.* Chicago: University of Chicago Press, 2011.

Rawling, Katherine D. B. "'She Sits All Day in the Attitude Depicted in the Photo': Photography and the Psychiatric Patient in the Late Nineteenth Century." *Medical Humanities* 43, no. 2 (June 1, 2017): 99–100.

Raz, Mical. *The Lobotomy Letters: The Making of American Psychosurgery*. Rochester, NY: University of Rochester Press, 2013.

Reidy, Joseph R. *Illusions of Emancipation: The Pursuit of Freedom and Equality in the Twilight of Emancipation*. Chapel Hill: University of North Carolina Press, 2019.

Ribovich, Leslie. "Saving Black Boys: Delinquency, Race, and the Institutionalization of Religious Practice at the Wiltwyck School for Boys, 1937–1942." *American Religion* 2, no. 1 (Fall 2020): 101–30.

Roberts, Dorothy. *Fatal Invention: How Science, Politics, and Big Business Re-create Race in the Twenty-First Century*. New York: New Press, 2011.

———. *Killing the Black Body: Race, Reproduction, and the Meaning of Liberty*. New York: Pantheon Books, 1997.

Robertson, Nancy Marie. *Christian Sisterhood, Race Relations, and the YWCA, 1906–1946*. Urbana: University of Illinois Press, 2007.

Rogers, George A., and R. Frank Saunders Jr. *Swamp Water and Wiregrass: Historical Sketches of Coastal Georgia*. Macon, GA: Mercer University Press, 1984.

Rose, Anne C. *Psychology and Selfhood in the Segregated South*. Chapel Hill: University of North Carolina Press, 2009.

———. "Putting the South on the Psychological Map: The Impact of Region and Race on the Human Sciences during the 1930s." *Journal of Southern History* 71, no. 2 (2005): 321–56.

Rose, Sarah F. *No Right to Be Idle: The Invention of Disability, 1840s–1930s*. Chapel Hill: University of North Carolina Press, 2017.

Rowley, Hazel. *Richard Wright: The Life and Times*. Chicago: University of Chicago Press, 2001.

Rubin, Julius H. *Religious Melancholy and Protestant Experience in America*. New York: Oxford University Press, 1994.

Sadowsky, Jonathan Hal. *Imperial Bedlam: Institutions of Madness in Colonial Southwest Nigeria*. Berkeley: University of California Press, 1999.

Santo, Alysia. "An Officer Suggested George Floyd Had 'Excited Delirium.' Experts Say That's Not a Real Thing." *Slate*, June 4, 2020. https://slate.com.

Savage, Barbara Dianne. *Your Spirits Walk beside Us: The Politics of Black Religion*. Cambridge, MA: Harvard University Press, 2008.

Scott, Daryl Michael. *Contempt and Pity: Social Policy and the Image of the Damaged Black Psyche, 1880–1996*. Chapel Hill: University of North Carolina Press, 1997.

Segrest, Mab. *Administrations of Lunacy: Racism and the Haunting of American Psychiatry at the Milledgeville Asylum*. New York: New Press, 2020.

———. "Exalted on the Ward: 'Mary Roberts,' the Georgia State Sanitarium, and the Psychiatric 'Speciality' of Race." *American Quarterly* 66, no. 1 (March 24, 2014): 69–94.

Shepard, George M. *Notes on Genealogy: Branches of Thrall Shepard, and Related Families*. St. Paul, MN: St. Paul Associated Letter Co., 1968.

Sidlauskas, Susan. "The Medical Portrait: Resisting the Shadow Archive." *nonsite.org* 26 (November 11, 2018), nonsite.org.

Smith, Gerald L., Karen Cotton McDaniel, and John A. Hardin. *The Kentucky African American Encyclopedia*. Lexington: University Press of Kentucky, 2015.

Smith, John David. *Black Judas: William Hannibal Thomas and the American Negro*. Athens: University of Georgia Press, 2000.

Smith, Leonard D. *Insanity, Race and Colonialism: Managing Mental Disorder in the Post-emancipation British Caribbean, 1838–1914*. London: Palgrave Macmillan, 2014.

Smith, Matthew. *The First Resort: The History of Social Psychiatry in the United States*. New York: Columbia University Press, 2023.

Sorett, Josef. *Spirit in the Dark: A Religious History of Racial Aesthetics*. New York: Oxford University Press, 2016.

Sparkes, Hilary. "Minds Overwrought by 'Religious Orgies': Narratives of African-Jamaican Folk Religion and Mental Illness in Late Nineteenth-Century and Early Twentieth-Century Ethnographies." *Journal of Africana Religions* 9, no. 2 (2021): 227–49.

Stacy, James. *History of the Midway Congregational Church, Liberty County, Georgia*. Newnan, GA: S. W. Murray Printer, 1899.

———. *A History of the Presbyterian Church in Georgia*. Elberton, GA: Press of the Star, 1912.

Stephens, Randall J. *The Fire Spreads: Holiness and Pentecostalism in the American South*. Cambridge, MA: Harvard University Press, 2008.

Strous, Rael D., Annete A. Opler, and Lewis A. Opler. "Reflections on 'Emil Kraepelin: Icon and Reality.'" *Journal of American Psychiatry* 173, no. 3 (March 2016): 300–301.

Sullivan, Laura. "Death by Excited Delirium: Diagnosis or Coverup." *NPR All Things Considered*, February 26, 2007. www.npr.org.

Summers, Martin. *Madness in the City of Magnificent Intentions: A History of Race and Mental Illness in the Nation's Capital*. New York: Oxford University Press, 2019.

———. "'Suitable Care of the African When Afflicted with Insanity': Race, Madness, and Social Order in Comparative Perspective." *Bulletin of the History of Medicine* 84, no. 1 (Spring 2010): 58–91.

Tate, Claudia. *Domestic Allegories of Political Desire: The Black Heroine's Text at the Turn of the Century*. New York: Oxford University Press, 1993.

Taves, Ann. *Fits, Trances and Visions: Experiencing Religion and Explaining Experience from Wesley to James*. Princeton, NJ: Princeton University Press, 1999.

Tevis, Britt P. "'The People's Judge': Jacob Panken, Yiddish Socialism, and American Law." *American Journal of Legal History* 59, no. 1 (March 1, 2019): 31–70.

Thomas, Todne. "James H. Cone and the Mysteries of Black Social Life." *Black Perspectives*, September 4, 2018. www.aaihs.org/.

Thompson, James Lawrence. *Of Shattered Minds: Fifty Years at the South Carolina State Hospital for the Insane*. Edited by Anita Wirick Roof. Columbia: South Carolina Department of Mental Health, 1989.

Thoms, Adah B. *Pathfinders: A History of the Progress of Colored Graduate Nurses*. New York: Kay Printing House, 1929.

Townsend, Craig. *Faith in Their Own Color: Black Episcopalians in Antebellum New York City*. New York: Columbia University Press, 2005.

Turner, Nicole Myers. "The Politics of Interdependent Independence in Black Religion: The Case of the Reverend George Freeman Bragg Jr., a Black Episcopal Priest." *Religion and American Culture* 31, no. 3 (Fall 2021): 419–54.

———. *Soul Liberty: The Evolution of Black Religious Politics in Postemancipation Virginia*. Chapel Hill: University of North Carolina Press, 2020.

Tyler, Lyon G., ed. *Men of Mark in Virginia, Ideals of American Life: A Collection of Biographies of the Leading Men in the State*. Vol. 5. Washington, DC: Men of Mark Publishing, 1909.

Vacek, Heather H. *Madness: American Protestant Reactions to Mental Illness across Three Centuries*. Waco, TX: Baylor University Press, 2015.

Walcott, Rinaldo. *The Long Emancipation: Moving toward Black Freedom*. Durham, NC: Duke University Press, 2021.

Washington, Harriet A. *Medical Apartheid: The Dark History of Medical Experimentation on Black Americans from Colonial Times to the Present*. New York: Doubleday, 2006.

Watts, Jill. *God, Harlem U.S.A.: The Father Divine Story*. Berkeley: University of California Press, 1995.

Weisenfeld, Judith. *African American Women and Christian Activism: New York's Black YWCA, 1905–1945*. Cambridge, MA: Harvard University Press, 1997.

———. *New World A-Coming: Black Religion and Racial Identity during the Great Migration*. New York: New York University Press, 2016.

Wells-Oghoghomeh, Alexis S. "'She Come Like a Nightmare': Hags, Witches and the Gendered Trans-Sense among the Enslaved in the Lower South." *Journal of Africana Religions* 5, no. 2 (2017): 239–74.

———. *The Souls of Womenfolk: The Religious Cultures of Enslaved Women in the Lower South*. Chapel Hill: University of North Carolina Press, 2021.

Wheatley, Jeffrey. "Colonial Governance of Superstition and Fanaticism in the Philippines." *Method and Theory in the Study of Religion* 30, no. 1 (January 2, 2018): 21–36.

White, Christopher G. *Unsettled Minds: Psychology and the American Search for Spiritual Assurance, 1830–1940*. Berkeley: University of California Press, 2009.

White, Deborah Gray. *Too Heavy a Load: Black Women in Defense of Themselves, 1894–1994*. New York: W. W. Norton, 1999.

White, James T. *The National Cyclopaedia of American Biography*. Vol. 21. New York: James T. White, 1931.

Willoughby, Christopher D. E. "Running Away from Drapetomania: Samuel A. Cartwright, Medicine, and Race in the Antebellum South." *Journal of Southern History* 84, no. 3 (2018): 579–614.

Wright, George J. "Theodore Diller." *American Journal of Psychiatry* 100, no. 4 (January 1944): 584.

Wright, Richard R., Jr., ed. *Who's Who in the General Conference 1924*. Philadelphia: A.M. E. Book Concern, 1924.

Yanni, Carla. *The Architecture of Madness: Insane Asylums in the United States*. Minneapolis: University of Minnesota Press, 2007.

Yenser, Thomas, ed. *Who's Who in Colored America*. 6th ed. Brooklyn: Thomas Yenser, 1944.

———, ed. *Who's Who in Colored America, 1933–1937*. Brooklyn: Thomas Yenser, 1937.

Young, Jason R. *Rituals of Resistance: African Atlantic Religion in Kongo and the Lowcountry South in the Era of Slavery*. Baton Rouge: Louisiana State University Press, 2007.

# INDEX

# ABOUT THE AUTHOR

JUDITH WEISENFELD is the Agate Brown and George L. Collord Professor of Religion at Princeton University. She is the author of *New World A-Coming: Black Religion and Racial Identity during the Great Migration*; *Hollywood Be Thy Name: African American Religion in American Film, 1929–1949*; and *African American Women and Christian Activism: New York's Black YWCA, 1905–1945*.